The House

Also by Anjuelle Floyd

Keeper of Secrets... Translations of an Incident

The House

Anjuelle Floyd

NOJ Publications Berkeley, California

Cover Created by:
Audria Gardner of Indigo Designs
www.designbyindigo.com

ISBN 978-0-9787967-2-3

Published by NOJ Publications
P. O. Box 9405
Berkeley, CA 94709
www.anjuellefloyd.com

Printed in the United States of America

All hold regret, and are seeking forgiveness.

Our salvation rests in the hands of others, most particularly the ones whom we love most, and who have treated us wrongly.

Chapter 1

Anna entered the office lined with cherry wood walls and built-in bookshelves, that of her attorney, Henderson Felterfield and marched straight to his secretary.

"Is Edward here yet?" She tapped her fingers on Claire's desk. Claire was on the phone. Halting her conversation, she placed her hand over the mouthpiece.

"Frieda's on the other line with him. Something's come up."

"Not again," Anna whispered. She ran her fingers through her hair, which had started to break. She needed to get a perm but funds were running short." This has got to stop."

For the past year, Edward and his attorney had fought Anna's request for a divorce. Edward had cancelled three times in the last month of the proceedings. As a result, her realtor had lost potential buyers for the house she and Edward had shared. *Time is money and money is time.* That's what Edward, also a realtor, always said. Now, as Anna's soon-to-be ex-husband, he was squandering away her time and money. Anna had entered the divorce process certain that Edward would welcome the end of their marriage. Now, fifteen months later she had grown weary of fighting to sell the house.

Anna was making her way to the leather sofa when her attorney walked up.

"I need to speak with you," Henderson said.

She followed him into his office. He closed the door behind them.

"Edward's stalling again," Anna said. "What reason has he given this time for not wanting to sell the house?" At age fifty-six, Anna had decided to move to the south of France. The only thing holding her back was the sale of the house in which she had raised their four children.

"We've got a problem," Henderson said. The morning sunlight enlivened his red tie and brown suspenders that were set against a white shirt and navy trousers. "David has retained an attorney. He's asserting that you're insane."

"The only insanity in my life is Edward. And now my eldest child has become like his father—only able to think of his own needs and desires."

"David's suing me, too," Henderson said. "He's claiming that I'm exploiting your debilitated mental state." Thirty-three-year-old David Manning had interned at Henderson's firm his first year out of law school.

Anna sighed.

"The suit is bogus," Henderson said. "David knows he can't get anywhere."

"But it's one more holdup. I *have* to get my house sold. I'm unemployed and running out of money." Again, Anna tore her fingers through her hair.

"The house is not yours yet. Edward still owns half."

"Then why isn't David suing *him*?"

"Because *you're* seeking the divorce."

"Where the hell was he with his legal skills when his father was having all of those affairs?" Anna said.

"He was a child."

8

Henderson drew close. His almond eyes set within his mahogany face softened. "David loves his father. He loves you, too. This lawsuit is his way of reacting. But, I don't think it was his idea."

"You're not going to tell me that Theo, Linda, and Serine are in this."

"If you ask me, Serine's behind it," Henderson said. "I think she and David have done this with Edward's blessings." Anna's youngest child, twenty-seven-year-old Serine, was a district attorney for Los Angeles County.

"Serine, of all people, should know how Edward's behavior has hurt us. All those nights away, the long, unexplained trips. She was the last one to leave home. I can't believe—"

"Regardless of all his philandering, Edward gave your children a good life. They saw him coming home to *you*. He was never violent or given to drink. You never spoke ill of him—"

"So, whose side are you on?"

"Yours, as always."

Anna clenched her jaw.

"I'll talk to David, check out my suspicions, but—"

"What about our meeting today?" Anna was coming unhinged. "How does Edward plan to use this *bogus* suit to fight the divorce, if he even shows up?"

"I'm not sure. But—"

Henderson's phone buzzed. He picked up the receiver.

"Yes . . . uh huh." A quizzical look formed on his rich, dark face. "Okay. Take him and Mr. Withers to the meeting room. We'll be right there." He clicked off and turned to Anna. "That was Frieda. Edward and Bryce have arrived." Henderson's eyes glistened. "Edward's also signed the divorce papers. Claire's making copies."

Anna's fingers grew cold.

Inside the conference room, Anna took her seat next to Henderson. Edward and his attorney, Bryce Withers, sat across from them. Edward gave Anna a faint smile then turned to Bryce who slid the open folder to Henderson. "As you can see, everything's signed," Bryce said.

Henderson began inspecting the documents.

Anna met Edward's gaze. Aside from the shock of his having acquiesced to the divorce, she noted tiredness in his movements. He seemed mournful.

"Everything's in order," Henderson said as he closed the folder. "And what about the house?"

Edward's shoulders slumped. His ruddy cheeks, normally full of fire and energy, lacked the red undertone that had so attracted Anna three and half decades ago. Her hands lay in her lap underneath the table. She pulled at her fingers. This is not like him. Something's wrong.

"I've signed over the house to Anna," Edward said. "It's hers."

Anna forced a swallow. In Edward's face was a sense of subdued penitence and clarity.

"Are you sure you want to do that?" she asked.

Henderson reached underneath the table and grabbed her hand to silence her. "When will we have the deed?" he asked.

"Claire's copying them as we speak," Bryce said. "I'll file them once we leave or—"

"If you don't mind, I'll submit it along with the divorce papers," Henderson offered. "I'm heading to the courthouse." He checked his watch. "I should be there in an hour." He gave a cordial smile, something Anna hadn't seen in the fifteen months of meetings.

Henderson stood and assisted her to join him. Bryce, then Edward, did the same.
"I'm glad we could work things out." Bryce reached across the table and shook Henderson's hand.

Edward extended his palm across the table toward Henderson, and said, "I've also spoken with David. He'll be withdrawing the lawsuit."

Refusing Edward's handshake, Henderson lifted the folder and said, "I'm going to file these." He left the room.

Bryce followed. The door closed. Edward proceeded to leave.

"Is everything alright?" Anna asked.

"Everything's fine." He turned and flashed a weak smile. His hand reached for the doorknob.

Groping to understand Edward's change of tactic, she parted her lips to speak, but he had slipped out the door.

Back in his office, Henderson closed the folder.

"Everything's as it should be, all as we requested."

"I'm worried about Edward." The flatness of Anna's words slid over her.

"*My* concern is *you*. I'm glad to see this come to an end, which happens when I file your set of the divorce papers." Henderson lifted the folder, checked his watch. "Eleven o'clock. If I leave right now, I can make it to the courthouse in time to have lunch by 12:30. Want to join me?"

Anna remained dazed by the turn of events.

Henderson walked from behind his desk, came around and leaned upon the front edge of the desk.

"Edward's behavior is not that unusual. I've seen this happen even in cases not involving divorce." He folded his arms.

Anna met the firm and impressive demeanor of Henderson's slim face molded around eyes perpetually hung in stolid sadness. She had not wanted to involve him in the messiness of her and Edward's private foibles. Yet, she had needed someone to trust, an attorney who would rein in the drama that was certain to erupt, and defend her with ultimate discretion. She had also wanted an attorney who respected Edward.

"Something's not right," she said.

"That may be. I have no idea why Edward chose to back down, and so abruptly," Henderson said. "But—"

"So you agree with me? This is out of character, even for Edward?"

Arms still folded, Henderson leaned closer. "There could be a million reasons why Edward changed his plan of attack. Perhaps he feels this is a battle he would do well to surrender."

Nausea ran through Anna. Henderson then said, "I can't believe he saw much prudence in David's decision to sue me— or you for that matter."

"Do you think David threatened to sue him, too, maybe his way of forcing us to stop the proceedings?"

Henderson walked to the coat rack beside the door, removed his jacket, and slid his arm into a sleeve. "We could have a wonderful discussion about this over lunch. Come up with an inordinate number of ideas as to why Edward has abandoned this cause." He buttoned his navy jacket.

"You think he has another motive?" A sense of dread glued Anna to the chair. It troubled her to think that Henderson didn't trust or accept Edward's actions. "You think he's up to something?"

"With Edward Manning, you never know." Henderson helped her up. They walked out the door, Henderson closing it behind them. "I think we need to be careful."

Again he checked his watch. "Meet me at Cesar's in an hour. It'll take me twenty minutes to reach the courthouse. If my friend is there," he tapped the folder tucked underneath his arm, "this will get placed at the top of the pile." Henderson Felterfield was known for his multi-level connections that simplified tasks requiring other attorneys what seemed like an act of congress.

Edward maintained those same types of connections. One of those had been with Henderson Felterfield, who until five years earlier, had served as Edward's expert on attorneys. Edward had sought Henderson's counsel when deciding which lawyers he would choose to oversee the various national and international real estate transactions Manning Real Estate handled. Henderson and Edward had also been good friends.

When considering Henderson to represent her in the divorce, Anna had asked him the reason for his and Edward's parting of the ways, both professionally and socially. "I didn't like the way he was treating you," Henderson had said. "I've always respected Edward's business acumen and all that he's accomplished in our community. But you deserved better. I told Edward that."

It hurt Anna to know that Edward's colleagues had seen through the pastiche of their marriage. Yet, Henderson's intimate knowledge on Edward Manning made him the only

12

person, in Anna's eyes, to represent her. They were African-Americans whose parents frowned upon divorce and saw it as a personal, social, and financial failure. Both parties lost when going their separate paths, much of what was sacrificed materially, emotionally, and spiritually never recovered.

"I'll be back in about two hours." Henderson informed Claire. "I'm going to the courthouse then lunch."

He and Anna walked out of the office and toward the elevator. The doors parted. Anna stepped inside. Henderson joined her.

"I don't want you to file the papers," Anna said once the doors were closed. Henderson's mahogany face went blank, and took on an ominous look of confusion. The muscles in his neck flexed. "Give me two hours, at least until four o'clock," Anna said.

"Three." Henderson held up three fingers. "I'll give you until three. By that time, *I'll* have figured out what Edward's up to."

Delivering the documents an hour before the courthouse closed would allow Henderson's friend ample time to work her miracle, a service for which Anna felt certain Henderson quite adequately compensated the young woman.

The elevator stopped. The doors opened. Anna stepped out into the ground lobby.

"I'll speak with you in three and a half hours," Henderson called out.

Anna left the building without looking back.

Chapter 2

Anna entered Edward Manning's office on Clay Street. His secretary, Philomena, was sitting behind her desk.

"I need to speak with Edward," Anna said.

"I'm not sure he's in." Anxiety filled Philomena's cinnamon face.

"Don't lie to me." Anna had caught her skirting the truth of Edward's whereabouts too many times. "I haven't signed the divorce papers. I'm still Edward's wife." Anna placed her hand on Philomena's desk. "I want to see h—"

"Edward's gone for the day. I don't know where he is." Bryce Withers came up the hall. His Italian-cut suit, a dark shade of brown, displayed the nouveau sense of style he had adopted from Edward.

"I need to speak to him," Anna demanded. "Where is he?"

"Is there anything wrong with the divorce documents? I think you'll find that he's been quite generous." *Generous* was not the word. Edward had been *cooperative*, a quality he did not display regarding his marriage.

"I'd like to speak to him," Anna repeated calmly.

"That won't be possible. I'll give him the message. Otherwise . . . " Bryce turned to leave. Fear toiled in Philomena's dark, brown eyes. She gave Anna a knowing look. Philomena had inherited her position as Edward's secretary from her mother, Wyntonia.

"If you don't know where Edward is," Anna called out to Bryce then halfway down the hall, "then how can you give him a message?" Anna walked toward him. "Either you know where he is, or you never plan to convey my message. In either case, you're lying."

A stern look gripped Bryce's auburn face. In manners, he was a perfect David, loyal and firm. Yet if he were to raise his eyebrows, shift the arch of his nose, and add a smile, he'd be a perfect physical rendition of Theo, Anna and Edward's second born. At thirty-five years old, Bryce Withers was two years older than David, and four years older than Theo.

During a meeting four months earlier, Bryce had manhandled Edward into submission after Edward had lunged across the boardroom table and tried to punch Henderson. As always, the inciting factor had been Anna's request not only for a divorce, but also her unrelenting determination to sell the house. She wanted no alimony, which Edward had offered, only proceeds from the sale of the house.

Bryce pocketed his hand. "Edward's *my* client. I'm not required to tell you *anything*."

"No you aren't. But you and I know that the Edward Manning you represented today is not the person he was a month ago."

Bryce's eyes grew sullen and angry, eager to spill over. He was holding a secret and shouldering a burden too big for his ambition no matter how sincere. The consequences for telling what he knew far exceeded the toll it took to maintain his loyalty to Edward. Edward asked this of everyone who worked with him. He demanded it of his family, too.

Anna had been the main puppet in his stronghold. As such, she suffered the greatest casualty, that of losing her dignity and the ability to speak up for herself. She had almost forgotten that she too held desires and passions.

16

Bryce turned toward Edward's office as if looking for an answer then went inside and closed the door.

Anna returned to Philomena. "Where did Bryce park his car?"

"Downstairs, in the garage."

"Does he still drive that black BMW?"

Philomena nodded. Her nervous look was calling out for help. Edward had entangled her and Bryce in his web of deceit.

Anna drove to the garage's entrance and turned off the engine. She was prepared to wait until three o'clock. However, moments later Bryce steered his black BMW sedan out of the garage.

Anna switched on her car and followed him to Highway 580, and then onto the Warren Freeway. She became curious when he took the 51st Street exit and started up Martin Luther King Boulevard toward Berkeley.

Edward had no contracts with properties in the City of Berkeley. He despised Berkeley for all its laws to create equality, appease residents, and control commercial encroachment. "It's always about the citizens of Berkeley, never about the businesses. How do they think they'll ever encourage growth?" Edward had always railed.

Moving at a comfortable speed, Anna's intrigue changed to confusion when Bryce turned onto Dwight Way. Anna had been certain Edward was some distance away. She followed Bryce through the intersection at Milvia. Slowing once more, he turned into the parking lot beside Hammond Hospital. Anna circled around the block to prevent him from seeing her.

Anna had delivered Edward's four children at Hammond. During ensuing years, the hospital merged with Berkeley General. Hammond now housed a cancer treatment center on the first floor and a small mental hospital on the three floors above. Twice, Anna had admitted Linda, their third child, to the adolescent wing. Edward had traveled tremendously at the height of his real estate career, much of that time spent out of the country.

At age fifteen, Linda, who was gifted with the ability to bring a violin to life, had needed both parents. She was sensitive and prone to depression that she expressed through intense irritability that bordered on violence. Linda directed her frustration toward Anna, and then at herself. Linda was also dyslexic. Lacking the ability to make straight A's like her overachieving siblings—their way of compensating for Edward's absences—Linda felt isolated. Nothing Anna offered could provide the balm that only Edward's presence could mend.

One weekend with Edward gone for nearly a month, and Anna questioning why she ever married him, Linda's emotions spun out of control. She cut her left wrist, and then somehow managed to slit the other. For what would be the first of three times, Anna had rushed Linda to Hammond Hospital where she remained for over a month.

Inside the hospital, Anna went to the information desk. "I'm looking for a young man, shaved head, black. He's wearing a tan suit and olive tie."

"Try the clinic." The young Korean receptionist pointed around the corner.

Inquiring of Bryce in the clinic, Anna learned from the nurse, "They've taken his father to the hospital."

"His *father?*" Anna was stunned. Bryce's father was dead, a fact that had drawn Bryce to work for Edward, who had become Bryce's mentor.

"Are you the young man's mother?" the nurse asked.

"Why, yes." Anna gathered herself and furthered the interrogation. "Is Edward not doing well?" Anna took a chance and used Edward's real name.

"Dr. Dana thought it best to admit him to Berkeley General." The nurse looked puzzled.

Anna failed at all the rationalizations she tried forcing upon herself while driving from the cancer center at Hammond Hospital to Berkeley General. Steeped in uncertainty, she walked off the elevator onto the fifth floor of Berkeley General Hospital concerned and fearful.

Had Bryce really come to see Edward? Perhaps Bryce was undergoing treatment, or maybe the nurse had been speaking about someone else, someone both he and Edward knew.

Anna walked to the nurses' station. "I'm looking for Mr. Manning's room, Edward Manning." Everything inside her hoped the nurse would say there was no Edward Manning on the floor.

Instead the nurse said, "He's at the end of the corridor. Last room on the right."

Anna's skin burned with fear and dread. Steadily she approached the door, her right hand clutching the strap of the purse hanging from her shoulder.

Her chest sank on hearing Edward's voice. "Get the fuck out of here! I don't want that shit. Get it away from me!"

"You've got to take this, Edward. Let them help you." It was Bryce.

"I don't have to let them do anything. And don't try that *Edward* crap with me. It's *Mr. Manning* to you. I'm old enough to be your old man."

"You are old enough to be my father. That's why—"

"Shut up and get the hell out of here."

Anna forced herself toward the hospital room. Reaching the doorway, she edged inside. A second, more intense, wave of nausea overtook her. Edward was lying on the hospital bed, his eyes full of fear and anger at being unable to control the situation.

All heads turned to her. A moment of silence passed. Glancing back at Edward, Bryce moved to stand, then said to the nurse, "This is Mr. Manning's wife."

"Ex-wife," Edward said as Anna flashed her palm to Bryce indicating for him to remain seated. "Anna is my ex-wife," Edward finished.

The young nurse with cropped sandy hair smiled and extended her hand to Anna. "I'm Rachel, Mr. Manning's nurse for this shift. I was helping him get settled."

"It's good to meet you," Anna managed.

Rachel turned back to Edward, and said, "I'll check on you later," then left.

Awkwardness set in. Bryce was avoiding Anna's gaze as she said to him, "Could I perhaps have a moment with my husband?"

Walking past her, he left, closing the door behind him.

Anna drew a chair to Edward's bedside. Moments passed as she considered the nature of their situation. Barely able to keep track of her thoughts, her mind settled.

"When did you think I would find out? Better yet, when did you *want* me to find out?" she asked.

"Never, if I had my way." Edward stared at the ceiling.

"Now that you *haven't* told me, what can I do to help?"

"Nothing short of making my chemotherapy work. Or take this cancer out of me." He turned to the window spanning the wall across the room.

"What are the doctors saying?"

"Six months, perhaps only three."

Anna caught her breath and fought back tears. Fifteen months earlier she had filed for divorce. With their children educated, working, and three of them married, she had wanted nothing more to do with Edward and the life they had created.

No more regretting that she had not applied to graduate school during her senior year in college, and had instead, married an up-and-coming real estate agent. That life was coming to an end, along with the hopes and wishes shattered by the disappointment of reality, and her new life was transitioning from wife to divorcee as Anna had configured.

"I'm sorry," Anna said. "I never wanted it to be this way.

"Nor did I," said Edward. "Neither did I." He continued staring at the ceiling, Anna wanting to hold him and say all would be okay, and yet knowing that it would not.

Chapter 3

Three hours had come and gone following her graduation from San Francisco State when Anna introduced Edward to her parents, Elena and Reverend Elijah Chason. The four had eaten dinner together; Anna to the right of her mother at one end, and Edward to the right of Reverend Elijah at the other end.

Edward conversed about his work in real estate since graduating Cal Berkeley two years earlier. Elena had said little. Her sharp eyes remained perched upon Edward as if she were an eagle, and he a fish that she was about to swoop down upon, lift from the river, and devour.

Moments after Edward had left, Reverend Elijah retreated to the bedroom for prayer. Anna went to her mother who was sitting in the living room. Elena had been crocheting, her thin fingers moving smooth and meticulously. "I'm going back to San Francisco in the morning, to the courthouse," Anna said. "I'm meeting Edward. We're getting married."

"I hope you're not pregnant." Elena's fingers never slowed, her eyes remaining focused upon interweaving the strands of white and yellow yarn with her needle.

"Why would you think that?" Anna lowered herself onto the chair next to her mother. The clear plastic that covered the chair crackled underneath her. Plastic also covered the sofa and the chair on which Elena sat.

"We all need affection," she said without looking up. " . . . *a show of love.*" Elena had no affection toward Elijah or Anna. Affection was a commonality that bound Anna to her father. Bitterness, anger, and resentment were cloaked in Elena's commitment to God. Anna had experienced her mother through a veneer of austerity that was stitched together by axioms such as *Pride goeth before destruction. Godliness is next to cleanliness. To God be the Glory. For I am nothing.* Elena crinkled her forehead. "I just hope you didn't marry for the sake of a child just to give a name to *someone* you hope will love you."

Child. Someone. Anna's head spun with the words. That's what she had been to her mother. She slid back in her chair. The plastic crackled once more. *Waste not, want not.*
Elena continued weaving the yarn as Anna took in the ordered fashion of the room.

The sepia-colored framed photo of Elena's mother was at one end of the fireplace mantel and a photo of Reverend Elijah's father at the other end. The oak floor, like the mantel, had been devoid of dust. The Bible had been carefully centered upon the coffee table.

Anna recalled meeting Edward. It had been mid-January 1971, nearly three years in the wake of Martin Luther King's assassination, and for African Americans—a decade behind their Euro-American counterparts—the dawning of their sexual revolution during which they had been exploring the limits of their power.

Twenty years old, Anna Nell Chason had been at a party hosted by a mutual friend when she caught Edward's stolid gaze across the room. One year after graduating Cal Berkeley, he had seemed self-absorbed, held hostage by whatever imprisoned his thoughts. The loneliness Anna sensed enshrouding him had awakened her own hidden ache. She had wanted to heal him. Anna transferred her hopes and wishful desires of passion, the show of love she needed from Elena, to Edward whose financial ambitions burned with a fire that was lit by the poverty of spirit that also dwelled in Elena.

Three weeks after they met on that cold, damp winter night in San Francisco, she and Edward began sleeping together. Anna had barely entered the spring semester of her junior year when she had placed her breast in his hands. Edward had settled his lips to hers, she supping, and he drinking to his fill from the river of unmet needs rising between them.

"I'm pulling out," he had said between kisses. He'd been referring to his decision to quit working for a San Francisco real estate company that had employed him since graduating college. The owner of the firm, a Jewish man who had escaped Germany during World War II, had mentored Edward during the last twelve months. Three weeks earlier Edward had received his license to sell real estate under his own name.

"Don't," Anna had not been speaking of the company. Edward plunged deeper into her, his life source feeding her desires and sealing their moment of closeness.

In the aftermath of their lovemaking, he explained. "I grew up not knowing what meal would be my last, and afraid that we wouldn't survive. Every day Mama came home with almost as little as she had when she left that morning. Seems like the rent was always due. She was always handing over her checks to the landlord.

We had no bank account. What little money, if any was left, went for food." The icy stoicism that had caught Anna's attention and drawn her to Edward overtook him. His body appeared to go hard like an arrow.

He clinched his jaw. "She worked for a doctor, cleaned his office, and the offices of the other doctors." Edward seemed sad. Then a bitter anger arose. "She was also his mistress, the doctor who hired her. He gave her drugs, prescriptions, to keep her going. She loved him."

The stimulants and relaxants Violet Manning received from the doctor delivered a semblance of balance in a world that was strewn with poverty, disrespect, and overwork, yet it never allowed her to reach a plateau of freedom.

"He got her other cleaning jobs. That's how we made it." The light that had burned in Edward's amber pupils from moments earlier when discussing plans for his real estate business drained from his eyes. Anna felt death sliding over her body.

Craving to escape her mother, she reached for Edward's hand, drew up the covers, and nudged into his chest. She kissed him. He entered her again. The more Anna received of Edward, the more she wanted. And so it continued until Anna's graduation.

Anna and Edward had been seeing each other for a nearly a year and a half when Anna graduated college. Anna's parents had headed back to their car once the commencement services were finished.

It was Mother's Day 1972 and Anna's heart was full of determination not to return to where she had started. An ache spread through her chest as she walked with Edward. He had sat in a different section of the stadium away from Elena and Reverend Elijah during the graduation services. He would be driving her home to meet them in an hour.

Anna had given herself to this man and revealed her vulnerability. With no job prospects, she would be dependent on her parents, something she hadn't thought of when committing to art history as her major. Still wearing her graduation gown, and with cap in hand, she said, "Where do we go from here?"

"There's not much I can offer you." Edward pocketed his hands and angled the heel of his right shoe toward the pavement. "I'm not what you think."

"I can't go back there," Anna said, speaking of home. "I won't."

"With this degree," Edward opened her diploma and perused it, "You could do a lot with a house."

Like turn it into a museum? Anna silently mused. Or make it a home. She had loved studying the art treasures of

Rome, Greece, and Northern Africa and the masterpieces housed in the Louvre of Paris and other museums around Europe.

"I'm not your father," Edward said. "I'm immunized against poverty. I may die poor, but it won't be because I haven't tried." Anna quelled the cautious excitement pouring into her stomach. "I'll give you a home," he said. "No matter what it takes."

We all need a show of affection, devotion, a home. Elena's words would remain alive long after Anna introduced Edward to her parents.

Throughout her marriage, with Edward away on long business trips, she would recall her determination not to return to living with her parents.

Chapter 4

A young man with the name Dr. Grimes embroidered above the pocket of his white coat entered the hospital room.

"This is my oncologist," Edward said.

Anna stood and extended her hand. "Anna Manning. Edward's wife."

"Paul Grimes. Pleased to meet you." The young physician's eyes glittered with surprise. He glanced down upon Edward lying in bed, and then back to Anna. "Will you be helping Edward in the coming weeks?"

"It's time for you to go, Grimes," Edward barked.

"As your physician, Mr. Manning, I have to ask these questions."

"Don't try that shit with me. *Mr. Manning* is for an old man. I'm not dead yet." Edward threw back the covers, swung his legs around, and placed both feet on the floor. "You'll get the answers when I give them." The contradiction Edward exhibited toward being called Mr. Manning surprised Anna.

"Okay, Edward, let's talk about what the next couple of months are going to be like in that—"

Edward stood. "You may be knowledgeable in what you're doing, but one thing you seemed to have forgotten, Dr. Grimes, is that this is still *my life*." Edward poked his forefinger on his chest pointing to himself. "These next few months are *mine*."

"I don't think he meant it that way," Anna chided Edward.

"The only way he can help me is to continue my chemo. And since he won't do that—" Edward brushed past Grimes and headed for the closet.

"Where will you go?" the young oncologist asked.

"I sure as hell won't die here." Edward began pulling his clothes from the hangers.

"Contrary to what you may think," Grimes said on approaching Edward, "I care about my patients, each and every one of them. I want to know what's going to happen to them once they leave the hospital."

"You mean you feel guilty for having failed at your job, giving me the death slip," Edward said.

"Mr. Manning, *Edward*, the chemo is not working." The oncologist spoke to Edward's back.

"I said I'd pay for more." Edward turned from dressing; fear shadowed the amber hue of his eyes. Edward was fighting a battle that neither his money nor his craftiness or expertise could help him win.

"I can't give the order for more chemo," Grimes said. "I won't."

Edward clinched his fist.

"Your system can't tolerate another round," Grimes said. "The chemotherapy is robbing you of valuable time. You may have already lost weeks. It's killing you." The oncologist's shoulders slumped.

A solemn silence overtook the room. Like Bryce and all young men who worked under Edward Manning, Dr. Grimes had submitted himself as one of Edward's followers. He revered Edward as a god. Now life had summoned the deity from his pedestal to enter the world of mortals.

What can I ever say to David and Theo? Anna pondered.

Outside Edward's hospital room, Grimes explained the prognosis. "Mrs. Manning, your husband—"

"Please call me Anna."

A faint smile stole upon Grimes' lips. The nametag above the pocket covering his heart seemed to pulsate. "Anna, your husband is dying from advanced stage gall bladder cancer."

"How much time does he have?"

"Five months at the most, six if we're lucky," Grimes said.

It was then late August. Anna took in a deep breath. Her heart settled.

"In my estimation, three is your safest bet for clearing up all financial and emotional matters."

Anna's hands grew cold. She felt even more nauseated. She looked at the nameplate beside the doorway, *Edward Manning*, then glimpsed at Edward back in the hospital room. He was fully dressed and ready to leave.

"This is hard work you do," she said to Grimes.

"Patients like your husband are the worst."

"You don't have to tell me that. I was married to him for over thirty years." Anna fought back tears with a bitter smile.

"I thought you were still married." Grimes frowned. "You said you were his wife."

"Technically, I am. We've been undergoing divorce proceedings for the last year." Anna glanced at her watch. Two-thirty. Henderson would be filing the papers at 3 pm. She needed to call him.

"I appreciate your honesty." Anna ended the conversation and started back to Edward's room.

"Anna," the young oncologist called after her, "what I said about Edward being the most difficult of patients—I didn't

29

mean that in a negative way." He walked toward her. "People like your husband have fight, spirit, and gumption. They're willing to work with their doctor." A misty sheen slid over Grimes' dark eyes. His brown face took on a sad glow. "But despite everything, I can't save them."

"I know." Anna touched Dr. Grimes' hand and left.

Nurses whisked past Anna as she moved in stride with the family members of other patients and continued toward the end of the corridor. Reaching an alcove, she sat on the couch and dialed Henderson.

"I was worried," he answered when Anna spoke.

"I'm here at the hospital with Edward."

"Hospital?"

"It's a long story. No, in fact, it's quite short. Edward is dying of cancer."

Henderson's silence revealed his shock.

"I don't want you to file the divorce papers," she said.

"Are you sure about this?"

"No. But I don't want you to fight me. You still have the papers?"

"I do."

"And you can file them any time?"

"Whenever you ask, but Anna—"

"Then, that's the way I want it. Don't tell Bryce. Don't tell Edward. Not even the children."

~*~*~*~

Bryce stood as Anna reentered Edward's room. Edward was sitting on the bed. Bryce and Edward were eyeing each other, waiting for the other to speak the next words in this futile battle.

"I should be on my way," Edward's young apprentice said. He appeared more frustrated than ever. "I have a couple of papers to file at the courthouse."

"Would that be Edward's will and trust?" Anna said. Bryce glanced over at Edward who had begun fumbling with his tie. Receiving no response, Anna said, "There'll be time for that later I suppose." Anna shuddered. A chill overtook her as she considered her words.

Bryce sighed and left. Edward unzipped the black duffel holding his clothes.

Anna closed the door, slid a chair to the bed, and sat. "Well, what do you want to do?" She interwove her fingers.

"For now, leave this place." He let go of the zipper of his duffel. "No one here seems to be willing or able to help me." He turned to the window across the room.

Joining him, Anna looked through the window to the garden beyond. A ring of stones encircled a bed of violets. Their bright purple petals shimmered in the Northern California sun now past its zenith.

"They're beautiful," Anna said.

"Hmmm."

"Looks like the garden that was outside my room at Hammond. It held geraniums," Anna said. "I promised myself after the birth of each one of the children that when I got home I'd plant some flowers, geraniums, roses, irises, pansies, whatever." She knew nothing about flowers or planting other than how to adore them. "A bed of flowers for each of the children, each with its own type."

"What stopped you?"

"Time. Never had enough. Someone always needed their braces tightened. There was a soccer match I needed to drive them to. Or a violin recital." Anna cringed at the thought of pain her children would feel when learning their father was dying. "I committed to giving," she said.

"It's your nature."

And yours was to take. Anna's heart pounded with the thought, old angers fuming to the surface. A wash of memories flooded her. I was a fool. I endured sleepless nights alone at home with the kids while Edward was in South America wining and dining the women he'd romped and played with. He was their greatest monarch.

Edward zipped his bag closed.

"What are you going to do?" She rephrased the question.

"I won't die here. Not in this hospital." The look in Edward's eyes became that of a little boy, not unlike David on the many occasions when Edward had been away and he asked, "Mommy, why are you crying? Do you miss Daddy? Why isn't he here? When I grow up, I'm never going to let you cry."

Minutes later Dr. Grimes returned. A young woman in a long, white coat accompanied him.

"Edward, Anna. This is Mrs. Reid, the hospice liaison," Grimes said. "She's going to talk to Edward about his plans at home."

"That's easy," Edward said. "I live in a two-bedroom apartment. I figure I'll pay someone to come in when I . . ."

"It's not that simple, Mr . . ." she thumbed through the papers in her hand.

"Manning," Edward said. "Edward Manning."

Anna stood and offered the hospice worker her chair. She went outside. Grimes followed.

"We do this with all our clients," Grimes explained. "It's hardest for the ones who live alone."

Anna considered what had once been their home. It was now a house filled with rented furniture staged to show potential buyers how happy they could be living there.

Anna scanned the white wall behind Grimes. The name beside the door, Manning, Edward, beamed ever brighter. She imagined the headstone Edward Manning April 30, 194__ . . . Life is strange, Anna conjured. I could die before him.

"I'll take him home," Anna said. "He can die with me."

"I thought the two of you were divorcing."

"I haven't signed the papers yet." Anna turned to leave. She needed to call the children.

"Anna." Grimes again caught up with her. She flipped her cell phone closed. "It's a lot to handle, caring for a person who's dying, the man you're divorcing, no doubt. Edward has less than six months, maybe only three, to live. If you think—"

"He's been my husband for thirty-four years. His fifty-sixth birthday is in February. And you're telling me he might not make it."

32

Somberness slid over Grimes' eyes. "Death does strange things to people."

"Are you speaking of me or Edward?"

"Both. During my training in the emergency room, I saw patients die suddenly. Their families were unable to say important things to them like 'I forgive you. Don't worry. Let it go. I love you.'

And then, there were those who died suddenly with everything said that needed to have been spoken. On the oncology floor, I see families come together and heal wounds that only the awareness of impending death can mend. I've also seen the opposite. Those who know their death is imminent, and denial is the only thing holding them together."

"Are you saying I'm in denial about Edward's condition?"

"Emotions influence how we see things," Grimes said.

A burning sensation rose from Anne's stomach. "Am I speaking to Dr. Grimes, Edward's oncologist, or the young man who has come to admire my husband?"

"Edward is dying. And you're about to divorce him. The last thing he needs is promises *you* can't deliver."

"And unless you can tell me without a shadow of a doubt that he has the slightest chance of surviving this—"

"I can't but—"

"Then let me, his wife, give him what he needs."

"For the last year, you've fought to leave him. What makes you think you can care for him now?"

"For the thirty-four years prior to this, I held down a home while Edward traveled the world and made love to any woman who suited him. I can handle this."

Grimes' nostrils flared as he inhaled. Swallowing, he pressed his lips together.

"Now if you don't mind, I need to speak with my husband." Anna eased back to the doorway where the voices of the hospice liaison and Edward grew clear and distinct.

"People find it difficult to contemplate their own death. Even those of us who work in the field," the social worker said to Edward.

"If anyone is to be prepared, I figured it would be someone like you or Dr. Grimes." Gone was the anger and torment in Edward's voice. A chord of acceptance had taken its place.

"None of us are ready, Mr. Manning."

"Please. Call me Edward."

A lumped formed in Anna's throat. She forced herself to breathe.

Chapter 5

Anna turned the key in the lock and pushed open the front door of the house she and Edward had shared for over three decades. They had moved there a year after David was born. She took a deep breath.

Closing the door, she wondered what potential buyers saw when entering. A vase of silk roses stood on the table against the left wall where David used to drop his books after school. The younger siblings, Theo, Linda, and Serine stacked theirs underneath.

When home and not traveling, Edward would stand his briefcase at the edge of their piles.

Anna removed her shoes and climbed the stairs at the end of the foyer. The newly shampooed carpet comforted her aching feet. Reaching the landing, she inspected each of the bedrooms also filled with rental furniture and arranged to the decorator's command.

"She knows what she's doing," Anna had said of the interior decorator when first seeing the layout of furniture in the house.

Elise McKinney, a childhood friend with whom Anna had graduated Holy Names High School, and then San Francisco State University, had recommended the decorator who staged the house. Elise was Anna's real estate agent. When Anna handed Elise the check to pay for the home staging service and the rental of the furniture, Elise pushed it back, gave Anna a smirk, and said, "Not until you've divorced Edward and this house is sold. Then you can pay."

Anna returned downstairs. Her feet soaked up the softness of the carpet as she tried to ward off the memories lying beneath. She was dialing Elise when the doorbell rang. With the phone to her ear, she ran to the door and opened it. Elise stepped inside, and dropped her bag on the foyer table. "My phone's ringing." She dug inside the bag.

"It's me." Anna closed her phone.

"Oh, you were calling?"

"Yeah." Anna padded back to the kitchen.

Elise closed the bag, removed her shoes, and followed. "So, how was the meeting this morning? Please tell me Edward and Bryce showed up."

"They did."

"Any progress?" Accustomed to the routine of Edward's stall tactics, Elise set hands to her hips. "Or what new rabbit trick did Bryce offer you and Henderson today?"

Anna removed one of the three glasses she had left in the cabinet by the sink, and filled it with water. Elise joined her at the sink. Anna sipped her water and took in the backyard swimming pool that had been drained. She had instructed Elise to include the patio furniture in the asking price.

"I guarantee if you fill that pool we can get ten thousand, maybe twenty more," Elise said.

Anna didn't respond.

"Anna?" Elise tapped her nails upon the counter.

Anna sat her glass on the cool, marble counter top. "I don't want to sell the house. Take it off the market."

"What did you say?"

"I don't want to sell the house. It's not for sale, at least not right now."

"Then, when?" Elise frowned against her voice rising.

"I don't know, but not now." She padded back to the foyer. "Send me a bill for your time, the decorator, and the rental furniture. I'll have Henderson cut you a check."

Again Elise frowned as she followed.

"Anna, what happened in the meeting this morning?"

Anna slid her foot into her shoe.

"Let's just say, I can't sell the house. Not right now."

"Why? What about all the bills you owe? Just yesterday you were dying to unload it."

The word *unload* tore through Anna's mind, bringing with it shocks of pain and joy that she'd experienced in the house. "This house is not a burden."

"Excuse me?" Elise knitted her brows. "But you've been complaining these last fifteen months about how Edward's been stalling with the divorce and holding up the sale of the house. Now you're giving in? What did he say to you this morning?" Again, she perched hands upon her hips. Elise never liked Edward. "Anna, what did he do?"

"Nothing. Except having signed the divorce papers."

"He signed the divorce papers and . . . ?"

"He also gave me the house."

"And why, pray tell, do you want it off the market?"

"Because, as I said, I don't want to sell it. I won't. Not right now."

"This makes no sense."

"I need it," Anna said.

"So Edward gave you the house." Elise brought her fingers to her temple. She began pacing. "You've decided to not sell it, at least not for now? What about France?" Elise whipped around.

"I'm not going. I can't. I've got to stay here and take care of Edward." The words slipped out.

"Edward?" Elise gestured with her hands and frowned, the lines deepening in her face. Elise had held Anna throughout bouts of depression during the time of Edward's constant absence when Anna felt overwhelmed with the children's needs. "What's he done now?" Elise asked.

"Nothing, except set me free."

"And you're choosing to stay in bondage?"

"I'm going to help him."

"To do what? Destroy you? That's all he's ever set out to do. Edward Manning's one intent is to make everyone he's around as miserable as —"

"He has cancer," Anna said. "Edward has cancer. He's dying."

"Serves him right." Elise pursed her lips and arched her thin frame.

"Elise, please."

Anna turned from her friend. She envied Elise's body, and regretted having given so much of herself to Edward and their kids. She had nursed the children from infant stage into toddlerhood and many times ate the leftovers of four- and five-year-olds rather than preparing a decent meal for herself. Eighteen months ago she had joined the gym.

Three months later, she announced that she wanted a divorce and retained Henderson to represent her. The slowness in shedding the extra pounds had forced her to continue exercising at the gym to relieve the stress of the divorce. Anna had entered her seventh month of exercising and was four months into the divorce proceedings when she'd met Inman Hayes at the gym. Just released from the hospital after a severe car accident, he'd come there for his first physical therapy appointment.

"Does Inman know?" Elise probed.

"No. I only learned two hours ago."

"You do plan to tell him?"

"I have to."

"You're playing a dangerous game. Inman loves you. He's offering you your first chance at happiness. Now you're turning around and—"

"Edward's dying."

"Let the dead bury the dead."

Anna arched her brows.

"I watched you make the horrible decision of marrying Edward Manning, and all that's resulted," Elise said. "None of us liked him. Least of all your mother."

"She was a horrible judge of character."

"And all of the rest of us were, too?"

Anna folded her arms and turned toward the window that opened onto the patio next to the empty pool.

"You think I don't know?" Elise grasped Anna's arms.

Anna shook her head in another attempt to free herself from what Elise was making all too explicit.

"You have spent your entire life trying to be with Edward Manning when he doesn't even know how to be with himself. He's arrogant and self-absorbed, has had more affairs than you have under panties, and he's still not happy."

Elise continued. "At least you took the time to wash your lingerie. He just kept moving forward, never looking back at the damage he caused. You had enough and broke free of him. Now with a chance at happiness and everything you've wanted, you're forfeiting it all for Edward?"

"It's not that simple. The children love their father," Anna defended. "I can't abandon him, not now."

"And you don't think they love you if you don't continue to sacrifice your life for Edward?" Elise touched Anna's shoulder and heaved a deep sigh. "The children need you. Thank God Linda found Brad and has someone to focus on her. You were so obsessed with Edward."

"I never ignored my children or their needs." Anna stepped back and steadied herself against the impact of Elise's implication. "I was always there for them, most of all Linda."

"If that's the case, why do you think she tried to commit suicide?" Elise asked. "And Serine—she was always crying and begging me to explain why you were so unhappy. Don't tell me it was because she was the last one home." Elise grasped Anna's arms.

Anna pulled away.

Elise said, "Everyone knew what Edward was doing. David, Theo, Linda, and Serine were well aware as children what Edward was putting you through by being away all the time—and with God knows who. It's amazing he didn't give you some kind of disease."

"That's enough." Anna whipped around.

"It was one thing for Edward to have all those affairs. Quite another for you to try and pretend he wasn't." Elise heaved a sigh. "If what you say is true, that Edward is truly dying, then you'd better toughen up, because you are all the children have ever really had."

Elise softened her voice. "Stop chasing a dream that'll never materialize. The children need you. *You* need you. Go through with the divorce, sell the house, take Inman, and leave for France the way you planned."

A knock sounded at the front door. Then it opened. Supported by his cane, Inman stepped in.

"What a pleasant surprise." Elise plastered a smile on her face. Anna took a deep breath and gathered herself. "I can't believe you're still using that thing." Elise greeted Inman with a light peck on the cheek.

"It's what keeps Anna around, and me in her good graces." He approached Anna.

"I was telling Anna—" Elise started.

"She was just leaving." Anna eyed her friend sternly.

"Fill that pool and—" Elise gave a crumpled smile. The house grew silent. Elise broke the stillness by glancing at her watch. "I do have to meet another client." She kissed Anna's cheek, and whispered, "Call me."

"And send me that bill," Anna said.

"Like I said . . . " Elise nodded her head, shook her forefinger at Anna, and left.

Anna walked through the open sliding glass door and to Inman who was leaning upon his cane as he studied the empty pool.

"Seems Elise has better plans for the house," Inman said.

"She wants to make a sale."

He brushed his cane beside the pool. "And you don't?"

"Not right this minute." Anna walked further onto the patio that was bathed in late afternoon sunlight and lowered herself into one of the chairs. Joining her, Inman laid his cane aside. Anna took in his smooth cinnamon face. His thick eyebrows and long lashes underscored his childlike eagerness to trust and attempt things new. Yet, Inman was no pushover. Nor was he naïve.

"You know how when you've always wanted something," Anna started, "and you were certain that if you got it, it would set you free? Everything would be right in the world, no more mistakes, no more wrong turns. You'd have figured out everything you needed to know, what you missed as a child. Then, you could live your life."

Inman smiled. His beige sweater swathed his chest and complemented his warm brown eyes. Anna's heart pounded. His easy manner and methodical caring always calmed Anna and left her feeling safe. She grew warm.

Inman said, "What is it you've figured out?"

Anna turned toward the pool. "I've never understood why I was so unhappy, what kept me from being like everyone else, forceful, ambitious, out in life accomplishing something instead of standing on the sidelines, deliberating, and fearful of making the wrong move."

Inman's smile remained.

"I'm still on the sidelines," Anna said. "I've yet to figure out what will make me happy."

Inman tugged at his chin, surveyed the grounds and then looked back to Anna. "How did the meeting go today with Edward and Bryce?"

Anna took in a breath and swallowed. "Edward agreed to the divorce. He deeded me the house. I also discovered he has cancer. He has six, maybe only three months to live."

Inman cast his attention downward.

"I want to bring him home, let him live out his time in the house."

"Has he agreed?"

"I haven't told him," Anna conceded.

"Do you still love him?" Inman turned to her.

41

"I don't know. Truly, I don't." Anna appreciated Inman and wanted all she could have of him, but she couldn't lie to him. She envied the calm silence displayed upon his smooth, brown face.

His sharp mustache reflected an old world air of distinction. She had imagined them walking the streets of Calais and Paris, and roaming the museums of Rome and Florence.

They would disappear into a new life, Anna leaving behind the pain of hers, and letting Inman love her. She had relinquished all hope of ever doing these things with Edward.

"What are you going to do about our plans?" Inman broke the silence.

Anna peered back into the kitchen, redolent with foaming memories that she wished to reach out and touch or transform. "I want to go to France. I want to leave all this behind and forget that it ever happened."

"But, you need to be clear about your life with Edward, your marriage, and what it never achieved."

Inman had raised Dancia, his daughter and only child after his wife abandoned them. Two years later, his wife was killed in an auto accident equal to the magnitude of the one he had recently suffered and survived. Inman had experienced the nagging doubt that slithered into one's life when destiny darted onto uncharted paths.

"I grew angry when I found out that Marian had been killed," Inman said. "I was angrier then than I was when she'd served me with divorce papers stating she didn't want Dancia. This wasn't supposed to happen to me. It couldn't. I rationalized."

Inman explained. "I'm a Wharton MBA with a great job and bright future. How could she leave me? She's not leaving me. She's a fool who doesn't know what she's got." Inman gave a bittersweet smile. "I used all the excuses I could find and concocted the ones I couldn't." He leaned back and glanced down at his cane.

"It wasn't until I had the car accident last year, two decades after Marian was killed, that I realized what had been there all along."

Anna bit her lip. Inman lifted his cane, stood, and then leaned over and kissed her. She wanted to pull him back, rip off his clothes and make love to him right there on the patio.

"Call me when you've done what you need to," Inman said. "Let me know when you've it figured out."

He went back inside the house, his limp barely noticeable, and saw himself out the front door.

Chapter 6

Anna was in Edward's hospital room. The shades were drawn and the darkness of night had descended.

"Edward," Anna called his name. "I want us to move back in the house. Let me care for you."

Edward appeared about to cry. "Thank you." His lips trembled.

Unable to witness his brokenness, Anna stood and said, "I'll let Dr. Grimes know—unless you want to tell him."

He shook his head no.

Later with Dr. Grimes, Anna explained. "He's agreed to let me take care of him. He seems relieved with the decision."

"I'll inform the social worker," Grimes said as he laid his hand upon Anna's shoulder. "I'm sorry for earlier. Dying takes a lot of energy and focus."

"I thought it was *life* that was hard." Anna blinked to fight back tears.

"It's hard to live knowing that the time is drawing near when you will no longer see your friends and family. Most patients don't want to know. Neither do their families."

"Would you want to know?"

"I'm not sure."

Anna frowned at Grime's words.

"I guess it depends on where you are in your life and how much you can handle," he said. "Then there's the nature of your relationships, most specifically the one with yourself. As for myself, I try to live each day knowing death is near, *and* that I have time." A crinkled smile formed upon his lips. "Some days I succeed. Others, well . . ." Again, he patted Anna's shoulder. "Edward's strong. And so are you. Call if you need anything."

Edward remained in the hospital from Wednesday night through the weekend. Anna split her time between visiting him and preparing the house for his return. Movers from the rental company arrived early Saturday morning and emptied the house of the various pieces of new and shiny furniture.

Three hours later, delivery men from the warehouse brought in bureaus, tables, and sofas from a life Anna had presumed gone. Under her careful direction, the warehouse delivery men returned each item to its rightful place, beginning with the upstairs and ending with the first floor rooms. Anna signed the service agreement and led the head warehouse delivery man to the door.

"Thank you," she said.

"Hope you have better luck selling your house later," he said.

She smiled and after shaking his hand, she closed the door.

Feeling an internal pull, she detoured from heading to the kitchen and instead entered what used to be Edward's study. Seated at the desk, she ran her fingers along its edge and observed the mahogany surface now void of papers and folders.

She grew sad as she recalled the loneliness that had filled the house and driven her to seek divorce. So many times she had wished to lay Edward upon the desk, climb onto his body, and force him to make love to her. His countless absences had fertilized her empty sense of longing that was rooted in her childhood with Elena. Anna yearned to greet love simmered by a flame of passion as intense as her commitment to giving.

Anna closed her eyes in response to her body growing moist and warm. During the last six months while feeling doomed to fighting Edward for the divorce and trying to sell the house, Anna had been intimate numerous times with Inman. Paradoxically, her body now ached for Edward. As a fifty-three-year-old mother of four and grandmother of two, she felt ashamed of the twists and turns of her desires.

Sixteen months had passed since Anna had last entered the study and observed Edward at his desk. She had brought him a cup of coffee, decaf since it was after dark, and lowered it carefully to the surface. Engrossed with the documents he'd been reading, he never looked up.

Neither had he acknowledged the coaster she had moments later slid underneath the cup just inches from his hand. He continued to review the documents, never thanked Anna. She had wanted so much for him to see her and the new negligee revealing her new figure minus the pounds she had worked hard to shed.

He stood up and announced, "I'm going to bed."

He had nearly reached the stairs when Anna called after him, "So this is just a holding place for you, this house?"

He stopped, and with brows knitted, turned and faced her.

"You know, like the airline clubs for frequent fliers, a place in the airport where you go during a layover. I hear they're very nice. None of the noise from the regular travelers. *Clean.* Members like you don't have to worry about running into anyone you don't want to see. Then, again if anyone you know is also a member—"

His amber eyes had grown cold, piercing like that of a hungry eagle holding a wellspring of anger edging toward the boiling point. Then, as if losing vitality, he resumed his trek to the staircase and started the climb.

"I want a divorce," Anna called out. "I want to sell the house."

"Don't even try." He whipped around.

"I should think you'd be happy to get rid of me and this prison, this holding cell. Then you can be—"

"I've given you everything I own. This house and the life in it." Edward rushed down the stairs. "This house is mine." He pointed to the floor and then aimed his finger to the ceiling.

"You're never around."

"There's nothing to be around for."

"More the reason I want a divorce and to sell the house."

"You won't sell a goddamned thing," he ranted, inches from her face.

"This house is part mine." It was the only thing Anna wanted money from. With their children now adults and either working or married, she needed no child support. She would work. Anna needed no alimony. She wanted a clean break.

"My blood, sweat, and tears went into this house," Edward said. "You will not sell it." He returned to the staircase, and with what seemed the sum of determination encompassing his life, started up.

"It would be nothing if I hadn't been here to maintain it."

"And whose money built, paid for, and maintained it?" Again, he whirled around.

"I'm through with this charade of a marriage. I want out and I want my share," Anna said.

"Then leave." He continued up. "But, you won't take the house." On reaching the landing, he headed down the hall toward their bedroom.

Anna spent the night in what had been Theo's room. A week later, and with Edward away, she asked Edward's former attorney and friend, Henderson Felterfield, to represent her in divorcing Edward.

"Say no more," Henderson had said. "Edward's my friend. We go back a long way. But he's done you wrong. I've watched you put up with his antics the entire length of this marriage. He's given more attention to the fine print of foreign land purchases than to your needs." Henderson's lips had been terse, the rich curves of his mahogany face appearing to hold a rage behind its placidity that both touched and struck Anna with awe. "He's disrespectful and unappreciative. At our ages, we have to start doing better." Henderson immediately served notice to Edward's office.

Edward arrived home at the end of the week to find a For Sale sign in the front yard and the locks changed. Irate, he made his demands known the next day through his assistant and attorney, Bryce. No divorce.

A month into the proceedings, Henderson informed Anna, "Edward's agreed to the divorce, but he doesn't want you to sell the house. And with you having refused alimony, a divorce without the sale of the house leaves you penniless."

Anna had resisted Henderson's urging that she allow him to pursue half the proceeds from Manning Real Estate to be paid either in one lump sum based on the worth of the business, or in monthly payments.

"I only want the divorce and half the sale of the house." Anna contended. "It's all I need to start over.

"But the alimony Edward's offering is worth much more than half the proceeds from the sale of the house, a hefty sum in and of itself."

Anna considered all the women with whom Edward had been, the anonymous phone calls, unexplained lingerie purchases, expensive meals that had fed more than clients and potential ones. "I want to be free of him and the house—its memories, joys, and hurts," she said.

The house had been a holding ground, a repository for what was to have been but would never exist. Her hopes had been born and lost in the house over which she and Edward had contended. Dashed by his unfaithfulness and constant absence— even when physically present—she wanted to be rid of the house and released from the prison in which she had been incarcerated during her marriage.

Henderson's eager willingness to help left Anna feeling his pity. Despite all her discretion and cool exterior, people knew of Edward's behavior and what she had endured. She had been the laughing stock of their community. Six weeks later and sitting in Henderson's office, Anna felt that same pity toward Edward when reading his demands as presented by Bryce.

Plaintiff agrees to wife's request for divorce. Plaintiff contests sale of house.

Three lines down.

Plaintiff states that house in question is the one and only home he and his children have known. Plaintiff wants to maintain house as a central meeting place for direct offspring and future generations that arise from his offspring.

"The kids have their own homes." Anna had lifted her head to Henderson. Edward's request left so much unstated.

Edward fought the divorce by making the sale of the house his battleground.

Once more, Anna ran her fingers across the mahogany desk and beheld her reflection on the surface. The last year had sped by. She was speaking less and less to her children, avoiding their calls, and not returning their messages. Eventually, they stopped calling. She had called each of them in between directing the movers on where to replace the furniture. She had told them, "Your father has cancer." She had explained the prognosis, then after their sighs, tears, and whimpers said, "I'm bringing him home day after tomorrow."

Now caught by the reflection of her eyes on the desk, she wondered, What will I say when they arrive?

Chapter 7

Monday morning, Anna drove her car to the front of Berkeley General where Edward sat in a wheelchair and a hospital attendant stood beside him. The attendant opened the door and Edward, on bidding him goodbye, got inside.

Back at the house, Anna unlocked the door. Edward stepped inside. "Where's the furniture," he said on taking a deep breath.

"It's all here."

"No, I mean the rental furniture." He turned to her. "The stuff Elise installed for potential buyers."

Anna wanted to ask how he knew about that. Instead, she headed for the kitchen. "I thought you might like some lunch. Are you hungry?"

"Not that much. The chemo leaves me without an appetite." Edward went to the table and sat.

"But I thought Dr. Grimes stopped—"

"I begged him for one last round." Edward met Anna's gaze.

She pulled away, went to the refrigerator, and lifted out two beers. She took one to Edward. As she opened the second one, he looked puzzled. "I know you're not going to drink that yourself," he said.

"And why not?" Anna hated the smell of beer. Yet she'd always wondered how it tasted. *Did he drink beer with his women?* She turned the bottled up and took a swig. Her tongue went bitter. Frowning, she placed the cold, green bottle on the table.

Edward sat his bottle beside hers. "Enough for me too."

"More effects of the chemo?"

"I lost the taste awhile back. Like a lot of other things." His voice trailed off.

Startled, Anna took the bottles from the table and emptied them in the sink. "I'd better start dinner."

"Did you have any plans for the day?" Edward asked. It was hardly past noon. He tapped the table.

"Not really. What about you?" Anna bent down and removed a pot from the cabinet beneath the range.

"I'm supposed to be dying."

She lowered the glistening stainless steel pot onto one of two back burners of the range. "What would you like to do?"

"I feel tired, but not enough to—" Edward stood and turned toward the sliding glass door. "I see you filled the pool."

"I thought you might like to spend some time out on the patio. It's early September. Indian summer is coming."

Edward's ruddy brown face glistened with vitality and hope. "Why did you do it?"

"Do what?"

"Bring me back here. *Why?*"

"I don't know." Those words would not suffice with someone as successful as Edward.

He pocketed his hands and stared at the floor. "Looks a hell of a lot different than when the children were here." He returned to his initial subject upon entering the house.

"In fact, this whole place looks different from when . . . " Fifteen months had passed since Anna had changed the locks and instituted new rules.

"They're coming next week," Anna said. Edward lifted his head and met her gaze. "I told the children about your cancer. They're coming home next Tuesday." David was flying from Detroit with Theo coming in from Chicago. "Brad and Linda are driving up. They should arrive that afternoon," Anna said. "Serine's due in that night."

"Why doesn't Serine ride up with them? They live on the same side of the city." Linda, Brad, and Serine lived in Los Angeles.

"Serine has a case that runs into the afternoon. She's taking a flight that arrives in the early evening. Linda and Brad are leaving in the morning."

"How is Linda?" Edward asked. "Have you spoken to her?"

"She's fine."

"And Brad?"

"You know Brad. He's steady."

"And everything's okay with the billing service?" Edward asked.

"Most of his father's clients are still physicians, but last I heard the company had entered a contract with a small hospital." Brad's father, Albert, a psychiatrist, had been the first to sign on for Brad's medical billing service.

"That should help the business, particularly in these times."

"Between Albert and his colleagues, Brad's got a lot of contacts." Anna filled the pot with water. "Brad's good for Linda." She noted Edward's brightening demeanor. "I haven't spoken to her in a while."

"Neither have I."

"But I don't worry." Anna placed the pot full of water on the eye of the stove that was glowing red and warm.

"With all that's been going on—" Edward grew silent. It was sad that they lived so close to their daughters and neither had much contact with them.

"But I don't worry," Anna repeated her words.

"I guess we've both been busy." Edward met her gaze.

Anna's hand stilled from shaking salt onto the surface of the water in the pot. The divorce proceedings, underscored by her effort at trying to sell the house, had consumed her life for nearly a year and a half. She slid the saltshaker back into its hole in the spice rack, then returned to the refrigerator and took out the roast, a bag of carrots, and two bunches of broccoli.

"What's that you're making?" Edward walked to the counter.

"A roast with vegetables." She closed the refrigerator door.

Again Edward glanced through the sliding glass doors. Sunlight beamed from the surface of the pool. The air of anxiety that had swarmed about him seemed less palpable. Anna's chest swelled with emotion.

"It'll be nice sitting out on the patio in the afternoons." Edward had spent little time in the house that he had fought to keep her from selling. She walked to the sink and turned on the water.

"I think I'll go and lie down." Edward stood then giving a slight cough started for the stairs.

"I did it because it was the right thing to do," Anna called out. "Me, bringing you back here."

Edward turned around. She beheld his familiar smile that reflected only half its usual glow.

Chapter 8

Oakland International Airport was crowded Tuesday morning when Anna arrived to meet David. As she stood waiting for him, an old friend chanced upon her.

"Anna?"

She turned on hearing her name. "Doris? Doris Martin?"

The woman smiled and embraced Anna. Both women had served as class mothers for Theo's third grade at Joaquin Miller School.

"How are you doing?" Doris relinquished Anna and stepped back. "You look wonderful," Doris said.

"Same for you."

"Looks can be deceiving," Doris said. "But that's another story." The sunlight pouring into the airport highlighted the brownish-red tint of Doris' hair. Anna presumed it was dyed. "What are you doing here?"

"Waiting for my son, David. Theo's coming too, later this afternoon. He lives in Chicago."

"Oh, my," Doris said, "he must be what, thirty, thirty-one?"

"He's thirty-one."

"That's right. Theo was only a few months older than Adrian. And what does he do?"

"He's in advertising. He has his own firm. It's small, but doing well."

"That sounds exciting and diligent." Doris smiled. "It's hard working for yourself."

"Yes. It is." Anna thought of Edward and all the miles he had logged in traveling around the world. "And Adrian, how's he doing? Where is he?" she asked.

Doris' face slid into a carefully contained somberness. "He died last year."

"I'm so sorry."

"Don't be." Doris shook her head. "It was for the best." Anna frowned trying to understand how that might be. "He was—" Doris started, and then her eyes brightened. Feeling a tap upon her shoulder, Anna turned around. Towering above her was David.

"David." Anna coolly greeted her eldest child. Thoughts of the lawsuit he had proposed against Henderson and the papers he'd filed in seeking to declare Anna mentally incompetent receded to the back of her thoughts. "How was your flight?"

"Early and crowded. I upgraded to first class. Though I couldn't tell the difference."

"Still—" Anna turned to Doris and said, "You remember Doris Martin?"

"Adrian's mom." David smiled and extended his hand. "Adrian was in the same grade with Theo. How's he doing?"

Doris exchanged a look with Anna.

"He's fine," Anna said.

Doris appeared relieved. "But not as well as you or Theo are doing." She opened her arms and gave David a long hug. Anna's heart ached for Doris' loss.

"Where are you living now?" Doris said to David.

"Detroit."

"Oooh." Doris gripped her arms and rocked back and forth as if to warm herself. "It's cold up there."

"And the summers are scorching. That's why I'm thinking about moving back here." He gave Anna a quick glance. Anna shuddered. David moving back to Oakland? She wondered what Heather, his wife of seven years, had to say about that.

"I'll let you get your things," Doris said to David, and then to Anna, "We can chat later. Call me sometime. I'm in the book." Again, she embraced Anna, this time lightly.

Anna and David went to the baggage carousel. "I'll bring the car around while you wait for your bags," Anna said. Painfully cognizant of Doris' loss, she reached up and kissed David.

"It's good to have you home."

Traffic was light on Highway 880, unlike at the airport.

"How's Dad doing?" David asked before Anna could thank him for coming.

"He seems strong," Anna said. "But then, you know your father. He's not one for complaining."

"About certain things." David leaned back in the seat and stretched his legs forward.

"Are you comfortable? The button's on the side. You can push your seat back," Anna said.

David slid his seat back.

Anna drove along with David's presence warming her— evidence that she had done something right. She refused to think about the lawsuit he had filed. However harsh and misdirected, David's actions paled in comparison to the death of Doris' son, Adrian. The Martins had divorced a decade earlier. Anna wondered if Adrian's death had been related to their split.

"So what's this I hear about you moving back here?" she asked.

"I'm going to do it."

"What does Heather think?"

David grew silent, interwove his hands, and closed his eyes.

Minutes later, Anna said, "You haven't answered my question about you and Heather."

"Heather's already out here," David said. An only child, David's wife was from Santa Rosa. "She, Josh, and Emily are at her dad's." Josh and Emily were David and Heather's children, ages four and three. "Heather's father's dying of cancer."

Anna's hand trembled upon the steering wheel. Heather's mother had died a week after Heather's birth. After three days of labor with a torn placenta, infection had set in and spread throughout her body. That Heather had survived evidenced a miracle.

"She's been out here for the past six months," David explained. "I've been flying back and forth every other weekend."

"You never called. Why?" Anna was bewildered and disappointed that David had been traveling so close to Oakland and never stopped to visit.

She exited off of 880 onto Highway 24.

"You and Dad were busy with the divorce—" David stopped short.

"Still, I could have gone with you sometime to help Heather with the kids." Anna's concern intensified. Her grandchildren had been so close. Time was precious. Upon entering her fight with Edward for the divorce, Anna had withdrawn from the children. There had also been Inman.

David said, "Emily was in pre-school before Heather left. Sometimes I take them back with me."

"Is everything okay with you and Heather?" Anna resumed her questioning.

"Heather's been worried about her father. He's all she has. It's obvious he won't make it." David breathed in. "She's depressed. And, when you called about Dad . . ." David turned toward the passenger window.

Anna reached over and patted his knee. "We're going to get through this." She sighed. "We'll make it," then, "We have each other."

Arriving home, Anna went upstairs and looked in on Edward, who was resting in the bedroom they had once shared.

"He's asleep," she said after coming back downstairs. "I'll get lunch ready for when he awakes." She went into the kitchen. David followed her.

He sat at the counter as Anna removed roast beef, bread, and mayonnaise from the refrigerator and brought them to the surface between them. She started making sandwiches as David watched.

Anna completed the first sandwich and placed it on a plate and sat it before him.

"I'm sorry about suing Henderson," David said. "I don't think you're mentally unstable."

"Did you conclude that before or after I decided to take care of your father?"

"I knew it all along."

"Then why the suit?"

"Because he needed you. I do, too. We all do."

Anna lifted another piece of roast beef and proceeded to make a second sandwich. David's attention followed her.

"Did you hear what I said?"

Anna sliced into the roast beef. Her eyes began to sting. The meat before her became blurry.

Edward entered the kitchen. David stood. Son and father eyed each other. Then Edward extended his hand and David rushed to embrace him.

Anna finished making the sandwich and rinsed the knife. "It's ready," she said of the sandwich. Holding back tears, she returned the ingredients to the refrigerator and slipped from the kitchen.

Anna entered Theo's old bedroom where she was now staying, closed the door, and went to the bed. She could not bring herself to sleep with Edward. Yet old fires burned.

A knock arose from the door. She turned from where she was sitting as it opened.

"Aren't you hungry?" Edward asked on entering.

"I just needed to change. Besides I still have to tidy up Linda and Brad's room."

Edward came around and faced her. "The room is fine." He reached out and attempted to touch her cheek.

"I'm sorry." Anna pulled away and whisked past Edward to the bureau.

Edward drew near as she slid open a drawer. "You never told me exactly why you wanted the divorce. The papers said irreconcilable differences, but . . . "

Anna's face ran hot with anger and with sadness. Nearly a year and a half had passed since the night she has asked for the divorce and Edward had refused. She couldn't believe they were discussing this, first *why* she brought him home, now the divorce.

"I thought you might have understood. All the women. You never at home. You weren't happy."

"But why did you wait so long? Serine had been gone for a decade."

"You thought I should have left sooner?" Anna whipped around. The conversation was devolving into a quagmire of confusion.

"I'm just asking why last year? Why the—"

"I'm not the one on trial here," Anna said. "You should be glad that—"

"Dad, Mom," David spoke from the hallway. "Linda just called to say—" David entered the doorway. Surprise registered on his face when observing Anna's things settled about the room and laid upon the bed, evidence that she had sleeping in Theo's room. "I guess Theo will be sleeping in my room like we did as kids."

Anna lowered her head in an attempt to avoid David's gaze. He turned to Edward standing somber, then left the room.

"I'll go set the table," Edward said.

After a momentary silence, Anna started past him. "You need to rest," she said.

"In a couple of months, I won't be able to do this." Edward reached after her. "I don't want to go to bed until I have to."

Anna felt weak at the brush of his hand. His choice of words strummed her heart. *I don't want to* versus *I won't.*

"I'm sorry," she said.

"Don't be. I got myself into this mess." Edward pocketed his hands and kicked his bare feet at the floor.

"You think you're being punished?"

"Why shouldn't I be? Look what I put you through. And my children."

Anna turned away and began reorganizing the clothes in the open bureau drawer. "It's just something we'll have to get through."

"I don't doubt you'll get through it. Nor that you'll stay strong for the children. You'll make sure they're okay. I know that," Edward said.

She leaned toward him. You should have taken better care of yourself and not traveled so much. Her thoughts listed everything that Edward had done wrong. She resumed her business of rearranging the disarray of clothes. Organizing and making sense of life's chaos was what Anna did best. The madness of what she was doing absorbed her.

"I'll miss you." Edward's voice cracked.

Anna's hands fell still.

"I'll miss you, too," she whispered.

Cognizant of what she had said, she slowly turned to face him. Edward had left the room.

Chapter 9

Linda and Brad arrived while David had returned to Oakland Airport to pick up Serine.

"I wish Serine had come up with you guys," Edward said as he grabbed Brad's hand and pulled him into an embrace.

He then kissed Linda. Anna was surprised that Linda didn't flinch. Rather, she embraced her father and whispered, "I love you."

When all was settled, Anna, Edward, Linda, and Brad sat around the kitchen table.

"So, Dad, what medications are you taking now?" Linda was intent on discussing the business at hand.

"Nothing," Edward said. "The chemo failed."

Brad took Linda's hand. With her other, she lifted her father's palm. Anna grew tense.

"It's going to be okay," Linda said. "We'll get through this. And so will you."

"For me, that means dying."

"That time's not here yet," Linda said. "Until then—"

"The roast is almost ready." Anna jumped up and went to the kitchen area. Sliding on her mittens, she opened the oven door, and removed the broccoli casserole.

"Need some help?" Brad joined her.

"The roast is done. I'll start the vegetables as soon as David arrives with Serine."

Anna pointed to the microwave, wondering what was keeping her younger son.

"When's Theo coming?" Brad looked at his watch. "It's seven o'clock."

"He said he'd be here by dinner. I told him we were eating at eight, but you know Theo." Anna caught sight of what she considered Brad's judgmental look about Theo and his tardiness. Still Brad had been good for Linda. Anna held no doubt that Brad Oliver loved her elder daughter.

Brad slid onto the stool at the bar.

"How's Linda?" Anna said.

Brad swiveled around to Linda and Edward at the table across the room. The two were in deep conversation. "She cried the entire night after you called with the news," Brad said. "Two days later, she saw her old therapist."

"She hasn't had to go back until now?" Anna asked.

Emotion drained from Brad's face, a mask taking over as if to shield his subdued anger. "Linda hasn't been in therapy for over five years."

Anna pulled out a drawer and lifted a knife. "I'm sorry. I didn't know."

"Perhaps if you called more." His words were soft, but firm.

"I'm sorry about that, too."

"Linda's been worried about you." Brad drew close. "She tries your cell phone constantly."

"I didn't want her or any of you to feel compelled to choose sides." Anna hadn't spoken to Linda in more than nine months, three months after she began divorce proceedings.

"We're all adults. And Linda was worried." Brad remained with his topic. "Eventually, she got a hold of Elise. She told us you were fine, that after moving into the apartment you only had the cell phone. Linda wanted to come up and see how you were, but I told her you needed some space."

Again, Brad shifted around to Edward and Linda at the kitchen table by the window and sliding glass door opening onto the patio. Linda was holding Edward's hand. He was speaking low and soft, his eyes searching as she listened intently.

"It's horrible that it took this for you to call," Brad said. "We're not just here for Edward. We came for you, too."

The kindness and civility of her son-in-law's words made Anna want to scream.

The doorbell rang. She went to the foyer, opened the front door, and saw no one. On her return to the kitchen, she heard voices. Serine was stepping through the entry of the sliding glass door with David following close behind as Brad slid the screen closed. David and Brad greeted each other with a hug. Anna's youngest child rushed to Edward who was sitting at the table with Linda. Edward stood and embraced Serine and held on to her for a long time.

"I'm going upstairs to freshen up," Linda said.

Serine took Linda's seat at the table.

"I'll help you get the bags out of the car and take them up to the room," David said.

The two men headed out the back door to Brad and Linda's car. Anna marveled at how cooperative the children were. Like other grade-schoolers, those younger and less experienced in life's trials, Anna's children had bickered at the slightest notion of life's injustices. Many a benign comment made by one sibling was blown out of proportion and caused the Manning household to become a war zone. Anna had spent much of her time directing her children's behavior, and micromanaging their actions. *David, don't judge your sisters. Theo, don't pick on Serine. Linda, it's not that way. No one's angry with you, Serine.* Sibling rivalry between David and Theo hadn't been an issue. Rather David and Theo had established a united front toward their younger sisters. At times, Anna had wondered if David and Theo had felt overwhelmed, three women to two of them. If Edward had been home more often . . .

A hand landed on her shoulder. "Need any help?" David was back from taking Serine's bags upstairs. Anna shook herself free from her last thoughts.

"I'm fine." She crafted a smile.

"Brad's upstairs taking a shower," Linda said upon joining David in the kitchen. "What can I do to help?"

Anna walked to the sink, turned on the faucet and then squeezing some dishwashing liquid into her palm, brought her hands under the stream of soothing, warm water.

"Like I was telling Brad earlier, everything's ready. The vegetables are in the— " She turned to the microwave then hesitated in her moment of thought, *I need to turn up the temperature on the water heater.*

Saying nothing she rushed past David and Linda down to the garage. Pulling open the door to the compartment housing the furnace and water heater, Anna increased the temperature on the thermostat of the water heater to its highest setting. Glad that she had thought of this now rather than when the showers ran cold, she turned back. On closing the door, she met Linda.

Anna froze.

"I didn't mean to startle you. Is everything alright?" Linda's voice was easy and sure—unlike Anna had ever heard it.

"I'm fine. Just wanted to turn up the temperature on the water heater. With five of you plus me and your dad, it's going to take a lot more hot water than usual."

Sadness slid over Linda's sienna face that, like Edward's ruddy complexion, held a red, almost orange, undertone.

"It's been difficult for you being here by yourself," Linda said.

"It wasn't like you all left home yesterday." Anna failed to avoid her elder daughter's gaze. "I've had time to adjust." Her chest sank. This was not a discussion she desired. Yet she felt close to Linda. Peace and calm, not evident before, entered their engagement. "I've missed you."

"Same here," Linda said. "Aunt Elise said you were fine, that you had a lot going on. I stopped calling because I didn't want to add to your burdens."

"You were never a burden," Anna said.

"Still it was hard on you," Linda said. "I haven't thought about suicide in five years." Her face exuded a warm glow.

Anna drew near. "Brad said you had stopped therapy."

"I realized I wasn't the cause of your unhappiness." She lifted Anna's hand. "I started loving myself."

Anna's lips trembled. She wanted to embrace Linda, and say she was sorry for retreating. Anna had needed to regroup. Memories of Inman and the smell of his damp and newly washed skin filled her nose. Her body grew warm and moist as it had when touching Inman's. She enfolded Linda's words into her heart. *I started loving myself.*

Linda turned and went back up stairs. A flurry of tears filled Anna's throat, she unable to heave or swallow.

Chapter 10

David and Brad arranged the plates and silverware on the dining room table. Linda placed the roast in the center.

"The vegetables have finished in the microwave," Anna called from the kitchen. She was standing at the sink and washing the dishes from lunch. "I wish Theo had told me how he was getting here." The clock on the range read 7:50.

"Don't worry." Linda lifted a bowl from the drainer, tore off a paper towel, and began drying it. "Theo always arrives, and right on time."

"For him," Anna said.

Anna had stayed in touch with thirty-one-year-old Theo. After he learned of Anna's request to divorce Edward, Theo—unlike David—called her every Friday evening. "I was wondering when you were going to do it," he said when Anna had told him that Henderson had filed the papers. Anna had been taken by Theo's awareness, and that he held no grudges. She was grateful for his support.

Theo added, "I'm glad you stood up for yourself. Dad put you through a lot." He then warned, "David won't be happy. Don't be surprised if he goes cool on you and stops calling for a while. As for Linda, she's known all along this was coming." Anna had cringed in both awe and embarrassment at the revelation of her children's depth of knowledge concerning the predicament of her marriage.

Anna never gave David a chance to grow cool. She withdrew first. The bogus lawsuit he launched against Henderson along with his futile attempt at establishing her as insane had been as much a response to her action of pulling away as her request for the divorce.

Wise to the ways to the world and the idiosyncrasies of his siblings, Theo had also said, "Serine, you've got to watch. She'll eventually come around. Until then, don't let anything she says or does faze you." Anna had wanted to ask the specifics of what he had meant. She wanted Theo to elaborate and explain, yet the act of breaking free from the mold she had cast for herself had taken its toll.

The façade she had worn for thirty-three years was falling away. "As children, we didn't understand," Theo said. "My own marriage has taught me a lot." Against her worries and concerns for Serine, and Theo with his own union, Anna put her own needs first. She chose to care for herself.

Anna walked to the kitchen table where Serine was sitting with Edward. Their heads were together, whispered murmurings flowing between them. Father and daughter could have passed for lovers. The youngest of their four children, Serine had been Edward's pet.

Where he had delivered gifts to the elder three on his return from business trips, he had mailed them to Serine before his arrival. Anna had always thought his actions resulted from guilt of often having stayed over an extra day or two for fun and pleasure and to spend time with his women friends.

Despite his compensation, Anna feared that Serine had surmised the truth about her father at a younger age than the others. The last one to leave home, she had known a difficulty in

Edward's absence that her other children had not experienced—one that Anna had failed to explain away.

Anna did not trust Serine's confident and strong demeanor. Her decision to become an assistant district attorney was but another extension of the influence of Edward's absence in her life. The lead district attorney had conveniently hired Serine an hour into her initial interview.

He would be her immediate superior and mentor. That was two years ago. Mother and daughter had spoken weekly then. Serine had described her experience of the achievement as a careful display of her ability to survive in a man's world, one where Edward had risen above his counterparts and foes.

Through listening and calm questioning, Anna saw her daughter unconsciously making known her need for a man in her life. A man, who despite *her* intelligence and strength, was emotionally available. He would protect her. The district attorney, Anna had concluded, was smitten with Serine.

Anna observed Serine sitting at the kitchen table and holding Edward's hand. "The others have gathered in the dining room," Anna said. Anger welled in Serine's eyes.

"We'll be there in a minute," Edward said.

Anna sat at the end of the oblong table in front of the window. David was to her right. The chair across from him and to Anna's left awaited Theo's arrival. Edward occupied his usual seat at the other end by the doorway where Anna had taken to sitting during her last months in the house, and when eating, nearly always alone.

Now with Edward back, and occupying that space, it felt strange sitting in the spot that she had held for thirty-three years, even on the many occasions when Edward had been absent.

Their plates full and the meal underway, her children ate and conversed.

"I'm really getting tired of the cold," David said to Brad on his right. "It'll be good to be back in California."

"I've never been to Michigan," Brad said, "but I hear the winters are brutal."

"Wicked is more like it." David cut into the slice of roast on his plate.

Anna had visited David and Heather over the seven years of their marriage, her trips increasing with and after the births of Emily and Josh. Anna liked Heather and found their home warm and inviting. David's sudden decision to return to California troubled her. Heather's father was ill and dying. David was saying little about the matter.

Unable to remember the last time they had eaten together, Anna observed her children around the table. Linda, at the other end, was again locked in conversation with Edward. She sat beside Brad. To the other side of Edward was Serine. Analytical and interrogating like her eldest brother, David, she took in David's conversation with Brad.

Anna turned to the empty chair on her left, and recalled Theo's words, *Serine you've got to watch. And David . . . don't be put off if he grows silent. Both of them like to control things.* She wondered when Theo might arrive and whether his wife, Millicent, would accompany him.

Explaining to which lake Detroit stood adjacent, David said to Brad, "It's all in the hand." He held up his left palm, and indicated how Michigan resembled the shape of a hand. He traced the slope of his finger down to his thumb. "Detroit is down here in this little corner." He tapped his palm. "All this is Lake Michigan."

"It's got to be difficult making that kind of move now," Brad said. "Then, again, better now than later."

"It's now or never," David explained. "I can't spend another year there. Emily and Josh are in preschool. And with Heather's father sick and terminal . . ." David halted. All conversation at the table disintegrated.

David glanced at Anna. Serine placed her fork on the side of her plate. After staring at her broccoli and carrots, Anna then cut into slice the roast on her plate. Brad eventually ended the awkwardness of the moment with, "Yeah, I see what you mean."

"So, it's definite you're moving back to Oakland?" Serine jump-started David's conversation with Brad.

"That or either some place down in the So Cal," David said.

"The firm I interned for is looking for someone with acumen and experience in wills and trusts," Serine said.

"Acumen?" Brad threw a smirk across the table at Serine. He exchanged looks with Linda, who, along with Edward, had been listening to David.

The legalities of family planning, trusts and wills, establishing, overseeing, and executing them was David's specialty. Yet as on so many occasions, and concerning other subjects, Serine's use of the word *acumen* had held an air of haughtiness.

"It's not simply about the knowledge," Serine explained while attempting to size down Brad's comment. "People are a ball of emotions when you're drawing up their trusts and wills. You've got to know how to handle them and their families. Especially when carrying out their wishes after they've . . . " Her voice trailed off. She turned to Edward.

Again the conversation halted.

"That's certainly true." Edward eyed Anna and then turned to David. "Bryce has brought mine up to date. I'd like you to look it over."

"Of course," David said. He reached over and patted Anna's hand. Softness covered his eyes. Her hand trembled.

David returned his attention to Serine. "L.A.'s a bit large for me, but I'd like to speak with your friend."

"I'll have him call you. It'd be nice to have you close."

"I agree," Linda intervened. She began rubbing her stomach. "But Mom might need you nearby," she said to David, then lifted Brad's hand.

"I was wondering the same thing," Brad said. "In fact—"

"You raise a point," Serine started once more. "Particularly with Mom being alone after Dad's—" Anna's youngest child threw her a pointed gaze. "Then again—" Serine started. She looked to Linda and Brad across from her. Linda massaged her stomach.

"I could use all the company I can get. With David and Heather in the same city, I'd get to see my niece and nephew. I like having family close by, unlike some people who don't mind living alone. And away from those they claim to love." The frustration intensified in Serine's voice as she again threw Anna a pointed stare.

Anna cut into her second slice of roast and lifted a bite of broccoli to her lips. Linda and Brad exchanged glances. They too lived in L.A., and had helped Serine settle into working there after graduating from law school.

David again patted Anna's hand. "Emily and Josh would love to see more of you. Not that Heather and I want to make you a nanny, but it would be good for the kids to see you more oft—"

"You might want to think twice about Mom being around to babysit," Serine said. "That is unless you're willing to send them abroad. Mom's moving to France." On registering Serine's words, everyone turned from Serine to Anna.

"Is this true?" Confusion and hurt filled David's face, a darker complexion than Edward's.

How had Serine learned of France? Anna had told no one except Elise and Theo. Of Inman, she had spoken only to Elise.

"I'd planned to," Anna said.

Edward's face, so often buffered against emotion, remained blank. Linda clutched his hand tighter.

"Before or after Dad got sick?" David asked as Serine observed intently.

"I found out about your father only two weeks ago," Anna said.

David took in a breath and exhaled as Brad lifted Linda's other hand.

"When were you planning to tell us?" Linda said. Unlike Serine, her tone was non-judgmental.

"After the divorce. When I'd sold the house."

"So, let me get this straight?" David gestured with his hands. "You were going to divorce Dad, sell the house, this *house*—" he made a broad sweep of his hand as if surveying the house, "—and move to France?"

"Yes. That was the plan."

"And what *is* the plan now that Dad—" David pointed to Edward, "—your husband, is sick and dying? Oh, but let me correct myself since you've already divorced him."

Stoic and calm, Serine turned to Edward. Anna stood.

"Are we to take this as a statement that you're still going?" Serine asked.

"I didn't know it was up for discussion," Anna retorted.

"Well, I, for one am not going to sit by and let you abandon Dad. Not like this." Serine stood.

David stood also. "If I didn't know it when I filed the suit, I know it now. You really are insane."

"That's enough!" Edward slammed his hand upon the table. Serine and David fell silent as Linda and Brad, still holding hands, lowered their gazes. Again, Linda massaged her stomach. Anna placed her hand on the back of the chair still empty of Theo's presence, and in the deepening silence, she left the room.

Moments later and in Theo's room, Anna sat folding bed linen and towels she had taken from the dryer. Following a soft knock, Edward peeked around the door.

"May I come in?"

Anna nodded and kept folding the towels. He entered. Reaching the bed, Edward lifted a pile of folded sheets and pillowcases and placed them in the chair by the night stand.

"Seems like you're always doing this."

"Someone has to." Anna was still fuming from the dinner conversation gone awry.

Edward lowered himself onto the bed, and brushed his hand across the plush, green comforter. "I've spoken with Serine *and* David. They were out of line."

"They're adults. And entitled to their own opinions."

"Some opinions are best kept to one's self," Edward said.

Anna laid a folded towel upon the pile in the chair by the night stand and lifted another from the pile on the bed.

"Perhaps like mine." Edward stared at her. She proceeded to fold the second towel.

"Let's not pretend that we're one big happy family."

Anna's hands fell still. She turned to Edward. "David and Serine are angry with me because I requested the divorce. You fed David's anger and encouraged him to file papers to have me declared mentally unfit and to sue Henderson. God knows what would have happened had you not agreed to the divorce."

"I warned David that if he filed the suit against Henderson or papers against you that I'd grant you the divorce. It's why I signed the papers."

"So David forced you to agree to the divorce?" The symbolism of David's actions had hurt Anna. That his actions had forced Edward into agreeing to the divorce further enraged her. "Henderson said the suit against him was bogus. No *sane* psychiatrist would grant the request after speaking with m—"

"That wasn't the point," Edward said.

"Okay, let me guess. You were also dying?"

The fading light in Edward's eyes dimmed another degree. Clinching his jaw, he stood and headed for the door. He was about to go through when Anna asked, "Why?"

Edward held the doorknob for a moment, and then turning back, he said, "You deserved better."

Anna breathed in his words not wanting to believe them, or that he had said spoken them.

"By the way, did you find a buyer?" he asked.

"A buyer?" She shook her head in an effort to clear her thoughts.

"For the house. A buyer for the house, this *house*."

"No."

His cheeks softened. He seemed sad.

"Tell Elise—I assume she's still handling the sale—tell her to call Bryce. He'll put her in touch with some of our contacts around California and abroad. People are always looking to move here. With five bedrooms and four baths, this is the perfect home for an executive and family relocating to the area. You'd be surprised how many people outside the country are looking for homes here."

"I'm sure they are." Anna took in a breath.

Edward walked through the doorway and left.

A few minutes later, she followed him to what had been their bedroom for thirty-three years.

"Why are you doing this?"

"You need to sell the house." Edward was in his pajamas and sitting upon the bed. His thin feet stood upon the floor. "There's no sense in you losing valuable advertising time while I'm here."

"And what if someone wants to see it? They just barge in on a sick man?"

"I'm sure Elise made pictures. If not—"

"No." Anna shook her head. "Why are you trying to help me sell the house? You battled for over a year, *fifteen months*, to prevent me from selling it."

"You're going to move to France, aren't you?

"Yes, but—"

"Then, you need to sell the house."

The words made no sense. That Edward had spoken them, defied conventional reasoning. But then their situation was anything but conventional.

"I don't understand why you're being so . . . .so . . . so *cooperative. Supportive.*" The onset and slow encroachment of Edward's death could not change the years of hurt she had experienced as his wife.

Anna pondered Edward's words hours after she had crawled into bed. *You need to sell the house.* And then, she mused upon her own continuing questions. Anna refused to trust what Edward said or did. Why was he being so amenable? Had he changed? How? Or was this simply another part of his plan to cheat death, or Anna?

During dinner, Edward had examined the palms of his hands edging toward frailness and trembling. His words *I could ask the same of you,* concerning Anna's change of heart, rang aloud in her mind. *Why had she stopped plans of divorcing him?* She had ordered Elise to take the house off the market. She had the men remove the rental pieces and return the furniture that had been in storage to their original positions around the house.

Anna had in effect re-established things back to the way they were, or could have been, before she chose to divorce Edward.

Why, she asked once more.

"Perhaps for the same reason you brought me back here. To let me die," Edward had said.

To let me die. His words resounded into Anna's sleep followed by her voice echoing, *I love you.*

Chapter 11

The next morning, Anna awoke to the smell of breakfast cooking. She showered and got dressed. Following the aroma of eggs and bacon, she descended the stairs. From the sound of the voices below, she concluded Theo had arrived.

"Well, hello stranger," said Linda.

"It's good to see you." That was Theo.

"It's about time." Brad teased Theo about arriving after everyone else.

"We were wondering where you were," said Linda.

Reaching the base of the steps, Anna crossed the foyer and stood by the kitchen door. Theo was at the stove hugging Serine as Edward looked on. David had yet to come downstairs.

"When did you get in?" Serine asked Theo.

"This morning." Theo turned back to the range and flipped the pancakes on the griddle. Then, he walked to the sink and began whipping eggs in a bowl. Theo's slow lope and careful ministrations reminded Anna of her father. Unlike Serine, the youngest, Theo had always been Anna's unofficial baby, the truly naïve one, who gave generously and from his heart without regard. Anna often thought Theo trusted others too much for his own good.

Anna entered the kitchen and walked to him. "Since when did you start making breakfast?"

"Since I realized that women weren't put on this earth to simply cook and clean." Theo ceased stirring the eggs, killed the flame under the pancakes, and embraced her.

"Sorry I'm late," he whispered.

"I'm so glad you're home," she whispered back.

Theo served breakfast to Edward, Serine, Linda, and Brad at the kitchen table then said to Anna, "Let's go into the dining room."

Hesitant and ashamed of her need for attention, she followed.

Theo sat in Edward's chair. "The food should keep them busy for half an hour or so."

"You mean before they miss us."

Theo smiled.

"Millicent didn't come with you?" Anna handed Theo a napkin. Reminded of his manners, he laid it upon his thigh.

Theo had dated many women throughout college, yet he had settled on fellow student Millicent Regarde when nearing the end of earning his MBA. Anna had never liked Millicent.

As the owner of a mortgage brokerage, she held too much in common with Edward. Anna found her to be quite aggressive, and she was quick to summon Daddy whenever the world presented its imperfections.

"She's merging the brokerage with her father's real estate firm," Theo said. "They're moving into his building this week." Millicent's parents, Thelonius and Henrietta Regarde, carried much distinction in black society of Chicago. Theo said little of Millicent when he called each Friday evening.

"I can't believe you've been married for five years already. How are things with you and Millicent?"

"She's busy finding new clients. With the recession, let's just say things have been better for the mortgage business." Theo wiped his mouth then let his napkin drop onto the plate. His love for Millicent reminded Anna too much of her loyalty and commitment to Edward.

"I mean *between* you and her." Anna clarified her question.

"That's another matter." Theo's lips appeared on the edge of trembling, or perhaps Anna misread them in her growing anxiety. She reached out and touched his hand. Theo patted hers, pulled away and then said, "So what's this I hear about David confronting you last night about moving to France?"

"It was Serine who raised the issue. Funny thing is I can't imagine how she learned I was moving."

"That would be Aunt Elise. Serine called her when Dad told us about the divorce and you stopped returning our messages."

"It was hard telling all of you that I wanted to leave your father, end the marriage. I needed room to think."

"I understood. So did Linda and Brad." Theo sipped his coffee. "Serine, on the other hand . . . well . . . she feels abandoned."

"I wasn't leaving her. Why didn't you mention this to me sooner? Although, you did warn me. I shouldn't have pulled away," Anna confessed.

"You needed to take care of yourself." Theo traced the rim of his plate with his forefinger. Unlike his siblings, he refused to accept Anna's silence. When the other three stopped phoning and leaving messages, he persisted in calling.

She sank back into her chair. "Are you angry that I'm moving to France?"

"No. I hope you're still going." Theo glanced back at the doorway leading to the kitchen where Edward was still sitting at the kitchen table with Linda, Brad, and Serine.

"I can't think about that now. Your father needs me."

"This is what I don't understand about you." Theo hit his finger upon the table. Confusion flooded Anna. "It was obvious to me and Linda that you needed to live your life. Dad couldn't support you doing that. In fact, I'm surprised you stayed this long."

"And why is that?"

"The man cheated on you. He was a constant philanderer. He was never around."

"He provided all of us a good life," Anna said.

"And you were unhappy."

"That was my choice."

"It affected us." Theo knitted his brows. "Do you know what it's like to see your mother never happy, always working, never smiling? It doesn't matter that the house you live in is large and beautiful and filled with toys you never play with, or that your father wears two-thousand-dollar suits and is respected, envied, or both for the work he does."

Theo drew closer. "It doesn't even matter that your mother acts like everything is fine, and never complains about her husband. You *know*." Again Theo touched his forefinger to the table.

Anna's eyes burned with a truth too large to encompass and with a boldness she could not ignore.

David entered the dining room. "Hey, bro!" Theo stood, David reached out, and the two embraced. "When'd you get in?"

"Early this morning. Around seven," Theo said. "I rented a car at the airport and called Linda and Brad to let me in."

"I didn't hear the phone ring," Anna said.

"I called their cell." Theo glanced back. Anna reminisced upon the days when there were no cell phones and she could decipher her children's lives by the calls they made and received.

Theo pointed to David's bag. "Leaving so soon?"

"Heather's dad just died." David looked past Theo's shoulder to Anna. His body held restrained sadness. "I'll be back as soon as I can."

"Take your time." Anna went to him. "Tell Heather I'm praying for her. If she needs anything—"

"I'll do that." David lifted his bag. Anna stretched up and kissed his forehead. The memory of accusations hurled the prior evening was a far-gone blur. David left.

Anna and Theo were back at the table when Serine entered the dining room. "So why are you two hiding in here," she said. Serine sat.

"We're not hiding." Theo smiled.

Serine threw Anna a cautious smile. "Everyone knows that you're Mom's favorite."

"I doubt that." Theo tapped his plate. "If memory serves me correctly, I received my share of banishments to my room and was grounded just as much as anyone. Now *you* on the other hand—"

"You have no idea what it was like for me here with Mom when you and Linda were away at college."

"I know enough." Theo smirked. "You got away with pretty much all you wanted."

"I beg to differ. But, being that you're so much *in-the-know,* has Mom given you the heads-up on her plans to move to Paris?"

"We discussed this last evening," Anna intervened. "And your father informed me he had spoken to you."

"He informed me that I was rude to you." Serine arched her back against the web of haughtiness spun by her words. "I'm speaking nicely this morning."

"What Mom does with her life is her business," Theo said. "If she wants to move to France, then—"

"So you knew about this?"

"Maybe if you bothered to call her, you would, too," Theo shot back.

"I wasn't the one who stopped calling." Serine's shoulders slumped.

"What's your point, Serine?"

"It's not just my point. David agrees, too."

"Well right now he's got other things on his mind," Theo said, "Heather's father just died. He's on his way up to Santa Rosa for the funeral."

"Heather," Serine murmured then slumped down onto the chair. "She can be a pain in the neck. Then again, what can you expect from a white woman?"

"What's that?" Anna snapped.

Theo rolled his eyes. "Here we go again."

When David announced his engagement eight years ago, it had taken the family a moment to adjust to the notion of his wife being white. Anna, Theo, and Linda had come to embrace Heather during the first year of her and David's marriage. While Edward maintained a cordial and cool exterior, Anna suspected he approved of Heather's devotion.

He had visited David and Heather many times in the last two years. Edward always returned singing Heather's praises. That troubled Anna. Like Edward, David could be headlong and stubborn. Anna worried that Heather was seeking to please David at the expense of her own needs.

"Heather is so unhappy," Serine retorted. "With her father dead, I doubt she'll be with David much longer."

"And how do you know this?" Anna asked.

"He told me," Serine said.

"When?"

Theo shifted to Anna. "They've been having problems for a while," he said.

"What kind of problems?"

"Well you know, David's busy at the firm. He comes home late," Theo explained. "Heather's not in the greatest of moods after being home with the children all day."

"I can certainly relate to that." Anna chuckled.

Theo continued. "Then with Heather's father getting sick and her traveling back and forth . . ."

"She's high maintenance," Serine blurted. She pursed her lips. "Always whining. Nothing like Millicent."

"Now wait a minute." Theo flashed his hand. "Raising two kids is hard. Heather—"

"Like you would know," Serine snapped. "Then again, Millicent isn't as eager to be barefoot and pregnant as Heather—"

"That's enough." Anna felt like a referee.

84

Linda burst into the dining room, "Daddy's fallen and bumped his head!"

Anna rushed upstairs. Theo, Serine, and Linda raced behind. "*Edward.* What happened?" She entered the bedroom and joined Brad who was kneeling beside Edward.

"I was dizzy. I'll be all right—" Edward moved to sit up.

"Let us help you." Brad supported his back. Theo bent over to assist. Edward batted away their hands. "I told you I'm fine."

Edward fell back upon Anna's lap. Theo and Brad exchanged glances then looked to Anna.

"Perhaps we need to clear the room." Linda said. She and Serine left. Theo and Brad helped Edward to the bed.

"I need to speak to David as soon as he reaches Santa Rosa," Edwards murmured.

Theo nodded.

"We'll be downstairs," Brad said. He and Theo moved to leave.

Edward lay down. Anna drew the covers onto him. "Yesterday was tiring. You were up late last night." Edward groaned.

"You need to rest," she said.

"I'll be fine." Edward tried to sit up.

Anna noticed the frailness of his neck and arms. Silent worry coursed through her. It was happening. *Edward was beginning to slip away.*

"I'm calling Dr. Grimes."

"And what is *he* going to do?" Edward caught her stare.

A slow burning sensation spread throughout Anna. "I'm calling him, and that's that." She hurried across the hall to Theo's room and dialed the oncologist.

"I've been waiting for your call," Dr. Grimes said when greeting her.

"He fell and hit his head. He was dizzy. It's only been three weeks," she said.

"How's he now?"

"Fine, but he's weak and tired. He's lost a lot of weight."

"That's to be expected."

85

"I thought you said we had three to six months."

"Each case is different."

"Is that how you see Edward, as another *case*?" Anna then recalled Grimes' concern about her re-entering Edward's life and caring for him. "I'm sorry. I didn't mean it that way."

"None necessary," Grimes said. "I can readmit him, but it sounds like you might need a hospice nurse."

"He's not bedridden. And, the kids are here."

"The first sign of the disease taking over is exhibited by stumbling and falling. My guess is that Edward has been feeling weaker than he's been letting on. While he hasn't taken to sleeping a lot, he's probably wanting to lay down more than he feels comfortable saying."

"And what is the hospice nurse going to do? Make him take naps? Sit around and wait for him to keel over?"

"First off, she's going to assess his energy level. Whether you know it or not, it's easier for him to tell the nurse how he's feeling than you. Edward doesn't want to let you or the children down. He's accustomed to you and them seeing him strong and independent. He's shedding that demeanor." Anna cringed at the word *shedding*. It made her think of a snake losing its skin.

"Anna, things are going to get messy. The Edward you know is changing."

"And whose side are you on?"

"Edward's . . . and yours. It's good that you've taken him home. Very few patients get that. But you and your children need to be prepared. My sense is that you are a large part of their preparation. Don't squander your time freaking out when things start happening. Instead, be available to him."

"Thanks, for the advice. I'll call you if anything changes." Anna wasn't ready for hospice.

Chapter 12

Anna left Edward's room. Theo met her on the second floor landing. "What did the doctor say?"

"Your father's sleeping," Anna ignored his words. "Get everybody and let's gather in the dining room."

They all filed into the dining room and took their usual places. Anna sat at the end of the oblong table in the chair she had occupied the prior evening. She placed her palms upon the table and glanced at the empty seat on the other end where Edward always sat.

"Your father's resting," Anna said. Those seated around the table remained somber. "I thought this was as good a time as any for us to talk."

As a way of grounding herself, Anna then repeated what she had said when she had called them about Edward's illness. She said, "Your father has cancer of the gallbladder. He was diagnosed last November. He underwent surgery then eight

87

months of chemotherapy. The chemo failed. Now he's dying. The doctor told me he had three to six months to live. Now this morning—"

Anna felt herself about to break. Theo stood and caressed her shoulders. She reached back and patted his hand.

"I just want to ask," Serine started, "did anyone know about this before Mom called? Or was that the first time you knew about Dad's illness?" She looked to Anna then surveyed the faces around the table.

Brad lifted Linda's hand then said, "Linda and I knew nothing until Anna called." Linda nodded in agreement.

Serine aimed her attention to Theo who stood behind Anna.

"I knew nothing until Mom called." His hands remained still on Anna's shoulders.

"I find that hard to believe," Serine said. "Everyone knows you and Mom talk all the time." Serine threw Anna a sterner glance.

"And what's that got to do with Dad and his cancer?" Theo said.

"You haven't answered my question," Serine fired again.

"I didn't give you the answer you wanted," Theo said.

"I can tell when people are lying."

"What is your point?" Anna asked.

Serine turned to Anna. "When did *you* find out Daddy was sick?"

"A few days before I called you."

Serine hit her with another piercing stare. "And just *how* did you find out?"

"We've had about enough of this," Theo intervened.

"No, let us finish." Anna waved him back. "I learned your father was dying of cancer the day he agreed to the divorce."

"And you didn't know until then?" Serine asked.

"No. I didn't," Anna said. "He had the surgery last January. Bryce said he would be away for two months, that it was for business." Anna had thought it was another stall tactic.

"And you never noticed him exhibiting any weakness from the chemo? Or were you so engaged in the battle of wanting to leave him that you never once noticed that he wasn't looking well?" Anguished fury seared in Serine's eyes, the same shade of light brown verging on amber like Edward's. "Maybe your plans for moving to France obscured your vision."

"What's your point?" Theo started toward her. Again Anna flashed her palm. But Theo continued. "This is not some courtroom with hoodlums off the street and you the prosecutor putting them in jail. This is Mom, our mother, in case you've forgotten. *When* she found out about Dad's illness has nothing to do with the situation at hand."

"And that situation *being*?" Serine smirked.

"That you seem intent on taking out your frustrations on Mom because things aren't going the way you want."

Brad and Linda exchanged glances. Linda massaged her stomach. Something was amiss. Placing his hand upon Linda's stomach, Brad looked to Anna. She felt powerless to say anything. So many times throughout her marriage she felt that her words didn't matter, particularly during Linda's adolescence. Perhaps Serine was right.

Again Anna met Brad's gaze, contemplative much like his psychiatrist father. She considered her son-in-law's words from yesterday afternoon when she had been cooking. *I wished you'd called more often. Linda was worried.* I've been callous and inattentive, Anna concluded.

Theo said, "I can't believe all the other garbage that's coming out of your mouth about Mom, and at a time like this. Then again, with what I know about you—"

Ignoring Theo's last words, Anna said to Serine, "I can understand that it was a shock for me to call with news that your father was dying."

"Never mind the fact that I haven't heard from you in months," Serine railed.

"I claim responsibility for that," Anna said.

"You're to blame for what's happening to Daddy right now."

"I won't accept that. I can't." Anna stood and flexed her fingers towards the table.

The tears and twists of frustration upon Serine's face pulled at Anna. The pain of being Anna's youngest child, the successful, twenty-seven-year-old prosecuting attorney who knew her trade lay hidden, but not quelled. Serine needed Anna to tell her that all would be well with Edward. Unable to do so, Anna felt as if she was betraying her youngest daughter.

Anna observed her left hand empty of the wedding band she had worn for over three decades. *I still love him*, she thought. But there were also the passionate nights Inman had given her. Why couldn't I have shared that kind of passion with Edward?

"What's going on in here?" Edward bellowed from the opposite end of the dining room. Everyone turned. He was wearing a bathrobe with pajamas underneath.

"Daddy, should you be up?" Linda went to him. Brad joined her.

Edward waved them back. He was using a cane to steady himself. Anna started toward him.

"I'm fine." He gestured for her to stay back as he made his way. Reaching the table, he lowered himself onto the seat he had occupied last evening.

"Let me get something straight here." Edward settled his attention on Serine, "No amount of bickering and bantering is going to take away what's eating me up inside. I have cancer. I'm dying. You all had better get used to that." He surveyed the faces around the table then stopped at Serine's. "I've had to."

Serine stood, pushed her chair under the table, and started toward the door. Edward reached for and caught her arm. She pulled away and left. He fell back in his chair, his eyes searching and dazed.

Theo frowned and broke the silence. "She's spoiled and wants her way."

"It's a little more than that," Linda intervened.

"And what might that be?" Theo asked. "We're all affected by this." Theo nodded at Edward. "He's our dad, too."

Rubbing her stomach again, Linda turned to Brad for protection from some powerful force. A knowing passed between them. Last evening Serine had alluded to needing family nearby. *I like having family around, not being alone, unlike some people who don't mind living away from those they claim to love.*

Linda and Brad lived in Los Angeles along with Serine. They had always been attentive to Serine, as much as she would allow. Anna wanted to ask what secret they held about Serine. Yet Linda's obsession with her stomach told Anna all she needed. Anna would not pry, but instead pray for the child she felt certain her eldest daughter was carrying.

"Will any of you let me know if David calls when he reaches Santa Rosa?" Anna said.

"He's already there," Linda said. "They're burying Heather's father tomorrow."

With one hand upon the table, Edward pushed himself to stand. He lifted his cane.

"Are you alright?" Anna asked.

"Nothing that some extra lease on life wouldn't fix." He maneuvered away.

Chapter 13

Anna rose early the next morning and went to the eight o'clock weekday mass at St. Maria's down the hill from the house. She and Edward had attended the parish on and off throughout their marriage. The children went sparingly. Though attending public schools, all had received their first communion at the parish, but none had undergone confirmation.

Raised a Baptist, Edward had thought little of Catholicism. His disinterest had not interfered with Anna's decision to have the children baptized as Catholics. Anna's mother, Elena was a Catholic.

She had converted to Protestantism upon marrying Elijah Chason, a young Baptist minister set on bringing souls to salvation before the flames of hell consumed them. Elena died seven days after Anna gave birth to Linda. The following year Anna had turned to her mother's religion.

As Father Richard offered benediction toward the end of the quiet ceremony, Anna slipped out of the sanctuary and into the chapel at the back. There, before the Virgin Mary, she knelt and prayed for strength to see Edward through his death, and to regain the respect of her children, most particularly David and Serine. As for Theo and Linda, she prayed, "Don't let me take Theo for granted, and please let me not forget Linda."

She was out the door and down the steps when Father Richard called after her. "Anna, it's good to see you. What brings you to mass early this morning?"

Surprised that he had noticed her, Anna turned and climbed back up the steps. The priest met her midway down the steps. Awash with various emotions, it pained Anna to consider how she appeared when Father Richard's warm hand landed upon her shoulder.

"Seems like you could use a good, strong cup of tea."

"I could," she conceded.

Inside the priest's spacious study, he handed her a warm cup of brew. Now free of his robe, Father Richard sat in the leather recliner across from Anna.

"Oooh. This is strong," Anna said after one sip.

"Assam, they call it. Father Will brought it back from India." Three years Edward's senior, Father Richard sipped his tea. "We Americans like our coffee strong, and our tea weak. It's just the opposite for the South Asians."

"Sounds like you know more than a little about teas, coffee, *and* India." Anna took another sip.

"How's Edward, and the children?" Father Richard asked. "I remember baptizing and administering first communion to each of the children. Time flies. Now, they're all married . . . I think."

"All except Serine." Ambivalence pulsed through Anna. She hadn't attended mass in three years. Most wayward Catholics returned for only two reasons, they wanted to re-marry, or someone had died or was *dying*. "They're fine. All at home," she said, the words shaking within. "Edward, well . . . Edward has cancer."

94

Father Richard's face remained kind and free of reaction. "I'm sorry to hear that."

"The oncologist says he has three months to live, six if we're lucky." Anger surged through her. "I'm not sure how lucky we may be. Edward fell yesterday. I spoke to Dr. Grimes afterwards. He urged me to contact hospice."

"How long have you known?"

"Two weeks." Anna explained that she had been pursuing a divorce, and then told him of the long battle that had ensued. "I found out he was sick and dying the day he agreed to the divorce. I took the house off the market and called the children. I told them they needed to come and see their father."

"How are they handling it?" Father Richard asked.

"David and Serine are angry. Theo and Linda seem to be okay. Linda's husband is supportive."

"She seems to have settled into a stable life," Father Richard said. Anna had consulted him during each of Linda's hospitalizations. Father Richard had also flown down with Anna and married Linda and Brad in the backyard of Brad's home.

"Brad is the best thing that has ever happened to her." Anna sighed. "David lives in Detroit, but he's talking about moving back here to Oakland. I'm worried about him and his marriage. Heather's father, Abraham, died yesterday from cancer. It seems to be going around."

Anna gave a bitter smirk. "For the last year, she and the children have been traveling back and forth between Detroit and her father's place in Santa Rosa. David said nothing about his decision to move or about Heather's father being sick until I picked him up from the airport two days ago."

"Hmmm."

"Things have been a bit strained for the past year with the divorce proceedings," Anna confessed. "I haven't been speaking to the children that regularly, except for Theo."

"Were the children upset about the divorce?"

Anna considered the depth of Serine's anger and her accusations. *I can't believe you didn't suspect something during all those meetings over the divorce. He was sitting right there in front of you, wasting away.* "After I told them that I'd asked

95

their father for a divorce, I didn't call them. I didn't answer their calls or return their messages. Theo was persistent. We talk every Friday night."

"Why did you step away from them?"

"I was ashamed."

Father Richard made no sign of judgment.

"After all these years, with everything we've been through, I was asking their father for a divorce." *And then there was Inman.* "I was tired and needed a break. I wasn't about to ask the children for what they couldn't give."

"And what was that?"

"Forgiveness for having lied to them about their father, presenting him as one person while he was really another. Edward went from one woman to the next over the course of our marriage. He never flaunted it. He also never made a secret of it."

Anna leaned back, and took in a breath. "He had a woman wherever he was overseeing a real estate project: South America, Panama, Portugal, Greece." Anna inspected the wedding band on her left hand and grew frustrated at how tight and awkward it had become. She had put it on that morning before leaving for Mass.

Father Richard remained quietly attentive. "The first affair was with woman in Rio de Janeiro. Edward had been flying back and forth for over a year, managing the construction of a hotel on a property he had purchased, and then sold to an American buyer.

I found the letter in the inside pocket of his jacket when I was dropping some of his things off at the cleaners. Stella was her name." Anna continued to stare at her wedding band. "I confronted him when I got home. He said it was nothing. That she was infatuated with him."

"Did you by any chance read the letter?" asked Father Richard.

Relieved that for the first time someone wanted to know—talking to Father Richard was like talking to her father—Anna said, "She never mentioned sex, though I'm sure there was some. Like most of the women whose letters I later found, she thanked him for listening to her, not looking down on her, and of course for giving her money. All the women with whom Edward was involved were poor and struggling, like his mother, Violet."

For the first time ever Anna considered how difficult life must have been for Edward and his mother. "She was grateful," Anna said of Stella. She lifted her head and looked across to Father Richard. "Like Esther and the others, she appreciated how kind he had been to them."

Father Richard and Anna both took a sip of tea. Moments later Anna added, "He never stayed with anyone of them more than two or three years." Again, Anna examined her wedding band. Now feeling slightly loose, she turned it around her finger.

Father Richard said, "How is it that you feel you misrepresented Edward to the children?"

"He's nothing like what they know of him—good father, wonderful provider, hard working. Edward was an adulterer, persistently unfaithful. A philanderer!"

"Are you certain the children had no idea? Better yet, how would it have benefited them to know?"

Again Anna fell sullen. "I suppose I didn't want them to see who I was or what I'd become. I was weak and disgusted with myself." Her thoughts halted preventing the word *adulteress* from slipping through.

She then said, "I've met someone at the gym. I'd been working out while battling with Edward over the divorce. He didn't want to let go of the house. That's all I wanted, no alimony, no part of his business, nothing but to sell the house and split the profit. Edward wouldn't hear of it. It's like the house was his heaven."

"Seems to me you stood to gain more money by accepting the alimony and a part of the worth of the business," Father Richard mused.

"I wanted a clean break, not some monthly installments that Edward could hound me about."

"Why didn't you ask for a lump payment? I'm sure your lawyers could have worked something out."

"I didn't want something worked out." Anna threw up her hands. "I wanted to be free of Edward and that house."

"The one you're back in, and with him and the children."

Again Anna glanced down. "I took the house off the market when I learned he was dying. I asked Edward to let me bring him home. He put up no fuss."

Her mind drifted back. "My attorney was eager to push everything through and file the papers. But I knew something was wrong. I haven't filed the papers. We're still married. The children don't know. Neither does Edward."

She held back tears against the rush of emotions. Pragmatism had allowed Anna to survive her time with Edward. Now parts of her were unwilling to accept that he was truly dying.

A wave of grief and disempowerment overtook her. Just as she had been unable to keep Edward home and faithful, she was now unable to save him from the cancer.

"What are your plans for the time you have left with him?" Father Richard asked.

"I was going to take my half of the proceeds from the sale of the house and move to France. I've always wanted to live outside the country. Anna did not answer Father Richard's question.

Instead she described her dreams of living abroad. "When I was in college I wanted to study abroad. Mama said it was unsafe and too expensive."

That's what white people do, Elena had said. Again she had been knitting. Like times before when stating her case to Anna, she had not looked up.

Elena's fingers had continued moving. *Your father's not made of money. He's a minister. And congregations don't want their preachers living like movie stars.*

Anna and her mother had been sitting in the living room the plastic encasing the sofa, on which Anna had been sitting, had crackled.

How she hated it. *The need to protect.*

Anna felt like that sofa, its cushions encased and unable to breathe.

She looked to Father Richard, sitting in the chair across from her, and she on the sofa much like she had been with Anna. "Edward gave me freedom, or at least the hope of it."

Still avoiding Father Richard's question, Anna said, "I majored in art history— something Mama thought was impractical. Thank God Daddy was paying the bills.

After the conversation with Mama I felt guilty. I didn't want members of the church thinking we were rich. But I felt stifled. And then there was the matter of leaving Daddy with Mama."

"Your parents didn't get along?"

"They were civil. Daddy loved Mama. But she always seemed unhappy, bitter. I don't know why." Anna took in breath. "I thought maybe when I graduated, I'd go to Paris on my own and get a job in the Louvre as a docent. Then I met Edward."

Anna laughed. "He was a year out of Cal, working in real estate, determined to make something of himself," Anna continued. "I envied that, his sense of purpose. Nothing was going to stop him."

Father Richard remained attentive.

"The day I graduated, I asked him what would become of us. There was no way I was going back home to my parents. Edward suggested we get married the next day. 'But we need a marriage license,' I told him."

Anna explained. "That's when Edward pulled an envelope from the pocket of his jacket and handed it to me. 'I've had it for a month,' he said. *'Will you marry me?'* His lips seemed to tremble, like the afternoon in the hospital when I asked him to let me take him home and care for him."

Father Richard repeated his unanswered question, "What will make of the time you have left?"

"I'll care for Edward, try to make him as comfortable as possible. I don't want him to die alone." Anna recalled Elena's last days. The Reverend Elijah had urged Anna to visit her mother. Anna had refused. "I was pregnant when Mama died. Edward and I were not having a good time of it." Again she stated, "I don't want Edward to die alone."

"I'm sure he appreciates that." The priest's words did not match his demeanor. He seemed to expect more from Anna. She grew anxious. He then said, as if knowing she needed to hear it, "You're a good woman, Anna. So many women in your position would gloat over the deck of cards life has dealt a husband like Edward.

Instead, what I hear from you is a fairly deep sense of commitment, and concern for a man who's done little to make himself available to you or anyone, even the women with whom he was involved. And yet, rarely are the things we do as humans completely altruistic."

"What good would it do for me to be angry with him?"

"Nicely put, but what is it you hope to gain by offering Edward an olive branch in taking him back, particularly since he has such a short time to live?"

"You sound protective of Edward. I mean him no harm."

"I believe you," said Father Richard. "But he *is* dying."

"Why is it so hard to believe that I want to help him and make his last days comfortable?" Anna thought of Inman. Will I lose him in the process of helping Edward in his last days? "Edward has no right to live the kind of life he has and then up and die like this. It's not fair."

"You say this despite having fought for over a year to leave him."

"That's not fair."

"Truth is not always fair and just."

And then the words, "I've been sleeping with Inman," slipped from Anna's lips. "He's asked me to marry him." It was a confession of sorts.

"How did you leave things with Inman?"

"I told him I needed time to take care of Edward and spend time with him. Inman seemed to understand. He's a widower. His wife was killed in a car accident two years after she left him and their daughter. That was twenty years ago."

"How were things with you and Inman before learning of Edward's illness?"

Again Anna shied from directness. "He's somewhat like Edward, determined and hardworking. But he likes being with me." Anna grew warm. "He's good in bed." Anna considered the last years of her marriage. "I can't remember the last time Edward and I made love before I asked for the divorce."

"Was that one of the things that prompted you to request a divorce?"

Startled at Father Richard's directness mixed with a lack of judgment, Anna settled into thought. She had endured three decades of infidelity. She said, "I'm not sleeping with Edward now that he's home."

"But, you're still married to him."

"What are you getting at?"

"He can't cheat on you now."

Why have you brought Edward home? The question hung in the chambers of Anna's mind.

The priest asked, "Is there anything you'd like to say to him?"

"There's a lot I could say. I don't know if it would be the right thing. He is dying."

Father Richard became thoughtful. He then said, "There's a group of Proverbs, African. They go like this. 'Death needs a strong heart. The goat says, Nobody willingly walks to his own death. If one could know where death resided, one would never stop there.'"

A lump formed in Anna's throat against the priest's recitation of truths that knew no denial.

"'Death does not sound a trumpet. When death holds something in its grip, life cannot take it away. Death is one ditch you cannot jump. Whatever you love, death also loves. Lie down and die. You will see who really loves you."

At that, Anna gasped and caught her lips. She began to cry.

Chapter 14

Anna arrived back home to find Edward lying upon the chaise on the patio. He was reading.

"Where are the children?" she asked.

"Theo, Linda, and Brad went to the grocery store. Seems they're preparing a special meal tonight."

I did that last night, Anna thought. "And Serine?"

"She's upstairs packing. Says she has court tomorrow." Edward didn't look up from his magazine.

"She just got here two days ago, and late at that. I need to speak with her." Anna turned to leave.

"Let her be." Despite his quasi-scolding last evening and yesterday morning, Edward appeared content to let Serine leave in what Anna considered a huff. His eyes remained glued to the magazine.

"I don't know how you can be so cavalier about this," Anna quipped.

"What do you want me to do?" He lowered the magazine and laid it upon the table beside him. "Tell her she can't go back to work because her father is dying of cancer?"

"I would think she might see the need to spend a little more time here with you. I'm not saying she has to quit her job." She considered Serine's berating, and then Father Richard's missive. *If you wanted a clean break, why have you brought Edward home, even if it is to die?* She took in Edward reclining on the chaise, the table to his right, and the pool on the left. He resumed reading his magazine.

The title on the cover read *Tricycle*. It was written in gold. Below it stood a Buddhist nun with a shaven head. She appeared to chide Anna toward compassion. What was it that had drawn him to marry her and then wander from one woman to another every five or six years? Anna labored to understand Edward.

"What did they have that I didn't?" The words eased from her lips. Again, he lowered the magazine, this time upon his lap. "Stella, Esther, and the others," Anna said. "What did they give you that I couldn't?"

Edward appeared to have stopped breathing, time was holding its own, marching to a beat outside of their hearts, and ticking toward an uncertain eternity held in the net of their mortality. He parted his lips and was about to speak when a crowd of voices rounded the corner of the house. Linda, Theo, and Brad stepped onto the patio. A fourth, unknown man came with them.

"Mom, Dad, look who we found," Theo said. He approached Anna standing by the patio table next to the chaise where Edward lay stretched. "Serine's fiancé."

Theo had told Anna that the person who gave Serine an engagement ring was named Grant. None of the children, nor Anna, had met him. Grant was the district attorney who had interviewed and hired Serine. She had spent half the meal listing the attributes of Grant Seifert, D.A. "There's a lot I can learn from him," Serine had said after two months on the job. "He's got some great ideas about the law and how to prosecute criminals. Whatever he shares will serve me well."

104

Anna extended her hand to the young man standing beside Theo. "Pleased to meet you."

The young man shook Anna's hand. His blue eyes sparkled. "Pleased to meet you, Mrs. Manning."

"I'll go let Serine know you're here," Linda said as she left. Brad lifted the groceries and followed her inside.

Theo introduced the young man to Edward.

"So you're with the D.A.'s office?" Edward sat forward as he laid the magazine on the table.

"Yeah, I guess so," he replied.

Donning a fresh tan, the young white man wore old, faded jeans and a shirt of similar quality. He could pass for a college freshman. Intuition and thirty years of living with Edward Manning told Anna that this young man was not a district attorney, but instead a person who had decided to wake up. A fiery sensation started in Anna's stomach and sank into her pelvis. This young man was not Grant Seifert.

"Would you like something to drink?" Anna asked. "Tea, soda, water?"

"Water would be fine," the young man said.

"Have a seat," Theo invited the young man.

"And have some lunch with us," Edward said.

"So, is Serine around?" the young man asked. He remained standing.

"She's packing." Anna returned to the patio with a tray bearing four glasses of ice, a carafe of water, and a pitcher of tea. "Seems as though she has court tomorrow." She sat the tray on the table, then eyed Edward.

"That's right." The young man pocketed his hands. He was pretending and posing as Grant, exactly as Anna had done with the receptionist after following Bryce to Hammond Hospital.

Edward lifted the magazine and resumed reading.

"So, Serine told you she was coming up here?" Anna asked.

"I was with her when you called," the young man said to Anna. He glanced at Edward absorbed in the words of the magazine. Anna wanted to rip the circular from his hand. A

105

charade rooted in Serine's misbehavior was occurring before their eyes and Edward acted oblivious.

"I wanted to come with her," the young man said to Anna. "I told her she should take some time off, and that I would drive her. She said she'd be okay, that she needed a day or so alone." The sparkle in his blue eyes dimmed with what appeared a sadness of knowing his own loss. "I was worried about her."

Anna was certain that Serine had spent much time speaking about, if not criticizing, her to the young man. Anna concluded the young man's visit had been as much an expedition to clarify facts about Serine's family or perhaps about Anna. Maybe it had been to discover who Serine truly was and what she was up to.

Serine's face went from placid dispassion to complete disdain and mortification as she passed through the entryway of the sliding glass door and onto the patio. Serine rushed toward the young man who was standing beside Anna.

"Why did you come here? I told you I'd been fine." Anna's youngest child bore the demeanor of guilt that Edward had worn for three decades.

"Grant's come to see about you," Anna said. "He was worried."

Serine shot her mother a cool glance of horror mixed with rage.

"I had to see for myself." The boy was no fool. Anna was about to ask his real name, but then a tall, muscled figure sporting a tailored navy suit, white shirt, and red tie emerged from around the corner of the house. His stride conveyed a manner of consequence and determination.

"Grant!" Serine ran to the dark-skinned man in the suit.

Last ebbs of color drained from the face of the young white man. A horrible wave of embarrassment swept over Anna. Relieved as she was that she had not misjudged her daughter, some parts of her wished that she had.

"You told me to come around the back way," the real Grant, tall and brown, pulled her to him and landed a light kiss on her cheek. Serine shuttled him to the far side of the pool.

The cold amazement on the face of the young unnamed man revealed that he had uncovered the very thing for which he had come hunting. Theo abandoned the fray and went inside.

Anna said to the young man, "Would you like to go inside, perhaps in the kitchen, and sit down?"

Emerging from what Anna could only imagine as the fathomless pits of whirling thoughts came the words, "Yes, I'd like that."

Anna placed the glass of water on the kitchen table and then sat adjacent to the young man. Edward remained upon the chaise reading, and sinking further into what Anna regarded as, *that infernal magazine.*

"How do you know my daughter?" Anna asked.

"We live together. Well, sometimes I spend the night with her." He lowered his gaze to the glass of water and stared as if he was unable to make sense of what was occurring.

A bit bewildered by his motivations that she was yet to tease apart, Anna yet respected and liked the young man. It took courage to drive eight hours into the unknown to seek out the truth. "What's your name," she asked.

"I'm sorry. It's Matthew." Again, he extended his tanned, pink hand, this time less warily. Again she shook it. "My friends call me Matt."

"I'm Anna. Always have been; always will be, Anna. At least in this lifetime." The two laughed.

Solemnity reasserted itself in Matt's demeanor. His body seemed to lose energy. He leaned back into his chair and attempted to straighten his shoulders.

"I love your daughter. But I don't think it's meant for us to be together, at least not in this lifetime."

Anna found the qualification interesting and profound. "Why do you say that?" she asked.

Matt remained focused upon Serine and Grant on the other side of the pool. He turned and said, "You mean other than the obvious?"

Chapter 15

Anna felt herself slipping back in time as Matt's gaze receded.

You know," Matt said, "I don't think the unfaithful are the ones at fault. It's people like me who won't give up, and refuse to see the futility of our hopes. We won't stop dreaming." He appeared to know much about the Manning family drama. Anna's intrigue of him deepened. "Hopes aren't always founded on solid experiences," he continued. "As my therapist explains, dreams compliment our waking experiences, the day-to-day reality we don't always like or trust. Dreams don't lie, ever."

Once again Matt turned to the sliding glass door, and observed Serine and Grant arguing on the far side of the pool. Edward, under the awing, and seemingly oblivious, continued reading.

"I had a dream right after Serine learned her father was dying," Matt said. "She was tending Mr. Manning in his last moments. She was crying, begging him not to die."

Feeling exposed, Anna grew anxious. The struggles of her family had spread beyond the confines of her and her children's emotions and were touching the lives of those on the periphery.

"He died," Matt went on describing his dream. "Serine lay on his chest, still and sad, her eyes glaring, seeing but not seeing, longing for what could have been, but never was."

Anna lowered her eyelids.

Moments later Matt said, "I'm a painter. I do abstracts. I met Serine when she came to one of my shows. I liked the way she interpreted my paintings. Or rather that she *didn't*. I caught her observing the centerpiece of the exhibit, the largest one in the show. I had painted the back of woman. She was nude.

In the top right corner the sun was setting in the west. In the bottom left side, another sun was rising. *Life and death, side by side*. Serine stood in front of the painting, observed it for a long time. I walked over to her, and told her I was the artist. At first, she didn't believe me."

"That's Serine all right. A prosecutor forever on the offensive."

"She never said like some people, 'Oh, I could tell you were the artist.' Instead, she explained, 'It reminds me how exposed I feel when I'm in love.'"

Anna's breath grew shallow and tense.

"I fell in love with her right then," said Matt. She had seen right through me. She knew how I felt when I was painting the woman. The painting was me.

Every person I paint is *me*," Matt said. I worked on the nude woman throughout the last stages of my mother's breast cancer. The woman was my hurt, the living and the dying, and the loss of my mother. The two suns were the freedom I felt when she finally died."

"When was the show where you met Serine?"

"About a year ago, late August, early September," Matt said.

"How prophetic," Anna mused.

Twelve months earlier she had entered the throes of seeking a divorce. She had notified the children. Serine was not

110

home when Anna had called. Anna had left a message. Days later, Serine called back saying that she didn't know how Anna could do such a thing. The conversation had continued with Serine launching intense accusations declaring Anna's lack of concern for the family and their needs. Serine ended the raw treatise with, "I'm engaged."

Through the sliding glass door, Anna saw Serine and Grant's argument had reach a head.

"Excuse me for a moment," she said to Matt. Anna walked past Edward still lying on the chaise and reading, and continued to the far side of the pool. Approaching Serine and Grant, she formed a cordial smile and extended her hand to Grant.

"Hello, I'm Anna Manning,"

"Grant Seifert." He shook her hand.

"I hope you're making yourself at home," Anna said, "—as much as you can." She eyed Serine standing beside him. Grant was as much a victim of Serine's emotional social play as Matt.

"There's some tea and water on the patio table." Glimpsing Edward still reading and seemingly unaffected by Serine's machinations, Anna grew angrier. "I wouldn't go inside," she said to Grant. "In fact, *don't* go inside." She eyed Serine, whose face swung between imminent rage and fearsome shame. "I need to speak with you," Anna said to Serine. Turning to Grant, she said, "Excuse me while I borrow my daughter for a moment."

Inside the house, Serine followed Anna into Theo's old bedroom. Anna closed the door.

"Care to tell me what's going on? Or would you rather leave it up to my intuition?" Anna asked.

"Why not your imagination?" Serine smarted.

"Believe me, young lady, my imagination could never have concocted a story of this proportion."

"Of this proportion?" Serine rocked her head left to right while mimicking Anna. "I'm dealing with this."

111

"Don't give me that. You're acting like a spoiled teenager rather than a responsible woman soon to be twenty-eight. Is this how you behave as a district attorney?"

"Assistant D.A.," Serine corrected, "—more to the point, the *assistant* to the *assistant* D.A."

"Oh, come off of it. And don't mock me." Anna bristled.

"Being a district attorney is not all it's cracked up to be." Serine meandered into discussing her world.

"Care to tell me why you took the job, or rather how much of you taking the job had to do with your attraction to Grant? I mean the *real* Grant?" Anna's words had carried a softness her opening question had lacked.

"I like Grant Seifert, but he frightens me." Serine's lips trembled. "He wants the whole nine yards, children, the house, commitment, the entire forever thing."

"But you're wearing Grant's engagement ring." Anna gathered herself. "Does he know about Matt?"

"He does now." Tears slid down Serine's face. "I told Grant that I've been sleeping with Matt since he gave me the ring."

"Oh, Serine." Anna' heart sank. She felt herself shattering within.

"Oh Serine, what? That I was betraying him or that I told him?"

"How about both?" While Edward had possessed his foibles, he had provided a home and security for which many would have died, if not killed. Anna could not understand Serine's actions or desires. What did she want or hope to gain from betraying both these men?

Serine said, "I'm not going to stand here and listen to you accuse me of what I've already berated and hung myself for." She moved to leave. Anna grabbed her arm. Serine's use of the word *hung* hovered in Anna's mind.

"We can get through this." Anna said.

"What? Me betraying Matt, and losing Grant, or Daddy dying?"

"All three. It's better to get these things out now rather than later."

"You mean after we're married, me and Grant, so that we won't become like you and Daddy?" Against anger moving full steam, Serine dried her tears.

"There's more than Grant to consider in this," Anna said. "Matt is a nice, young man."

"He's just a *fuck buddy*," Serine spat.

Anna slapped her youngest child's cheek. Quickly she grasped her lips then astonished at what she had done, murmured through her fingers, "I'm so sorry."

Weeping once more and trembling, Serine jerked open the door and ran to her room.

Chapter 16

W ithout knocking, Anna barged into Serine's room across the hall. "We're not finished talking."

"You don't *love* Daddy. And you *hate* me. You—" Serine hesitated. Anna breathed in and forced down her hurt and anger as Serine laid out her dilemma.

"You didn't *like* Daddy either. I *like* Grant. I *love* Matt." Serine said, "Problem is I don't love *and* like either one of them. I want to like *and* love whomever I sleep with. But I *can't*." Penitent, Serine slumped onto her bed.

Anna felt shameful for having slapped her daughter. Her efforts falling short of answering Serine, Anna then considered Inman and berated herself for giving into her passions and needs. She trudged back to Theo's room where hollowness engulfed her.

Anna lay upon the bed. Fumbling through remnants of memories. She was deep in thought and holding her arms when after a knock sounded from the door, Linda entered.

"Dad's not feeling well. Brad's bringing him up."

Reaching the landing, Anna saw Brad and Theo helping Edward climb the stairs.

"I'm just tired," Edward said as if to calm her.

You were only reading, Anna thought.

She turned to Linda. "Where are Matt and Grant?"

"I'll see to them." Linda started downstairs. Serine was still in her room sulking.

Anna went inside the bedroom where Edward lay on the bed. She closed the door as Theo and Brad left, then proceeded to tuck Edward under the covers.

"It's some mess we've gotten ourselves into," he murmured as she propped his head upon the pillow. "Our children are lost," he added.

"They're fine," Anna said. She gave the covers one last pull.

"This is not something you can clean away or that can be ironed out in the dryer." Edward's words shocked her.

"The way you appeared on the patio seemed to indicate you had full confidence in our children." She went to the closet and pulled down another pillow.

"I'm a fool," Edward said. "Or rather, I've developed the uncanny ability to convince people I'm stronger or less affected, or that I don't know any better."

"Like me." Anna returned with the pillow hugged to her chest.

Edward regarded the pillow. "You could smother me you know? I couldn't stop you."

"Was that supposed to be some kind of sick joke?" Stunned, Anna took a moment to register the words, their meaning, and then on bolstering his pillow. "Sit up," she placed the pillow under his head.

"I'm serious," Edward egged on while obeying her.

"You want me to smother you and go to jail?" She stepped back. "What good would that do?"

"Maybe get out some of your anger."

She sighed.

"I just want it to be over," Edward stated blankly. "Actually, I'm scared."

"I need to see about Matt and Grant, and dinner." She walked to the door.

"It's going to get messy."

"It's been messy all along." Anna turned back.

"Not like now. This time I won't be coming back."

Anna wanted to lunge herself upon Edward, shake him and scream, How could you do this? Instead, she pulled the door open, and was about to exit when Edward spoke.

"About Stella and Esther?" The door wide open, Anna slowly turned once more. "They had nothing on you," he said. Edward's amber eyes appeared lost and dazed—a feature she had never seen nor associated with *the* Edward Manning with whom she had become accustomed. Something had happened over the past year.

Anna steeled herself against a torrent of emotions brewing to a boil. "I was scared," he said. Edward lowered his head.

Anna breathed in the hurt she so wanted to relinquish, feelings of betrayal she had hoped to abandon while moving through The Louvre and The Hermitage museums of Paris and St. Petersburg while viewing the works of art they housed. Calmly, she walked to Edward.

"You were arrogant and self-serving just like our youngest daughter." Matt's soft pink face came before her. *I don't think it's meant for me to be with your daughter in this lifetime . . . We won't relinquish our dreams.* "Your behavior has been abominable," Anna continued. "It hurt, terribly. Most of all, it affected these children, our children. *Your* children."

Edward examined his hands and pulled at his fingers. He still wore his wedding band. A roller coaster of memories reeled across her thoughts. She considered the late night breast-feedings of David, Theo, Linda, and Serine. As infants in her arms, their tiny lips explored her nipples. Edward was either absent or watching from a distance, heated anger writhing within his stare.

117

"What was it about me becoming a mother?" Anna asked. "What turned you away when I gave birth to your children and loved them?" She had only been trying to give them what she had not received from Elena, and what Violet had lacked, irrespective of her intent toward Edward. *A show of love. Someone.*

"I envied them," Edward said. The sorrow of his admission overtook the room, and ripped away one more layer of the dank, sordid history standing between them.

"You were jealous of them? They were babies, infants— *our* children." Anna's chest sank.

"I was jealous of *you*." Edward lifted his head. And for a moment, Anna beheld the hurting child he had been when he confronted the doctor with whom Edward's mother had had a long-standing affair. She recalled Edward's fury at Violet's grave site. He had caught the doctor kneeling at Violet's casket about to be lowered into the ground.

"You killed her," Edward had said to him. "You killed her more than the drugs you prescribed for her."

"I loved your mother," the pale-skinned doctor had said.

"You're a liar. An absolute, fucking, liar."

"Your mother meant everything to me."

"Then, why didn't you marry her?"

"I asked and she refused. She said she could never trust a white man."

"You're a goddamn lie!" Edward punched the man and knocked him to the ground.

Anna rushed to Edward and pulled at his arm as others looked on. "We should go," she whispered.

He pushed her away, his attention fixed upon the doctor lying in the dirt. Placing his foot upon the man's neck, he riled, "Don't ever come near my mother's grave site again. If I suspect, or even wake up from a dream where I see you here, I swear I'll hunt you down, and kill you, piece by piece."

The same rage that welled in Edward's eyes that day three decades earlier had swirled in Serine's when she described Matt as nothing but a sexual toy. Matt's dream of Edward's dying body upon the bed came into focus then dissipated.

The memory faded. Settled back in the present moment, Anna took in Edward lying upon the bed. Death was encroaching upon his weak body. He was shriveling. Slowly, she returned to the door, walked through, and pulled it closed.

Chapter 17

Grant Seifert had removed the jacket to his suit when Anna approached him on the patio. He was standing by the pool with his back to her, his hands pocketed as he observed the water.

"It's normally full of trash this time of the year," Anna said on reaching him, "I'm usually biting my nails and trying to decide whether to continue with the weekly cleanings or to close it for the winter."

Grant turned to her, removed his hands from his pocket, and gave a half chuckle. "My mother always had the same problem."

"What does she do now?"

"Nothing presently. She's dead."

"I'm sorry." Anna glanced down at the water.

"Don't be. She's in a better place."

Where Matt was soft spoken and direct in his questioning, Grant Seifert wanted to convey that he possessed all the answers. Anna took in Grant's chiseled, athletic face and wondered had his mother's death been sudden. "Were you with her when she died?"

"As a matter of fact, I was in Europe. She was in a car accident." Grant sighed. "It paralyzed her from the neck down. She was on a ventilator."

"How long did she survive like that?"

"Three days. My plane landed six hours after she died." A melancholic smile assumed control of Grant's all-about-business demeanor. His shoulders became curved and human-like rather than square and soldierly as if prepared to fight the enemy of the ubiquitous and ever present criminal. "My father was with her when she passed."

"That was good," Anna said, "—that she wasn't alone."

The brightness went from Grant's eyes. Yet they remained sternly attentive. "My mother was a strong woman. What white people term a *loner*. She kept the truth about herself and who she really was close to her vest."

A chilly sense of self-recognition rushed through Anna. She lifted her hands to her chest. Realizing what she had done, she let them fall to her sides.

"I don't know what it is with you women," Grant said, and then on catching the harshness of his words, "Excuse me, but I need to be frank." Anna recognized that beyond outward appearances that Grant needed Serine more than the reverse. "Why isn't it enough for us to love and need you? Why can't you lean and depend on us, and let us take care of you?"

"Perhaps it's because too many of us have been let down and disappointed."

"We're not all the same." Grant clinched his jaw. He had connected with Serine's goodness, what was hidden and protected by her anger.

Anna considered Stella, Esther, and the three or four others with whom Edward had been involved.

"I want to give myself to Serine, all of myself, not parts like that artist fellow."

"I don't know if that's a correct assessment of Matt's intentions." Anna's identification with Matt went deep. "Perhaps the better question is why did Serine let it happen?"

122

"She was confused," Grant said. "Your decision to divorce her father was tearing her apart, upsetting her. Her father had been unfaithful to you many times, but she couldn't understand why you waited so long, and after so much had gone on."

That seemed to be the sixty-four-thousand-dollar question. Anna calmed herself. "Sometimes it takes awhile to realize that not only are we unhappy but what we might do about it."

"Thirty-three years?" Grant frowned. Anna sensed that Grant's interest in why she had chosen to divorce Edward somehow trailed back to his mother's death. "Why do you stay with the ones of us who mistreat you and don't give you what you want and need, but leave those of us who love you, open our hearts, and pour out all we have?"

"Is that what you view me as having done?" Anna considered her words to Inman when telling him of Edward's illness and wanting to care for him. *I need to be with him*, to which, Inman had replied, *I also need you to be certain of what you feel for me.*

Grant's countenance turned sad. "My mother left my father for a man half her age, and with none of my father's integrity. I was in law school, studying in Budapest at the time. Mama and I talked often. I was an only child. She never said anything about why she had ditched Dad—even when I told her that I knew, and questioned her. I found out through my grandmother, her mother, that she'd left my father. She never told me she was leaving, or *why*."

"Perhaps she didn't know why."

"Oh, she knew alright," Grant said. The prosecutor driven by the young adult searching for answers had returned. "She knew her answer betrayed her guilt and would never measure up. My Dad was innocent." The force with which Grant spoke launched a blast of insight.

Anna saw herself not only as like Grant's deceased mother—some part of her dead and another part dying—Anna also felt a kinship with Grant's father, the part of herself that possessed no voice, or rather refused to speak. "No one's innocent in a marriage," Anna said. "Guilt is always shared. We are not what we think, you, me, Serine, Edward, Matt, my children, your parents." Anna was amazed at the level of honesty with which Serine had spoken to Grant of Edwards's dalliances. It revealed a depth of truth unblemished by youth and innocence.

Matt's a fuck buddy; that's all. Again, Anna trembled at having slapped the most vulnerable of her children.

She said, "For the past year, I have been engaged in trying to divorce Edward. I've wanted my freedom for a long time. And now that Edward is dying and has maybe less time than the doctor says, I'm afraid. I'm afraid and angry that death is taking him from me."

Anna had never realized until she met Matt, and was now speaking with Grant that without Edward in the world, as unfaithful as he was, she would be alone.

"I would expect you to feel vindicated." Grant's eyes receded as if recalling his father's loss—the anger and hurt he might have felt when his wife, Grant's mother, died.

"For thirty-three years I've been having an affair with my loneliness and private frustrations," Anna said. "They've been with me all my life. It's drew me to marry Edward. I wanted to escape myself, who I was, what I hated."

She forced a bittersweet smile, and staved back tears. "Now I won't have him abandoning and frustrating me with his self-absorption and perpetual traveling. When he leaves this time, he'll never return."

Chapter 18

Anna's conversation with Grant awakened within her a nest of questions buzzing for answers. She drove to the cemetery behind the *Chapel of the Chimes*. The quietness held within the high stone walls surrounding the graveyard against the bustle of the streets beyond delivered a tranquilizing effect as she walked between the headstones of the dead.

Anna slowed in nearing the markers bearing her mother's and father's names: Elena Chason and Reverend Elijah Chason. Kneeling at the marker, she recalled her father's words when learning of Elena's prognosis. *Your mother's dying. I don't know what I'm going to do.*

"You'll be fine." Anna had said. They were at the old Providence Hospital; her mother was in a room a few steps beyond where she and her father stood. She had placed her hand upon Elijah's trembling shoulder. His face was blank; his eyes were empty pools of misery. Anna wished she could have entered his eyes then traveled the banks of his memory and uncovered why and what had ever drawn him to her mother.

"I love her," he said.

"I'll drive you home,"

"But my car," Elijah said. "How will I get it home?" He had come hours earlier. After speaking with Elena's doctors, he had called Anna.

"Edward and I will come back for your car."

"Is he home?"

"Yes," Anna said.

Reverend Elijah seemed surprised. He handed over the keys to his car. She accompanied him downstairs and to the garage.

Minutes later and moving down Telegraph Avenue, he asked, "Are you happy?" The Reverend had seemed more bereft in asking that question than in telling Anna of her mother's prognosis.

"Yes," Anna said. Pregnant with Linda, she still held hope for her marriage.

They reached her parents' home on Union Street in Oakland. She took him inside and prepared dinner.

"I doubt I'll be able to eat anything." Elijah moaned. One day Elena had been ironing his shirts for Sunday services; the next she'd been unable to get out of bed. Her illness had shocked him. *Brain cancer last stages*, the doctors had said. Anna set the plate on the table. "What will I do?" Reverend Elijah had asked. He looked to his only child.

"What you've always done." Anna sat next to him. "What *we've* always done. Pray." But she hadn't prayed in a while. This would be her first time in years looking to God for help. Not even Edward's malfeasances had forced her to look outside herself for answers.

The approaching death of Elena Chason, stalwart helpmate of a minister, and a mother with little show of affection, had drawn on Anna's vulnerabilities. *My mother's dying. Daddy is losing his wife. We don't know what to do. Help us, oh Lord, to see this through. Help us.* And, there was the church where Elijah had ministered for more than thirty years. *Guide Daddy in what to do.*

During the last five years of occupying his position, Elijah had been reticent to share his duties with a younger assistant who would eventually take over and make it difficult to attract another minister.

Anna began washing the dishes.

"Daddy, you need to think about finding someone to help out at the church," she urged. "Not that they have to completely take over, but you need someone to preach at least two Sundays a month."

"Delivering the word of God is my way of life." Elijah sighed. Still at the kitchen table, he leaned back in his chair as if acquiescing. "Without your mother around, not preaching would be like—" He turned to Anna. "It would be like you losing David, Theo, and the baby you're carrying, no clothes to fold, no one needing your food, or *you*. With Edward away all the time, you'd lose hope."

Anna realized that Elijah knew of the problem plaguing her marriage, Edward's unfaithfulness.

Back at home, she told Edward of her mother's condition. "Mama's dying and Daddy doesn't know what to do. I'm worried about him."

"Then, bring him here," Edward said as he undressing.

"I don't want to move him here. And, besides, he wouldn't come."

"Why not? The house is plenty big enough. We have five bedrooms." Edward had begun plans for a house when learning that Anna was pregnant with David two years earlier. Violet had died the afternoon Edward was meeting with the architect.

"I don't think it would be good to uproot him. Two losses might topple him over."

"Suit yourself. The offer stands."

Fuming at Edward's callous response, she turned from the closet, and walked to him. "If you really want to know why I don't want Daddy here, it's because I'm ashamed for him to see me here alone with you away all the time."

"I work," Edward snapped.

"Yes, you work. But you also play quite rudely and very dangerously." Anna wondered if any of the women with whom Edward had affairs were married or had boyfriends.

"Come off your high horse, Anna. You have everything any woman could need or want."

"Except you."

He got in bed. "You have me as much as any woman can expect to have a man when he's working to provide for his family."

"Did you give Stella as much as you give me, David, and Theo?" Anna had massaged her abdomen containing Linda.

Edward rolled over and turned away from her.

"I told you that was over."

"And, I don't believe you." Anna had seen letters from Esther.

"That's *your* choice. As long as I provide for you and David, I'd say you have little to grumble about."

"I deserve better," she spoke to his back then hit his shoulder. He whipped over on the bed and grabbed her wrist. "This is the only way I can get you to touch me."

Edward dropped her hand. He lay back down, and again turned from her.

"What's wrong with me, Edward? Surely it's not because I'm pregnant, that I'm a mother—*the mother of your children*? My mother is dying. My father is out of his mind with worry. Soon he'll be alone." Anna didn't know quite what it was that her father would miss about her mother. What had drawn him to marry such a cold and soulless person?

"You're just like her, the two of you cut from the same cloth, you and Mama."

"I thought you said she didn't like me?" Edward popped up. Redness filled the whites of his eyes surrounding his amber pupils.

"Takes one to find one. One thief always knows another."

Edward jumped out of bed. "If I'm so much like your mother, why'd you marry me? The way you're describing us sounds like you've got a fair amount of her in you."

"She *is* my mother."

"So what are you saying," he yelled, "that you married me because I reminded you of your mother? Or of *yourself?*"

"I'm saying I'm tired of being here alone while you travel around the world. Why can't you focus on real estate here in Oakland, Berkeley, or San Francisco?"

"And there aren't women here, too?" A light flickered in Edward's eyes and quickly died.

Anna recalled how he had said, *I'm not like your father. I'm immunized against poverty. I can't promise much. I'll give you a house.* When learning Anna was pregnant with David he had stated, *I won't have my son growing up in an apartment. We'll need a house, a home.* Propelled by the memory, Anna had asked, "What is it with you and things—money?"

"It takes money to keep this house and allow you to stay home and care for my sons. And in case you haven't noticed, we have another child on the way."

"These are my children."

He looked to her bulging stomach with what seemed vehement and disappointment. "Ownership does not bequeath capital. It takes capital to live."

"And what is our capital?" Anna asked. "Why aren't we living as man and wife rather than as a two people under the same roof?"

"Thank God we have one."

"But what keeps us, going as we do, under it?" Anna drew near. "Don't you want something better?" Again she grasped her stomach, fearful of how all the negative energies between her and Edward would affect the child she was carrying. Despite the anger and frustration, she had grown warm and moist between her legs. There was something about Edward when angry that rendered him vulnerable—and *attractive.*

"And what the hell is *better?*" Edward sat up and raised his arms as if to encompass the house. "This conversation is ridiculous." He got out of bed and headed for the door. "Your

129

father's welcome to live here whenever he likes." He pulled open the door and left.

Anna ran her fingers across the name etched into the headstone, *Reverend Elijah Fredrick Chason. Loving husband and father. Dedicated minister. Servant of God. 1910–1980.* As the memory receded from the shores of her mind, Anna removed her wedding band. She considered burying it in the dirt near the headstone. But she could not. Instead, she placed it in her pocket and drove home.

Chapter 19

The water kettle let out a piercing cry as Anna entered the kitchen. She slung her purse onto the chair at the table.

"Want some?" Theo asked. He turned off the flame and poured steaming water into a mug.

"Hot tea on a warm afternoon in Indian summer?" Anna walked to the counter.

"It calms the nerves," Theo said.

Yours or mine? Anna wondered.

Theo filled a second cup and smiled then said, "You look like you could use a tranquilizer." He went to the table and sat. Anna lifted the second mug from the counter, filled it, and joined him at the table.

"I assume that since the house is still standing, Matt and Grant never crossed paths," Anna said. She stirred her tea, lifted the bag from the mug, and laid it on the saucer between them.

"Oh they crossed paths all right. But I think by the time they did, it was obvious Serine had duped both of them." Theo sipped his tea.

He's just a fuck buddy. Anna pushed Serine's words into the back of her mind. "I can't believe that girl. I've a good mind to—Where *is* she?"

"Save your strength. Brad and Linda drove her to the airport. She's headed back to L.A.," Theo said.

Anna blew across the brim of the mug. "Just like her father, running away from the consequences she created."

"I think she calls it being fair and staying neutral."

"On what?"

"She didn't want to give either Matt or Grant any ideas," Theo said.

"More than wearing Grant's engagement ring? I'd never speak to her again if I were either of them. She'd better hope neither one kills her."

"I doubt that. They're too much in love with her."

"Don't you mean to say they each realize how much a waste of time she is?" Theo stared at her, as even Anna did not believe her own words. "I'm embarrassed," she said.

"From a man's perspective, both Grant and Matt knew about Serine long before today. There's no way each of them couldn't have known the other existed, unless they didn't want to."

"But Serine accepted Grant's ring."

"Still, you can't *not know.*" Theo held to his point.

"So he's battling for her, Grant?"

"Or he's avoiding something within himself, same as Matt."

"Like me with the women with whom your father was involved?"

"Dad was your husband."

"He still is," Anna said. "Only I refused to see who he really was."

"You said that," Theo said.

Anna flashed her left palm for him to remain silent. Theo noticed she wasn't wearing her wedding band. Her words had revealed, and exposed, more than she had intended. Grant's words returned. *Serine was hurt that you decided to leave her father after all these years.*

Anna observed the surface of her tea, and wondered what it was about Theo's marriage to Millicent, that allowed him such wisdom, and he was unwilling to see.

"You've become a regular chef." She decided to take the conversation in another direction. "Every time I look up, you're in the kitchen."

"It calms the nerves."

"Like tea." Anna took another sip, then sat her mug on the table. "Seriously. There are two reasons—no excuse me, *three*—that a person spends a lot of time preparing food. One, they're a chef and truly love cooking. Two, they cook for their family because without them, everyone would starve. Or three, it provides a distraction, or calms the nerves, as you say."

"How about two and three?" Theo said.

"Besides the merger of Millicent's brokerage with Thelonius' real estate company, how's everything with Millicent?"

"It's beginning to get hard to tell." He took a third sip then sat his cup on the table.

Thelonius Regarde, Millicent's father, had never seemed fully pleased with Millicent's choice of Theo as a husband. It was as if Thelonius felt his one and only child had settled for less than she was worth. For this, Anna had not forgiven Thelonius, not that he had felt the slightest bit of contrition.

Theo said of his wife, "She's always held a rebellious streak toward her father's demands. That's what I liked about her. Not that I want her to disrespect him. But now it seems she admires his success so much that she's trying to emulate his every move."

Anna grew anxious. Besides her dislike for Thelonius, whom she regarded as a variation of Edward, Anna always feared Millicent would eventually evolve into a variation of her father, in short another Edward. Like Edward Manning, Thelonius Regarde had led a vibrant extramarital life, by which his wife, Henrietta, seemed unaffected. This had been the initial reason Anna had been against the marriage.

"Thelonius recently apologized to Millicent's mother," Theo said. "Unlike Dad, he didn't have to get sick to see the light. He's admitted his past mistakes and made amends. But it's presented a funny sort of twist in Thelonius wanting to bond with Millicent. It's like she's fallen in love with him. She's got a new man in her life."

Anna's younger son leaned back in his chair and sighed. "As for me, I'm steady Eddy. Why should she worry about me? I've no intentions of going anywhere. I come home every night at the same time, prepare dinner, and wait for her to show up."

Anna inhaled as her son described occupying the same role she had played with Edward.

"Millicent and Thelonius spend hours and hours talking. First, it was to get to know him better. Now that they've merged the brokerage with Thelonius' real estate company, she's got the best explanation in the world for being with him. *I was at work.*"

"Only work is with Daddy," Anna mused.

"Yeah. It's like *they're* having an affair," Theo said.

And they are. Anna knew it was figurative, symbolic of something deeper. Still she felt her son's pain.

"Have you spoken to her about it?"

Theo chuckled. "About a dozen times each week. Like you, I've become accustomed to eating alone." Theo gave a weary smile. His finger traced the edge of his cup. Fridays are the worst. Sometimes she doesn't get home until three in the next morning, Saturday."

"This is why you call every Friday evening." Anna grew sad. "Where are they?"

"Always *Saturno*'s, the restaurant where I took Millicent on our first date. It's open all hours on Fridays and Saturdays." Theo turned to Anna.

The hurt in his dark brown eyes deepened. "I worry about her coming home so late. Millicent says, 'I'm just getting to know him.' I tell her that we need to focus on *our* family. She claims that by knowing her father, she'll be ready and prepared to settle down and be there for our children."

With Millicent spending so much time with Thelonius, Anna wondered how Theo and Millicent would ever have time to conceive.

Theo said, "I never realized until after we were married that as a child, Millicent was really close with her godfather."

"The godfather who missed the wedding?" Anna recalled the stir that erupted at the event around his absence. Millicent had wanted the mysterious man to give her away. When he didn't' show, she became despondent, almost calling off her the nuptials. Anna, Edward, and Theo had not met Millicent's godfather; they didn't even know his name.

"She's always been tight-lipped about him," Theo said. His eyes receded, revealing that the subject of Millicent's godfather was a heavily discussed and threadbare topic between him and Millicent. "In our five years of marriage, she's never told me his name. But I can tell they were close."

"How so?"

"We can't go anywhere in or around Chicago, and particularly if we're having fun, without her mentioning, 'Oh, yeah, my godfather and I came here one time. Or, I first came here with him.'"

"Have you ever asked of his name?"

"I'd be intruding if I did." Theo turned to her. "It's the same way with Thelonius and Henrietta. I never heard of her godfather before the wedding. Then, when he didn't show, here she was about to call off everything for a man I didn't know, and have never met. I sensed Henrietta was relieved he didn't come. As for Thelonius, I've never seen him so hurt."

Anna had never heard about the matter in such detail.

"Henrietta later told me that Millicent going through with the wedding in her godfather's absence was a testament that Millicent truly loved me. I think about that now when I'm home alone," Theo said. "Henrietta and Thelonius never mention Millicent's godfather. And Millicent wouldn't think to bring him up in their presence. The matter of his absence at the wedding nearly toppled Thelonius. He was afraid. Millicent apologized for her behavior after we returned from the honeymoon. I think that's why she's so happy and willing to be with Thelonius now." Again Theo turned to Anna. "It's like there's this secret between Millicent, her mother, and father. It centers on Millicent's godfather. The three have an understanding *not* to discuss it."

Theo finished off his tea, and went to kitchen. Tired and angry, Anna joined him at the sink where he was washing his cup.

"This charade I've played with your father has hurt you, your sisters and David," Anna lamented.

"Leaving him wouldn't have changed his behavior." Theo held his cup under the stream.

"But it would have signaled that I had more self-respect than to let him trample over me. It would have shown that I had confidence."

Theo turned to her. "Do you have more now that you've chosen to divorce him?" *Confidence* is what Anna surmised that Theo needed so he could leave Millicent. "Leaving Dad would have put you and us in a precarious position. It's not easy as a single mother to make a living, certainly not one as prosperous as Dad's."

Had Anna left Edward when her mind first contemplated the thought, when she had learned of his first affair, the one with Esther, Anna would have never conceived Theo. She swallowed and forced herself to hear Theo's take on a rationalization that had played all too many times in her head.

Theo said, "You stayed, not because you were a martyr for justice or a glutton for punishment. You stayed with Dad because it was practical. You had four children who needed food, a roof over our heads, and schooling. Dad gave us the best."

"I stayed because I needed someone, a family, purpose. You, your sisters, and brother gave me that." Theo's problems with Millicent left Anna feeling she had failed at demonstrating what a healthy relationship truly looks like. "The *best* that your father provided hasn't made you kids happy. If anything, it's made you less sure of yourselves." Long ago Anna had

136

determined that a person like Millicent would exploit such a gift as Theo. Anna wanted Theo to leave Millicent. But Theo loved her.

Theo confessed, "On my better days, I think I'm envious of what Thelonius is giving Millicent, what he's done with Henrietta. That if I had my way, Dad—"

"—would do the same with me. Admit he was wrong," Anna said."

"Yeah, for starters, anyway," Theo said. "Now that he's sick and dying."

"There's always hope." Anna considered Edward's words in light of the recent change in behavior. *I was scared. I envied your ability to give so much of yourself, and to love. It's undying, never changing, what I'll miss when I'm gone.*

"Maybe now he will." Theo said.

Anna's heart sank in considering all the recent drama, most particularly with Matt and Grant. Serine's lies had ensued from Edward's infidelity and also the fact that Edward was now dying.

She said, "You and Linda have always been the forgotten two. Linda cried out in her suicide attempts. But you, you've always been my good child." *Lord, help me not to take Theo for granted.*

"I'm sure Serine and Millicent would disagree with you sometimes," Theo chuckled.

"I love Serine. But like your father, she's drawn to infidelity and drama," Anna said. *Millicent too.* "She's remade herself in his image."

"Serine needs you, Mom. And, from Millicent's perspective, I'm sure she'll tell you I've got my moments. I have two parents. I'm not all you. And you are by no means a pushover. It took strength to stay with Dad despite his maneuvers."

If you only knew. Anna felt horrible that her pregnancies with Theo and his sisters had stemmed from having sex with Edward while fully aware of his unfaithfulness, attempts at gaining a commitment that Edward was unable to grant.

"I'm sorry," Anna said.

"Don't be. I'm glad I'm here, that I was born. Theo stroked her cheek. "I'm also proud to have you as my mother."

Anna leaned her head upon Theo's shoulder and held him tightly. *Would you say that if you knew about Inman?*

Chapter 20

Anna slid under the covers. She was mournful and embarrassed that her children, specifically Theo, knew so much about her low self-esteem and lack of confidence. It touched her that despite her foibles, Theo held a wisdom that understood and appreciated her battle to save her marriage.

If only she could translate that strength into mending her life. Anna would help Theo thrive beyond the storm of Millicent. She would help Serine and David survive Edward's death. Despite Brad's obvious devotion, she would not forget Linda. Forever mothering.

Anna's mother, Elena, had hung on for eight weeks after surgeons had found the brain tumor having sown its seeds of death throughout her body. Anna had delivered Linda, Elena's first granddaughter, a week before Elena died.

During Linda's turbulent adolescence, Anna feared Linda's penchant toward ending her own life lay rooted in the chaos of Elena's sickness and the problems of Anna and

Edward's marriage. Anna drove her father to and from the hospital each day during those last two months of Elena's life. Fearful of the evil spirits she sensed lurking in Elena, Anna did not go inside the hospital and visit Elena. Elijah had been unrelenting of Anna's avoidance of her mother.

Anna was driving him home one day after visiting Elena at Berkeley General when Reverend Elijah said, "She's asking about you. Why won't you come to see her?"

"You need your time with her," Anna said. She slowed the car to a halt at the intersection of Telegraph and Alcatraz Avenues.

"I've had my time. She wants to see you," Elijah said. The light turned green and she turned onto Alcatraz Avenue. The Reverend placed his hands upon his daughter's full and pregnant abdomen. He said, "I hope this one is a girl."

"I don't."

Her father tilted his head to the side then turned toward the passenger window. "I wanted more children. Your mother didn't."

"Why?" Anna's fear and dislike of her mother drove her to uncover what made Elena tick.

"She said she had only enough love for one child," Reverend Elijah explained. "That you were a girl made it all the more difficult." Knowing that Elena had wished for Anna to be a boy made Anna all the more determined not to see her mother.

She would not be a portal for Elena's anger, and malcontent to enter the baby she carried inside. Anna sought to protect her child. She did not know she was carrying a girl.

Upon reaching home, she switched off the ignition. Her father opened the door and was about to get out when Anna asked, "Why did you marry Mama?"

"It's what we did back then." Anna's father spoke a truth evidenced by the creases deepening into his dark, brown face upon a body that no longer stood straight and tall. "It's all we knew, what was expected of us, to marry and have a family."

"Did she ever seem to love you?" Anna had always been certain of her father's love for her mother. "Was she different back then?"

"She was more honest," Reverend Elijah said. "Your mother was very clear. She hated life with her parents. They had been Louisiana sharecroppers who owned less than the beans they picked. She said she couldn't go back home, that if she did, she would die either by God's will, or her own hand." Anna's father began to cry. Holding back her own tears, Anna reached across the seat, and enveloped him.

I can't go back home. I won't. Anna had spoken similar words to Edward on the day she graduated college. She married him the next day. Those same words crisscrossed Anna's mind as she writhed in the throes of delivering Linda. Edward had been in the Mediterranean overseeing the sale of some resort condos on the coast of Cyprus when she entered labor.

Anna called their neighbors, Doris and Charles Martin. Doris drove Anna to the hospital while Charles remained at the Martin home with David and Theo, then ages four and two and a half, playing with the Martin's son, Adrian.

Charles had helped Anna into the car before taking the boys back to their home. Rattled and knocked by the spasms of contractions rippling through her during the drive, she had contemplated the warmth and support of Charles' hand to her back. She had wondered what woman Edward might have been with.

The memory of Charles' hand brought comfort to the pain and ache of Anna's loneliness when hours later she fought to give birth to Linda, her third child. She concluded it similar to what Edward provided the women with whom he slept.

Following the delivery, and with Linda's tiny infant lips sucking from her breast Anna again considered the warmth of Charles' palm and what the women in Edward's life, and whom she had never met, provided him. Anna's mother, Elena, lay three floors above ebbing toward death.

The madness rooted in Elena eventually blossomed in Anna as a well hidden, but no less powerful, obsession with Edward's unfaithfulness. Anna's ruminations on the women with whom he transgressed his marriage vows both consumed and fueled her instincts toward mothering.

The commitment to giving her children what she never received from Elena grew stronger. Anna's determination toward loving her children without condition became a vicious cycle propagated by Anna's attempt to shield herself from the hurt of Edward's absences. The more she gave, the less of herself remained in the marriage. Edward would not notice should he ever discover his way back home.

Anna's children had survived Edward's long absences to which she offered no excuses or explanations beyond, "Your father is working." While her statements held substance and carried weight against David and Theo's minds fast approaching adulthood, Linda had thought otherwise. She was suspicious of their father's prolonged time away.

When Linda was fifteen, Edward brought his new protégé home to dinner. Gabrielle was her name. Thirty-years-old, she sat at the other end of the table adjacent to Edward. Hurting and angry, Linda was upset about having to sit next to the woman she considered an enemy. Anna had prepared a special meal, despite her suspicions of why Edward was bringing Gabrielle into their house.

The entire family sat around the dinner table eating when nineteen-year-old David, a college freshman, reported with serious demeanor and controlled pride, "I aced my calculus test." As a philosophy major, math had not been his strong suit. With his sights on entering law school, he had been worried about the test.

"Wonderful. I knew you would do it." Anna had patted his shoulder then asked him to pass the bread.

"Thanks, but I had to prove it to myself." David handed her the basket.

Like his father, Anna thought as she buttered her roll then eyed Edward cutting into his trout.

"If I can keep this up, I'll be finished with an A, or at least a B," David said.

"You will." Again Anna touched his shoulder. "Please pass the potatoes." She didn't worry about her weight at that time.

Theo blurted, "Charles and Doris, I mean Mr. and Mrs. Martin, are getting a divorce." Their son, Adrian, attended high school and played on the local soccer team with Theo.

"Who told you?" Anna asked. Serine, then twelve, and at the other end of the table quietly observing Edward rapt in conversation with the vibrant Gabrielle. No one except Anna appeared to have heard any of what Theo was saying. "She's been upset about something." Anna didn't mention that in the past month she had given six of her own Valium to Doris.

Sandwiched uncomfortably between David and Gabrielle, Linda picked at her food.

"Are you alright?" Anna asked. Linda placed her fork on the side of her plate and drank some water.

"Adrian says he's going to live with his mom," Theo continued. "His Dad says that's better since he doesn't have time to take him to school and soccer practices."

"Well he's only got this year, really three months, before he's on his own," David offered. "When school's out in May, he can get a job and save up money. Then he won't have to bug them and he can stay out of contact while they're hashing out everything. After his freshman year in college, he can get a job on campus and never have to come home again."

"It's not that simple, Mr. Philosopher," Theo bit back. "College costs money." Even at seventeen, Anna's younger son showed signs of the deep but practical thinker.

"Unless Adrian wants to spend the rest of life stuck between his parents bickering, he'd better toughen up," David said. "He's on his own now."

Serine remained mesmerized by the circus at the table. Linda, across the table, continued picking at her food. Theo and David continued their discussion of the Martin's divorce. Edward shot a glance at Anna, and returned to conversation with Gabrielle. Edward and Gabrielle were quite animated in discussing plans for Gabrielle's place at Manning Real Estate.

Anna hadn't felt the kind of excitement that she imagined was flowing between Edward and Gabrielle in a long time. Gabrielle was his protégé and new interest. Gabrielle lived in America. There would be no leaving her Anna suspected; no sadness or depression after he departed and began a new round of selling foreign properties. Slowly, she began to ponder and imagine that the beautiful, lithe Gabrielle was perhaps the woman for whom Edward would leave her when the right time came.

A divorce would destroy the children should Anna request or Edward demand one. Anna grew fearful that Edward would announce plans for a change both in his business and his marriage that night.

Again, Anna met Linda's gripping gaze. Hurt and betrayal flowed through, emotions that were and should have been Anna's, but that she could not accept and allow to surface. She remained calm as Linda's frustration bubbled.

Theo admonished David. "The key to Adrian surviving the breakup of his parents is more than gaining entrance to a good college. Life as he knows it is gone. It's dead."

Anna's heart sank upon hearing those words. She glanced at Edward deeper in the throes of discussion with the beautiful Gabrielle and Serine, who could have passed for Edward and Gabrielle's daughter. Serine watched, ever more mesmerized by the two.

Theo said of Adrian, "He's worried. And scared."

"He told you that?" David asked.

"No."

"Then who?" Though he would eventually settle for aspects of the law that required little or no time in the courtroom, David was already displaying lawyerly tactics of demanding answers.

"The counselor at our school," Theo said. Even then, he had the ability to see between the carefully structured lines of life. Serine remained fascinated and glued to watching her brothers battle within the discussion. Only Linda seemed to realize that the argument was not simply about the Martin's divorce.

Anna, fearing and realizing that Theo knew something she didn't want any of her children to know, whispered to her younger son, "You went to see a counselor?"

144

"We all need counseling," Linda said with her eyes fixed upon her plate full of food uneaten and growing cold.

David turned to her. "What did you say?"

"We all need someone to talk to. Everyone in this family," Linda said.

"About what?" David asked as if he had destroyed all memories of Linda's problems. He had been away at Stanford in Palo Alto when she had taken an overdose of pills the last time. Dread moved through Anna like a tidal wave overtaking an island.

Linda said, "We're like the Martins." She lifted her head and added, "Mom and Dad are just like Mr. and Mrs. Martin. Dad doesn't love Mama and she—"

"What did you say?" Edward stopped talking to Gabrielle.

"You don't love Mama," the words fell from Linda's lips like water from a jagged cliff.

"Don't embarrass your mother like that, or me."

"You embarrass yourself and Mama, by bringing *her* in here." Linda pointed to Gabrielle.

"Close your mouth." Edward hit the table.

"It's true." Linda lowered her head. "You don't love Mama. And you don't love us. That's why you stay gone all the time. You only love the women that you're with." Linda pushed back her chair, wobbled to her feet, and left the table. Her unsteady gait revealed that she had taken one of Anna's Valium again.

Naked we come into this world. And naked we shall leave.

Seven days after Linda entered the world, Anna stood at her mother's grave site. As pallbearers had lowered her casket into the ground, Elijah Chason recited scripture amid the hundred or more mourners in attendance of Elena's burial.

The Lord is my shepherd. I shall not want. He maketh me to lie down in green pastures. He leadeth me beside the still waters. He restoreth my soul . . . Yay, though I walk through the

145

valley of the shadow of death I will fear no evil. The Lord is with me . . .

Anna recited those words, and others under her breath half a decade later and while observing Edward assist other pallbearers in lowering Elijah's casket into a rectangular space cut into the ground beside Elena.

Where can I go from your spirit? Or where can I flee your presence. If I ascend to heaven, You are there; If I make my bed in Sheol, behold, You are there . . . If I dwell in the remotest part of the sea . . . Your hand will guide me . . . .Surely the darkness will overwhelm me, And the light around me will be night . . . Anna had spoken little to her father in the years following her mother's death. It was not due to distance. He lived across town in North Oakland near the church he had ministered for three decades.

Elena's death had hewn a large hole in Elijah Chason's life. Anna had tried filling it with dinners she prepared and daily phone calls that waned to every other day, and then once a week. Soon, he refused to eat the meals, and Anna eventually saw that it was best to leave her father to his loneliness and let him suffer in silence.

She finally settled on calling him each Sunday after she returned from mass. Having delivered his sermon at Roadside Baptist Church, two blocks down from Union Street, he would have arrived home.

The time eventually came when Reverend Elijah no longer gave sermons. Anna's patience never strained. She continued to call, Elijah sometimes not answering. Anna took to leaving letters in his mailbox. Answering machines, voice and e-mail had yet to arrive. Though Anna seldom ventured to her childhood home on Union Street, her will to connect with her father while staying outside the net of his misery remained strong until his death.

Naked we come into this world. Naked we shall leave. Anna now lay in bed wondering what she would utter to herself, hold as comfort, and offer as prayer when others would lower Edward's casket into the earth.

146

Chapter 21

Anna awoke the morning after Grant's and Matt's departures feeling vague and tentative about her ability to adapt to Edward's dying. Like her eldest and youngest, David and Serine, Anna would have to stretch beyond her means, exit the known and enter a zone of discomfort, a place she had successfully avoided.

She had married Edward in order to escape the misery of her mother, Elena, and her inability to hold intimate relationship with her family. Anna married Edward prepared to love and grow close with him. Now that he was dying, she mourned, not simply the closing of his life, but the death of hope and the loss of what could or might have been.

The aroma of bacon and eggs drew Anna from her bed. Venturing downstairs, she entered the kitchen where Theo turned to her with a smile and said, "I wondered when you might be getting up."

"What time is it?"

"Half-past eleven."

Shocked that she had slept so late, Anna was even more disturbed that Theo seemed untroubled that she had done so. Their conversation last evening had overturned rocks of truth and shattered boulders of long-held beliefs deposited inside Anna.

It also troubled her that Theo had usurped the kitchen, her area of expertise and escape, and made it his place of calm and safety. This was all Millicent's doing, Anna silently grumbled.

Theo handed her a plate of eggs, bacon and toast.

"Thanks." She took her plate to the table and sat.

Theo joined her. He had been cooking all morning. "I got excited when I heard you in the shower. This is fresh, just for you and me."

"I guess we could call you the resident chef," Anna said.

"I suppose so. And I hate to eat alone." He smiled.

Again Anna thought of Millicent and silently groaned.

Theo brought some eggs to his mouth, chewed them, swallowed, and said, "Linda and Brad have gone for a walk. They ate earlier." He sipped his coffee. "How did you sleep last night?"

"Fairly well." Anna grew awash in the shame at how much she relished her son's thoughtfulness and caring. She drank some coffee.

"I think you should know that Serine's been involved with both Grant and Matt for the last two years. I spoke with her this morning." Theo explained, "She's back in L.A., was on her way to court. She's pretty shaken up. I told her she at least owed you an explanation."

"She's got to choose. At least give back Grant's engagement ring." Anna shook her head.

"Like I said last night, Matt and Grant have known about one other." Theo finished his eggs, and sipped his coffee. "As for Serine's disjointed perspective on the matter, you might want to speak with David about that. Serine looks to him for guidance."

Anna lowered her fork onto the edge of her plate. She sighed and leaned back in her chair.

"David left a message on Linda's phone," Theo explained. "The funeral was yesterday." Again Anna sighed. It was all too much. Theo continued, "Heather's going to be at her father's for another week or so cleaning out the house, and packing his things." Anna stared at Theo's smooth, dark face. "David will be back late tomorrow, or the following afternoon. He has a fair amount to attend with Heather's father's estate."

"I can imagine." Anna wondered when David would be called to do the same with Edward's belongings. In light of David's statements at the dinner table nights earlier, Anna debated how much she wanted to involve her eldest son in handling Edward's estate. She would need to speak with Henderson about that.

"I'd like to know how the service went," she said. "I should have been there. In fact, why isn't David sharing some of this with me? I am his mother." The brunt behind her words hit Theo like a cold gust of wind. Glimmer dimmed in the eyes of her younger son. "I guess I'd like to know I'm still needed."

"David is a thirty-three year-old man," Theo said. "You've given enough of your time, and yourself to him and all of us."

Lifting her cup of coffee, Anna asked, "Is that why *only you* persisted in calling when I stopped?" Anna had at one time wondered how Theo's persistence in calling involved the other three. Now she knew it was personally driven.

"You were hurt," Theo said. "You need to let that go."

"You mean the *hurting*," Anna corrected.

"It pained you to ask for a divorce. Even more since Dad was fighting not to give it to you. Like always, you pulled away from us." But this time Anna had not been living in the house with her children.

"I didn't want to involve you."

"We were already involved. He's our dad. You're our mom."

149

Anna stared at the food growing cold upon her plate. Her mother's voice arose. *Waste not, want not.* The futility of all Anna had dedicated her life to—remaining faithful, and honest to Edward, their marriage, and their children cut at her heart. Despite Theo's understanding, and forgiveness of her actions, Anna felt she needed to explain why she had withdrawn.

The silence between them pulled at her. It pained Anna that she *could not* explain what she had hoped to gain from not speaking to her children. She also felt ashamed of what she *had* experienced with Inman, passion and intimacy, and beyond that, the hope of being loved.

Yet on learning of Edward's terminal illness, Anna had quickly retreated back to the house where she would care for him. Did she love Edward, or not? The love she had held onto throughout their marriage died fifteen months ago.

Anna looked at her coffee and recalled how Edward had never looked up when she placed the cup of decaf on the desk beside him. He had continued scribbling furiously across the document representing the lucrative sale of a property.

Anna now wondered of her ability to hold fast to the all-encompassing love she had nurtured and spread upon her children. She felt proud that as adults living in the world under their own steam, they sought and received comfort from within their own ranks.

It also shadowed her with a sense of having been excluded, even though she had instigated the estrangement by withdrawing. Anna sensed that her children, like her, held questions not simply about her marriage, but about her as an individual, who she was, and who she had become in seeking a divorce from Edward.

Words she had spoken to Edward filled her head. *I hate you for what you've done. You've hurt me. More than that you've hurt these children. You took away their innocence. I'll never forgive you for that.* Her thoughts shifted to Inman. Would the children accept him after Edward had died? Would she even want to be with Inman and face that challenge?

The cumbersome questions threatened to overwhelm her.

"Your father hurt me terribly," Anna said, "but I've yet to divorce him." Theo seemed surprise and yet not so. "That morning," she explained, "the day I found out that he was sick and dying."

"The day he agreed to the divorce, and your selling the house," Theo interjected.

"Yes. That morning, in the meeting at Henderson's office would have been our last time together," Anna said. "Your father had given me my freedom. He deeded me the house. I knew something was wrong. All through the meeting he didn't seem himself. He was not the Edward I knew."

She said, "He was not the man she had loved and depended upon as a constant in her life. Neither was he the Edward Manning she had grown to hate. "I asked Henderson not to file the divorce agreement," Anna said. "I haven't told your sisters and brother."

"Does Dad know?"

"Yes."

Theo remained still with his hands on his lap.

"But you're no longer wearing your wedding band."

"It was all coming to an end. My world, the way I wanted it, had come as I requested. I was terrified," Anna tried explaining her actions and the contradiction of remaining married but having removed the symbol of unending commitment. "I was also angry, still am, but—" Tears threatened to spill over. Her vision blurred.

"And what about when you learned Dad was sick and dying?"

Anna's chest cleared and lightened. "It was strange. I knew somehow that I hadn't lost him. And then when he agreed to let me bring him home, I . . . I . . . I felt hope." Lines formed upon Theo's forehead. "I have him now," Anna said. But he's dying. Now death is the other woman."

151

Chapter 22

Anna was standing at the counter lost in the oblivion of cutting carrots when the patio door slid open, and David entered. She laid down the knife. Torment and anguish filled his eyes. He dropped his bag, and approached the counter.

"How was the service?" Anna asked.

David slid onto one of the stools. A shadow of shame gripped her elder son's face, for what Anna suspected was the way he had spoken to her three nights earlier. Anna proceeded to the refrigerator, took out some ham, bread, and mayonnaise. David needed distance.

"It was nice," he said of his father-in-law's funeral. It's not what I want for Dad."

"And Heather?" Anna was back at the counter. "Will she be coming here?" Anna was not ready to contemplate that far ahead. She began making a sandwich.

David tugged at his fingers then twisted the wedding band on his left hand. Emptiness hung in his eyes. "I think she wants a divorce."

"Are you sure? What has she said?" Anna lowered the knife to the counter.

"She's met someone. He lives next door to her father."

"Who?" Anna pursued.

"His name is Rob. He helped Mr. Matthews during the early stages of the cancer by driving him to the oncologist and the chemotherapy treatments. He knew a lot of what was going on. He called Heather each week and gave a report. When the calls came more often, sometimes every day, she decided to come back and stay."

"What makes you think she wants to leave you for him?" Anna finished making the sandwich and placed it before David.

"She's tired." David fingered the sandwich. Despair was written and etched in every curve and crease of his forehead, and face. "Her father's death has taken everything she's got."

"Can't you help her? Don't you want to?"

David leaned back in his chair. "I work every day, bring home all I have, and give what's left to Heather, Emily, and Josh." Anna grew frustrated and angry. David sounded like Edward when Elena had been dying.

David started, "Now with Dad dying . . ." He furrowed his brows. "What is it you wives want from us?" His words again echoed Edward's contempt during Elena's last days. Yet David appeared sincere in his desire to understand.

"We just want a friend," Anna said. The conversation had devolved to a variation on the theme of her conversation with Edward decades earlier. Anna felt trapped. Her eldest son, and child in whom she had put many of hopes, now held a need to know. David's soul was seeking liberation and the peace that *passeth* all understanding.

Linda entered the room. With Serine gone, she had been upstairs all morning with Edward. "I think we need to call hospice."

"What's happened?" Anna said. David stood.

"Daddy says he's really tired. He wants them."

154

David went upstairs. Dread filled Anna against the glow of serenity draping Linda's face. Theo, who had been outside by the pool, entered the kitchen through sliding glass door.

Linda lifted the cordless phone. "Dad gave me the number to hospice," she said then displayed the crumpled piece of paper.

Anna started upstairs. Theo followed. He grasped her hand when she reached the landing. "I'm here if you need me."

Anna patted his fingers then continued to Edward's room.

~*~*~*~

The hospice worker's visit that afternoon ran matter-of-factly, eerily so. Anna found it surreal as she watched Edward listen, and then speak with the woman about the services they offered.

"I don't want to put my wife at a strain," he said, "When the time comes that I can't do for myself . . . " Brad was already assisting Edward to the bathroom, and then waiting until Edward signaled he was ready to get back into bed. Unable to witness and hear any more, Anna stood and left.

In the downstairs study that used to be Edward's office, David and Theo quietly discussed varied matters. Linda and Brad, for whom Anna envied their closeness, had gone for a walk. Of all Anna's children, who would have thought Linda would become so stable in adulthood?

In the kitchen, Anna removed a glass from the cabinet and filled it with water. On the way to the table, she glanced at the pool. The sun was glistening upon the water's surface. Moving through the sliding glass door, she stepped out onto the patio and lowered herself onto one of the cushioned chairs. She lifted her head and took in the awning that extended ten feet or so.

Edward had installed it, saying, "Then you can sit underneath, and watch the boys swim up and down the pool." Anna had spent many afternoons watching David and Theo swim the of the lanes of the pool, while she was shaded by the

155

overhang attached to the home and hearth over which she held dominion, and within the kingdom Edward had established, guarded, and maintained.

Protected under that same measure, from the hot rays of a late September mid-afternoon, she now recalled Edward taking the children to swim lessons at the Oakland YMCA. On the weekends when he had not been away, Edward had walked, stopwatch in hand, alongside David and Theo swimming laps.

The sun had beat upon Edward's ruddy face and cast a tan that lasted long after Christmas, and into the heart of winter. His voice had been encouraging as David and Theo pulled on their strengths to reach the length of the pool and back.

Anna lowered her eyelids and tried to imagine the time when Edward would no longer leave for a business trip in Brazil, Greece, Egypt, and Panama during which he would extend his stay only to return home with an even deeper tan. Edward's death would invoke a time when darkness would descend and he would be forever gone from Anna, the earth, their marriage, and the *house*.

Anna smoothed back tears, left the cushioned patio chair, and walked to the pool. Crouching at the edge, she lowered her fingers into water and considered going for a swim, one from which she would not return. The water would have transformed her through a baptismal of sorts. Arising from the waves she would experience resurrection with Edward.

Linda emerged from around the corner of the house.

"There's someone here to see you."

Brad accompanied her as they both approached Anna. Behind him came Inman. Anna's heart raced. Linda's eyes sparkled the same as when Brad, Theo, and she had led Matt onto the patio. Anna calmly stood and walked to Inman.

"It's nice to see you," she said.

Inman did not move to kiss her cheek. She smiled in thanks.

"Linda, this is a friend of mine, Inman Hayes. Inman, this is my daughter, Linda, and her husband, Brad Oliver."

"Pleased to meet you." Inman smiled. "I've heard a lot about you."

Linda and Brad took turns shaking Inman's hand. Anna had never spoken to her children of Inman. She mused on her future, the possibilities that stood distinct from probabilities, the hopes that she was frightened of holding.

"Can we offer you something," Linda said, "Iced tea? Water?"

"Thanks. But, I'm fine." Inman gave a slight wave.

Linda and Brad went through the open sliding glass door into the kitchen.

Inman's gaze then slipped toward the house and settled upon a place that had become familiar to him over the past year. He had often met Anna there on Friday afternoons before or after she met with Elise when trying to sell the house. One time, he had asked Anna why she was in such a rush to sell the house.

She explained that she needed money and that even though Edward had offered to pay alimony, the paperwork would take time. She wanted her freedom so she could move to France.

Inman had asked, "Is this your way of letting me down easy?"

"You can join me," Anna had retorted.

"I'd love to." Inman's quick answer had surprised and frightened Anna. She had interpreted Edward's absences and self-absorption as evidence of her flaws, that she was damaged goods. But things had changed. *I was scared, Anna. I am scared.* Never had she considered that like her, Edward held his own demons of self-loathing.

Elena's words haunted Anna. *Everyone needs affection. A show of love.*

She loosened up on her walk toward the house with Inman.

"I'm glad you came," Anna said. He followed her inside to the kitchen.

"So this is how it was before." Inman remarked on the old furniture replacing the rental pieces. The wonderment held upon his face seemed to ask if there was a place for him in Anna's life, or if she was just using him to reach a more desirable destination.

157

Anna removed a pitcher from the refrigerator and poured him a glass of water. She put it on the counter near where he sat.

"I started to call," Inman said. "And then, I thought someone might—"

"Don't worry about it," Anna said. Inman's presence brought to light how much she had missed him and the person she became when in his presence. She rested her attention upon his eyes.

"How's Edward doing?"

"It's only been three weeks. Now, he's upstairs talking with a hospice worker."

"Death condenses time." Inman sat his glass upon the table.

A sheath of guilt cascaded Anna. "I thought we'd have more."

Inman's lips parted. He was about to speak when Theo, followed by David, entered the kitchen. Inman stood. Again Anna made introductions. The differences lay stark between the way Theo and David greeted Inman.

Reserved and wary, David offered a light grip, while Theo, open and eager, gripped Inman's palm between both hands. Unlike with Linda, Inman said nothing of having heard about them. Anna had spoken about her children to Inman. And he had talked of his daughter to Anna.

Inman glanced at his glass of water standing on the marble counter, then said, "I only wanted to check on you to see how all was going. Now that I've done that, I should let you go."

Lightly, he kissed Anna's cheek then hugged her, a fearful, yet welcomed surprise. Anna lost her breath on letting go. Inman's cologne, a mixture of Japanese cherry blossom and spice had enlivened her senses. Her breast tingled against his chest. She grew wet. The children, most specifically, David, would never understand.

Anna saw Inman to the door. On returning to the kitchen, she stepped through the sliding glass door and saw Theo and David sitting at one of the tables shaded by the awning. Both moved to stand on her approach. Their father taught them their manners. She waved her hand indicating for them to remain seated. Anna sat.

"I was saying to Theo," David started, "—that since Dad is making plans with hospice, perhaps you need to speak with him about finances."

"I'm sure your father's insurance covers this sort of care. If not, then I know he has—" Anna said.

"We're not talking about the cost of hospice. Somebody's got to pay for the running of the house." David surveyed the patio, the pool, and the house.

"There's no mortgage," Theo interjected as if to prove a point he had raised during their private discussion in the study.

"But I'm sure you incurred some costs with Elise trying to sell the house," David said to Anna.

The house. The words filtered through Anna's mind as she eyed Theo.

"We were just thinking," David started again. Theo looked to Anna as if recalling what she had told him. *I haven't divorced your father. No one knows but you.*

"I know what you were thinking," Anna spoke. "But, I'm still married to your father. I haven't divorced him."

"I thought—" David started.

"I know what you thought. Perhaps more consideration toward your own marriage might help your cause. She stood and left. Anna was angry. *But at what?*

She couldn't quite decipher. It didn't matter. Inman's presence had renewed in her what the last few days with Edward and her children had drenched. Some parts of Anna were dying. Others were coming to life.

Chapter 23

Days passed. The week ended and a new one began with David, Theo, Linda, with Brad hovering around Edward, seeing to his every need and allowing him, at least from Anna's perspective, little time alone to contemplate his approaching death.

While thankful for the children's presence, she wondered how Edward might handle their leaving. David needed to get back to his law firm in Detroit. Anna worried that he had not said anything of delays for getting clients' work done. She had not seen him make one phone call back to the firm. Then again, he had his cell phone.

Neither has she seen him at the computer checking his e-mails, nor had he mentioned needing to do so. Of Heather and the children, Josh and Emily, David had spoken little except for snippets concerning the funeral for Heather's father, and his forgone conclusion of Heather wanting to divorce him for Rob.

As for Theo, Anna concluded that Millicent would keep the household going whether he was present or not. Only God knew what Theo would find on his return to Chicago. Anna was beginning to consider that it was perhaps a good thing that Theo and Millicent had no children. Yet David and Heather had Emily and Josh, whom Anna had not seen in a little more than a year.

Six months in her battle for the divorce, matters had crested to a point that Anna almost relinquished the need to sell the house. The week following an especially heated meeting in Henderson's office—Bryce had pulled Edward from trying to punch Henderson—Edward had flown to Detroit, and visited David and Heather.

Anna had learned of the trip a week later when she received a call from David, during which David describing how Edward had played with Emily and Josh. Anna now surmised that Heather's father would have been sick during this time. Edward too would have been undergoing chemotherapy. Had *David known of Edward's illness?* And if so, how much*? Why had he not said anything to Anna?*

Edward's words returned. *I warned David not to sue Henderson. And trying to have you declared insane made it easier for me to give you what you wanted. I would never let him do that to you. David's actions made me see who I was, what I had become.*

Anna sighed as she pulled the sheets, towels, and pillowcases from the dryer. Two decades earlier, this kind of work had been one of the many banes of her existence, a necessary task for a mother of four. The amount of laundry dwindled as each child left for college. Anna's loneliness rose with each departure.

She considered all that Serine had seen during those years while she had been the last at home; Linda was at Fresno State, and David and Theo were in graduate school. With Linda continually upon the edge of depression and anger, Anna had made constant trips to Fresno.

During Linda's junior year, Edward, having had enough of her outcries, removed Linda from school and brought her back to Oakland. Through some business connections he got her admitted into St. Mary's College in Moraga. There on the

162

campus of a college overseen by the 300-year-old Catholic order of the Christian Brothers, Linda had met Brad Oliver. He seemed to care little that depressive thoughts and a desire to commit suicide plagued her. In his mind, all Linda needed was love. And he would give it to her. Brad's father, a psychiatrist, relished the idea of transferring to his soon-to-be daughter-in-law what he had for thirty years given his clients.

Linda's voice pulled Anna from her tower of thoughts. "Mom."

A familiar term, the word, *Mom*, had grown stale in Anna's memory over the last decade. She both missed the nostalgia of hearing it, and experienced relief in the lack of its echo. At fifty-five, Anna Manning was growing old and selfish. Time for her, like Edward, was running out.

She turned to Linda. "How's your father?"

"He's resting. Theo's with him." Linda reached down for the basket of clothes. "I'll help you fold them."

The two went into Theo's old room. Linda closed the door. The two sat on the bed. Anna started folding towels. Linda folded a pillowcase into a neat square and laid it upon the bed.

"Brad's leaving day after tomorrow," she said. "I thought I'd stay and help if that's okay."

"There's hospice, you know. Your father arranged for a worker to begin coming next week."

"Are you okay with that?"

"I'm fine."

Linda folded a second pillowcase then gently lowered it on top of the first. She clasped her hands, laid them in her lap. "I'm pregnant, four months."

Warm relief filled Anna's body. She had sensed something about Linda's quietness, the protectiveness and care she had shown her stomach. Brad, always loving, had been ever more affectionate.

"I'm so happy for you." Anna reached across the pile of folded towels and pillowcases and hugged her elder daughter.

On seeing that Linda had yet to smile, Anna asked, "Are you afraid you'll have to go back on the medication or that the pregnancy will take you into a depression?" At one point Linda

163

and Brad had decided against having children due to the constant round of daily medication Linda took. That had been at the beginning of their marriage.

"No." Linda shook her head. This was the first time since Linda and Brad's arrival that Anna had witnessed or sensed any inkling of the melancholic and pessimistic Linda. "It's just that I want Dad to see my child."

Anna shuddered. In her joy, she had forgotten that Edward would most probably not be alive to witness the birth of his third grandchild. "Have you told your father?"

"No."

Again Anna embraced Linda, this time shoving aside the folded towels and pillowcases. She held on tight to her daughter. What had once separated now bound them. Anna pulled Linda's head onto her chest and stroked her cheek. She looked at the towels and pillowcases yet to be folded. They were laying beside the folded ones. By-products of family. Women's work, she thought. What keeps the life force going, and maintains the cycle of humanity.

"Do you know what it is?" Anna asked of the child that Linda was carrying.

"A boy. We want to call him Edward. Edward Manning Oliver."

"I think that would be a fine name." Anna refused to allow her tears to intrude upon her daughter's moment of joy.

Linda left Anna's arms and wiped her face.

"Edward Manning Oliver," Anna repeated. "It's a lovely name."

Linda beamed. Then for a third time Anna reached for her daughter.

~*~*~*~

Anna was sitting at the kitchen table and drinking tea when the phone rang. The joy and anticipation of Linda's addition to the family juxtaposed to Edward's terminal illness pulled at Anna's extremes.

David came to her with the cordless phone in his hand.

"It's for you. *Inman*."

Anna took hold of the phone, missed the look of serious questioning on David's face as she turned and headed toward the sliding glass door.

"How are you?" She stepped outside on the patio and slid closed the door.

"I called to ask you the same," Inman said. Three days had elapsed since their last meeting.

Anna lost her smile. The warmth of hearing Inman's voice faded.

"There's a lot going on."

"Seems that way."

"Why do you say that?" Anna said.

"Which son was it that answered the phone?"

"David."

"Your eldest," Inman said.

"Why?"

"Just asking. "He's the taller of the two," Inman said.

"Did he say anything to you?" Anna grew anxious.

"No."

At some point she would need to tell the children about Inman. *At some point*. Not now. "I miss you," Anna said. She fell prey to desires suppressed upon returning to her role of wife and mother. "I wish I could be with you."

"Is that wise?"

Anna whispered, "I feel like I'm an alien." She glanced back at the house. The kitchen was empty. "I know so little of what goes on in my children's lives. They call one another regularly, but on their cell phones."

"Why don't you tell them that? Say you want to know more."

"I've always tried not to call on them, or interrupt their lives with the foolishness in mine."

"You can't have it both ways." Inman's words stung Anna. "At some point you've got to tell them about us. Unless that is—"

"You don't understand," she said. "I've always been there for them. I've also tried to give them their space. I never begged them to come home when they were at college. I supported them in going out on their own. Never asked them to look back."

"Anna, why did you bring Edward home and halt the divorce proceedings?"

"Is this why you called me? Is that why you came over last week?"

"I actually wanted to see if you were up for dinner," Inman said. "But since you've raised the issue—"

"Then, how the hell did we get so off course?"

"I asked you how you were doing?" Inman said. "You followed with, 'A lot's going on.'"

"You sound as if I don't know how to handle my children. That I'm ashamed of you. This is not like it was with Edward and his women," Anna said.

"Are you so sure it's not, at least in your mind?"

"Is that how you feel, that I'm keeping you hidden?" Anna's body was hot. "Do you know what it's like to live over thirty years with a man who's been unfaithful? It's hard, particularly when you're trying to maintain his image as a loving father so that the children don't judge him erroneously and think that just because he didn't love you—"

Feeling a presence, Anna stopped short. The soft approach of footsteps softly fell silent. She turned back and met Edward's gaze. He was within arm's length. Her hand went numb. She nearly dropped the phone.

"Anna, what's wrong? Who is it?" Inman's voice trailed up the receiver.

"I have to go." Anna murmured. Her eyes never left Edward. "I'll call you later," she said to Inman." Edward drew near.

She clicked off the cordless and laid it upon the patio table. "Why are you out of bed?" Anna asked.

"I'm tired of lying down. I need some air." He was wearing a cotton robe over a white t-shirt and a pair of burgundy plaid pajamas. The robe was rumpled as if he had been sleeping in it.

Anna tore her gaze from his and started past him toward the kitchen. "Would you like something to eat?" she asked.

Edward caught her arm. "I'm fine."

Anna turned toward him. Softly, he stroked her cheek. Pangs of guilt threaded through her. She lowered her head. Was this how Edward felt on his return home and facing her after having been with the women? Anna hadn't made love to Edward in nearly a decade.

Softly he asked, "Are you alright?"

"I'm fine." Anna would not look at him.

"You didn't sound fine on the phone. Was it Elise bugging you about having taken the house off the market?"

"No," Anna mumbled. Her lips trembled. How much had he heard?

Edward pulled her close. His slowing breath swept her face. Anna leaned upon his chest. He caressed her head, ran his fingers through her hair.

"Oh, Edward," she moaned.

"We'll get through this," he said then kissed her cheek.

Anna whimpered silently. The image of Inman lay upon the surface of her thoughts.

Chapter 24

Anna entered Scott's Restaurant in Jack London Square. Spying Inman at their usual table by the window, she informed the maître d' that she had located her party. Inman rose from his seat at the table that could seat four, and greeted her. He did not kiss her. She sat across from him.

"I'm sorry for hanging up on you." Anna laid her purse on the seat of the chair beside her. "But Edward—" Shame overtook her once more. She wished she could return home, erase the last three decades, and start over.

Inman joined her in sitting.

"Did Edward overhear you speaking to me?"

Anna nodded. "How much, I don't know."

"Did you tell anyone where you were going?"

"No. Just that I needed to go out. Like Edward often did, I suppose." She seethed. Inman remained calm, further irritating her. "You take this as some kind of game."

"No. Your husband is dying. Your four children are home. It's not been easy."

"Scratch that. Three. One left the other day in a huff." Anna explained the foray with Serine's suitors. "It was horrible. Both Matt and Grant were at the house. Serine was in her room hiding from what she had done. Add to that, she's engaged to Grant and wearing his diamond."

"It certainly adds spice to a situation brimming with a harsh dose of reality," Inman said. Anna stared at him. His smile faded. "Did Serine ask the guys to come?"

"No. But she must have indicated that's what she wanted. Why else would they have taken time from their jobs, driven and flown up here?"

"Perhaps they truly care."

"That's what I'm afraid of."

Inman appeared to understand, condone, Serine's behavior. Anna's anger percolated. "It's scandalous. She called Matt her fuck buddy. Serine used that word to describe him."

"It generally means—"

"Please." Anna flashed her palm. "I know what it means. I'm appalled that a child of mine would think of someone in that way."

"So noted." He gave a light smile of agreement.

"Serine knows better. I taught her differently. Perhaps you don't mind Dancia using that kind of term, but I do."

Inman's smile dissipated "Should Dancia use the word, I'd be more concerned about what drew her to speak of someone that way."

"Serine's obviously gotten off track. I should have—"

"I don't know that you could have done anything."

"It's because of Edward's behavior over these years," Anna quipped. "I'm certain of that."

"You think you should have left Edward sooner?"

Anna stared at Inman. "Perhaps it's the way I am now, who I've become, what I've done this past year." She recalled Edward's words when he interrupted her conversation with Inman. *We'll get through this. We will.*

"Edward's dying."

"So, that makes it alright for us to be together?" Anna was furious. "If Serine knew I was here with you now, she would say I was behaving no differently than Edward. I was committing adultery, the very thing that Edward—"

"Okay, then introduce me to your children." Inman had told his daughter, Dancia, of Anna. "Bring me out of the shadows. Tell them I love yo—"

"Didn't you just hear me? Never mind their father is dying."

"Which you just found out."

"And now that I know about Edward, I'm trying to do the right thing." Anna grew more frustrated trying to explain her dilemma.

"Never mind he spent the last year fighting to keep you from divorcing him by trying to stranglehold you into not selling the house." Now Inman was angry. "Putting your life on hold won't save Edward. If he's really sick and dying—"

"Are you saying you don't trust him, or what the doctor says, that this is all a hoax?"

Inman furrowed his brows. "That sounds more like something you'd accuse Edward of doing." Anna sighed. Inman surveyed the table between them. "Anna, we've been seeing each other for the past five months. Many of those weeks we've spent three to four nights at either your apartment or my house in Berkeley. Now that Edward's terminal—"

"He's not dead yet." The finality of the word terminal shook Anna. She lifted her purse and made to leave. Inman grasped her wrist.

"Then why aren't you wearing your band? Why did you remove it? Anna, at some point you're going to have to tell your children about us, me."

"Yes, but not now. Not at this moment." She shook her head.

"Then when? Have you never considered we'd get this far? Or had you planned to use me like Edward used his women?"

Anna wished for Inman to caress her as Edward had done earlier that afternoon. She pulled back, attempted to free her hand from Inman's grasp—her weak attempt at resisting what her body so desired.

"I won't let you go," Inman whispered.

Anna's heart sank at how she would choose the words to tell her children of Inman. "I didn't rush to introduce you to the children because of the divorce. It was hard enough for me to even reach the point of asking for it. Telling the children was a nightmare."

"And you survived it."

"But at what cost?"

Inman frowned as he sought once more to grasp her attention. "You don't believe that asking for the divorce caused Edward's cancer—that you made him sick to the point of dying?"

"That's absurd." Anna snapped. But Serine's logic had concluded just that. "Serine accused me of ignoring Edward's suffering. She questioned how I could have fought for the divorce all these months and not been aware that Edward was ill."

"Serine is a daughter who's losing her father to cancer," Inman said.

"Precisely my point. I have to tread carefully."

"Somewhere along the way, you've got to start living the life you want, Anna, and making your own joy."

Her cheeks ran hot, and her ears burned against the sad medley of Inman's questions. Again, the chorus of Edward's voice arose. *We'll get through this.*

Over her entrée of salmon with green beans and rice, Anna explained each one of her children's dilemmas. She listed reasons beyond Edward's dying as to why now was not the time to tell them of Inman's role in her life.

"Two days ago, David buried his father-in-law in Santa Rosa. He died of cancer. David's just back and he's certain that Heather is having an affair with the neighbor who helped with her father. Theo, on the other hand, seems in no rush to get back to Millicent in Chicago."

"*Millicent*, did you say?"

"Yes, Millicent Regarde." Anna disliked calling the name. This was her first time discussing her daughters and sons-in-law with Inman. "I never wanted him to marry her," Anna said of Millicent.

"Why?" Inman seemed intrigued and invested in hearing Anna's reasoning.

"Millicent Regarde is an absolute *b-i-t-c-h*. Forgive me for spelling it out like that, but she simply doesn't love my son. In fact, I don't think she can love anyone but herself."
Inman's cinnamon face twisted against its usual calm. "Why do you say that? What evidence do you have?"

Anna wanted to ask him what was wrong, but instead remained with her frustration. "I saw it the first time I met her. Never mind what Theo's told me since being home." No longer would Anna, as she had done throughout her marriage, make excuses and try justifying her feelings and opinions.

Let the dead bury the dead. For Anna the dead had more to do with her mother, Elena, Edward, and now perhaps, Theo's marriage to Millicent.

Anna said, "Millicent is a near perfect replica of Edward. She's having a love affair with her father, Thelonius."

"You know this for a fact? Have you ever met these people?" Inman's demeanor became like stone.

"Thelonius was a philanderer like Edward," said Anna. He was never around, always off playing with other women, his gift to himself for having made millions. Millicent told Theo. Her mother, Henrietta—"

Anna bristled with shame and anger at the thought of another woman, like her, accepting her husband's behavior with little fight and stamina to leave. "Let's just say that Theo and Millicent's shared experience of witnessing their mothers' pain attracted them to each other. Only now Millicent is following in her father's footsteps."

"By having an affair with her father? That's preposterous." Inman was indignant. "It would be incest."

"I'm speaking figuratively. Apparently, Thelonius has begged Henrietta and Millicent's forgiveness. Millicent has merged her mortgage brokerage with Thelonius' real estate firm. She's enthralled with the attention Thelonius is giving her."

"You don't think he's sincere?"

"Why should he be? He's probably afraid that something will become of him like with Edward."

"Is it so bad to change your habits to make life better for yourself, and the ones you love?" Inman knitted his brow and drew Anna's ire.

"I doubt if he's sincere."

"Were you sincere in taking Edward back home to die? Or did you simply want to watch him suffer?"

Again Anna moved to leave. Inman missed catching her hand. When he arrived outside, she stood waiting to get into her car that the parking attendant had driven around.

"Anna." He caught her shoulder as she moved to get inside. Anna turned around, and made to slap him. Again Inman caught her hand. He drew her near, settled his lips on hers. And there they lingered long and warm.

Chapter 25

H ours later, Inman kissed her lips as he had done in the parking lot, and then her breasts. Anna lay in bed with Inman at his house in the hills high above the campus of UC Berkeley.

"I'm sorry," she said.

Inman touched his forefinger to her lips. Slowly she closed her eyes. He moved his lips to her stomach, abdomen, and womanhood. Anna lost track of her anger and vulnerability. She relaxed her head into the pillow.

Inman eased his body on top of hers. The feel of his skin against her chest, as on so many occasions during the last six months, enlivened spaces left long dead by Edward's absence.

Inman merged his body with hers. Slowly, carefully he entered the temple of her repose. Love, complete and pure, engulfed Anna. Long-erected barriers and defenses fell away. She forgot the pain of isolation.

Anna's yearning for things to be different with Edward seemed not to matter. The hope of what might have been had Edward touched her in all the right places, the fear of what could have occurred hours earlier—*We'll get though this*—slipped underneath the fullness of Inman's arms encompassing her.

Inman massaged the areas within Anna's emotions that Elena had never caressed during Anna's childhood. His lips reached into the forbidden places of Anna's body, the tributaries feeding into her soul, places that Elena had taught Anna to scorn.

Men. They take everything, and give nothing.
Falling in love breaks your heart.
The best women live without them.
Never become dependent.
Men demand change from a penny. As far as love, well .
. .

"Mama, do you love me?"
What is love?
The only thing you truly own is your mind . . .
Anna opened her eyes and met Inman staring upon her. She had fallen asleep after their lovemaking.

"Do you love me?" She breathed in and held her breath.

"As much as you'll let me."

Anna turned her head upon the pillow. The twist of anguish on Inman's face when she'd spoken harshly about Millicent formed in her mind.

Anna said, "I don't hate my daughters-in-law." Again, Inman seemed perturbed at Anna's return to the subject of Theo's wife. Of Heather, she said, "Believe me, I was as surprised as any black mother when David brought Heather home. I hadn't counted on my sons, least of all David, being interested in a white girl. Perhaps Theo, but not David.

"What bothers you about Millicent being married to Theo?" Inman directed the conversation back to the subject of Millicent.

"I don't want my son hurt. Theo's so much like me. He gives so much, too much. And Millicent, she's a taker. She's like her father. And Edward."

"Theo is Edward's child too." Inman's voice was kind and guiding.

"But, it's people like Millicent, Thelonius, and Edward who run the world. They're the ones who get what they want, no matter how they have to go about it, or who they have to step over."

"And what is Millicent taking from you? What has she taken from Theo?" Inman said. "More importantly, when are you going to give yourself permission to have what you've always wanted?"

She looked to him. Their brown bodies were naked except for the sheets wrapping them in the darkness. Anna sat up. "I realize Millicent may just want to reconnect with her father," she said. "But Theo is her husband. He wants to start a family."

"Maybe Millicent is spending time with Thelonius trying to iron out their difficulties, at least some of them, before having her own children."

"That's how Theo says she explains it."

"Perhaps that's the way she intends it. Or at least that's what she hopes time with Thelonius will yield."

Anna wondered what Inman had surmised about Millicent's difficulties with Thelonius. The death of Inman's wife, who had abandoned him and their daughter appeared to have left father and daughter close.

Inman spoke of Dancia with the care and concern of a loving father, but also with respect and admiration of the young woman she had become despite having one parent. Anna envied the closeness she sensed between Inman and his daughter. He seemed to know so much about women and their desires, especially Anna's.

"Time with Thelonius doesn't change what he did."

"Then why did you bring Edward home to die? So that Serine won't become like him, or you?"

Inman's allegory left Anna dazed.

177

Chapter 26

Anna returned to the house well past three in the morning. On entering the kitchen, she flipped on the light. David's face came into view as her eyes adjusted to the brightness.

"Did you have a nice time with Aunt Elise?" he asked, his arms folded. Anna had told Linda she was going out to meet a friend. She had hoped Linda would assume the friend was Elise.

Anna removed a glass from the cabinet and filled it with water from the faucet, her modus operandi when anxious and avoidant. She had spent the last six, nearly seven hours with Inman, much of that time in his bed. The drive home had not provided sufficient transition. Drinking water gave her time to think, plan, and conjure a response.

David's arms remained folded across his chest. "I don't suppose your friend was Elise?"

"I'm still your mother, twenty-four years your senior," Anna said then proceeded upstairs.

"Dad was calling for you in his sleep," David said. Anna turned back. "I think he was having a bad dream." David unfolded his arms and let them hang.

"What else did he say?"

"He just kept mumbling your name. Linda had given him something to help him sleep."

Morphine. It's happening.

"Moments later he cried out," David said. "I went in and tried to wake him."

Anna trembled. Dr. Grimes warned it would get messy. "How long has he been taking something to help him sleep?" she asked.

"The hospice worker left it. She showed Linda how to give the injection."

"Linda needs her rest." Anna again started for the steps.

"She's pregnant."

"I've congratulated her. But you need your rest, too." David followed her. "Linda and Brad are worried about you. So am I." Anna turned back this time unable to avoid her eldest child's gaze. "You don't think Dad will want us to euthanize ..."

She covered her mouth to stop the tears. David drew near as if to take her into his arms. It was so unlike him. Awash in the shame of having been with Inman, Anna backed away and continued upstairs. Her face grew warm, began to burn as always when Anna felt bewildered, afraid, and guilty. Last embers of what she had shared with Inman—what had healed and assuaged her pain—fueled resentment of the dilemma she now faced.

Anna eased the door open and slipped into what used to be her and Edward's bedroom. She lowered herself into the chair by the bed. Despite her sweater, she felt cold. Edward was asleep. He did not move. Pushing aside plaguing thoughts, Anna longed for the Edward Manning of the past. The one who had been strong and certain. Often she had wished a bit of his determination and potency to drain into her. During their

180

lovemaking, Anna had been drawn, if not addicted, to the intensity of Edward's thrust.

Edward had been nothing like Inman who was soft and never aggressive. Edward had been forceful, as if fleeing something, or parts of himself. The muscle of Edward's soul coming through when he made love to Anna left her bruised. Or had it been love?

Anna drew the sweater tight around her shoulders. She leaned back and considered the ease with which she had received Inman hours earlier. Slowly she lowered her eyelids and recalled the emptiness that he had filled.

Chapter 27

During the rise of his career, much of Edward's work had taken him to South America where he had sold properties to Americans. One night, having returned from a two-week trip in Brazil, Edward arrived home from SFO past midnight. The children, ranging from ages twelve to six, had been in bed for hours.

Anna had served Edward filet mignon with pearl onions, asparagus, and wild rice, a far cry from the hotdogs and French fries she had fed the kids and the chicken she had eaten. Despite his repeated wishes for only a sandwich—she had kept his meal warm—Anna heaped large portions onto his plate. "It's nice.

But after eating all of this I won't be able to get up tomorrow morning. Never mind the jet lag," he complained. Anna hadn't wanted Edward to go to work the next day. She wanted him to lie in bed while she drove the children to school, and then upon returning home, make love to her.

Anna, who had never traveled beyond the U.S., considered the women like Stella more beautiful and confident than she. Anna felt certain Stella's sensuality and sexual appeal had attracted and kept Edward returning to her for six years. But with Edward now home and fed, Anna would make him happy.

Her heart pounded that night as Edward removed her clothes. A mesmerizing heat bonded them. Glad to have him home, she had pushed back the thoughts of Stella, the Brazilian woman with whom she was certain he had been with while on his trip.

Anna and Edward engaged in torrid sex, Edward pulling at her hair, Anna gripping and sticking her nails into the skin of his arms. It was almost masochistic. And then suddenly, Edward pushed her aside.

"I can't do this." He crawled from on top of her.

Anna sat up. Edward's back was to her as he sat on the edge of the bed facing the door.

"I can do anything they can," Anna said.

He tore his hand through his hair and sighed. "You're not like them."

"You don't think I'm good enough?"

Edward stood and went to the bathroom. Anna restrained herself from following him. The shower went on. She lay back upon the pillow thinking of the madness in which they had been about to participate. If only he had given me a few more minutes, she thought.

Edward returned nude and dripping wet from having showered. His body, then cool, had smelled of Dial soap. His arousal lay at bay. She looked to his body, lean and trim, his manhood dead. Anna wished to revive it. She reached for his penis.

"You're not that to me." He brushed back her hand.

"I'm your wife."

"You're the mother of my children."

"But I need love and everything you give Stella and the others," Anna said.

"You don't need that." Edward's words echoed through the darkness. It was as if he were a Greek deity come down from the heavens, the outline of his body distinct against the moonlight, and everything about him was exposed. And yet . . .

Again she reached for his penis. This time he grabbed her shoulders, and lifted her upon the bed.

"Life is filthy," he whispered. Anna felt him resist her and his own needs. A tide of emotions flowed from his hands into her. She craved the hidden parts of him that he gave the women. "Not like this," he said. "You're better than them." He pulled away.

"But, I'm your . . ."

She reached out. He was gone.

Anna laid in bed that night, darkness surrounding her as she wondered why Edward would not make love to her. With each child she gave birth to, Anna lost a piece of what had drawn her to Edward. He was stepping away and taking parts she could never reclaim. Her hope for intimacy began to shrivel.

Anna woke the next morning to an empty bed. Edward did not return for three days. She called the office each day with Philomena's mother, Wyntonia, stating that Edward had not been in. When Anna called the third day of his absence, Wyntonia repeated what she had said on previous inquiries, this time adding, "I don't know when he will arrive."

Frustrated despite sensing that Wyntonia was tired of the phone calls, Anna blurted, "You're his secretary. Don't you know anything? How does he run a business like this. What do you tell his clients?"

"The same as I tell you," Wyntonia said, then followed with a more piercing additive, "*They* seem to understand."

"And just what is it that I'm to understand?"

Wyntonia's sigh siphoned through the phone as if to say, Edward is not faithful. And most likely never will be.

Anna confronted him on his return the following day. "You've made me a laughing stock. Even your secretary sees me as—"

"Perhaps if you didn't call so much," Edward said. Again, he had arrived home long after the children had gone to bed. When they had asked about their father, Anna had as on other times, told them he had been delayed due to work.

He turned to Anna. "Don't ever call my office again, not like that." Edward had received Anna's message. With the bottle opener, he flipped the cap from his beer. Liquid bubbled up and fizz drained down the sides of the green bottle. The bottle slipped through his fingers, hit the floor and shattered. "Damn!" Edward cursed.

"I was worried and didn't know if you were okay, or whether the boyfriend or husband of any of those women had—"

"If I want you to know where I am, then I'll tell you; otherwise—"

"Why can't you be faithful?" Anna asked. "Am I not exciting? Am I *that* dull?" Edward silently removed his tee shirt, stepped out of his trousers, and was about to enter the shower. "Don't you hear anything I'm saying? Don't you care?" She walked to him as she had done three nights earlier. "Edward?"

"This is who I am." He turned around and tapped his chest.

"Well, why didn't you say that before we married and had children?"

His eyes seemed to roar against the dim lighting of the bedroom lamp. "It was never my idea to have four children. One would have been enough." He threw his hand. "But oh no, you kept wanting more. More." He raised his voice, then mimicked Anna by speaking at a higher pitch. "Let's have another child, Edward. Let's have another. I want a little girl. Let's try for a girl."

Anna slapped him. Edward went to the bathroom, closed the door, and showered. Later, he eased into bed. Anna's back was to him. He touched her shoulder. Anna resisted moving. She could not believe the level to which she had fallen. She *yearned*, was begging in her own feeble way, to be touched and held, for Edward to make love to her.

Casting your pearls before swine.

Waste not, want not. I hope you're not pregnant.

Men never love a woman who is pregnant.

A mother can only bear children—never give love or receive it—at least not with the father of their children.

They give so little and steal our lives.

Men.

186

I am a servant of the Lord.
God is my lover.

Anna wondered what her mother had thought of the state of her marriage to Edward. While she had never raised the issue of Edward's philandering with Elena, Anna was quite sure that, like Elijah, her mother, had been aware. Unable to stir the fires of passion between her and Edward, Anna chose to maintain herself and her children in financial comfort by remaining in a marriage where her husband engaged in behavior she considered pornographic with other women.

Ignorant to the ways of the world, Anna longed for the intimacies she imagined Edward to have experienced with those women. Over time, Anna made the children her focus. She took refuge in the house in which Edward had placed her. *The house* was her mainstay, heaven on earth encased by the hell of her marriage.

Slivers of morning sunlight pierced the window shade. The clock read 6:00. Anna was sitting in the chair next to the bed where Edward lay. His breathing was calm and peaceful, unlike throughout their marriage wherein fits of anger seemed to direct his inhalations and breathing out. At times, he called out the names of the women with whom he shared himself in ways that Anna now realized even he abhorred.

What kept you at a distance? She wondered. Anna leaned forward and touched his shoulder. Moments slipped by, his breathing remained calm. She removed her hand.
Anna leaned back, was about to close her eyes. Edward opened his. She could not avoid his gaze.

"What is it, I never understood. What did they have that I didn't?" she whispered.

As if holding no answer to her question, Edward closed his eyes and went back to sleep. Once more, Anna pulled the sweater upon her shoulders, this time wishing to rent a hole in it with her nails. Instead, she let go. Anna closed her eyes. Hot tears seeped through and onto her face. She did not wipe them.

Chapter 28

Anna had almost finished her coffee when David pulled out a chair and joined her at the kitchen table.

"Has Dad said what he's going to do with the business? He was the center of action at Manning Real Estate."

"Bryce." Anna thought aloud. "I haven't talked to him since I first saw your father in the hospital."

"He hasn't called?" David asked.

"Bryce is going through his own turmoil and grieving. Your father was like his surrogate dad."

"Do you have his number?" David seemed perturbed.

Anna went upstairs and pulled her cell phone from her purse. Back at the kitchen table, she scrolled through the list of names and numbers in the cell phone address book.

"Here it is, Bryce's cell." She recited the numbers. David wrote them down. As David lifted the cordless from its cradle on the counter by the range to dial Bryce, Anna slid open the glass door and stepped onto the patio. She considered Inman and the hours she had spent with him before returning home early that morning. Against Edward's missive, *We'll get through this*, Anna missed Inman.

David walked toward Anna, who was standing by the pool. He had ended his call with Bryce.

"Bryce says he's spoken with Dad three times since he's been home."

"When? How?" Anna asked.

"He's got his cell phone upstairs."

"Your father was always a master at keeping things to himself." *Hidden.* Anna simmered with annoyance at the memories.

"Bryce said he was waiting for you to call him," David said. "He wants to meet with you, today if possible, at Scott's."

"Did you tell him that your father wants you to oversee the execution of the estate?"

"Yes."

Anna's mind flitted back to last evening and eating dinner with Inman. Memories of lying next to him, Inman making love to her swept across her thoughts. The essence of his passion swarmed through her and overshadowed the torrid memories of painful times with Edward. I'm behaving like Serine. She failed to dismiss the thought.

David said of Bryce, "I told him you'll call back to confirm."

Edward's virility had been on the wane as he sank from the pinnacle of his manhood into middle age. His present transformation asked more of Anna than any of his past antics. Honesty. Perhaps if she could present her truth about Inman to the children. Anna was determined to offer an example that Serine could follow. Once more David called Anna from her ruminations.

"He's dying. I'm losing my dad."

Anna touched her eyes, still sore from crying earlier in the chair beside Edward's bed where memories swirled above, and below.

"I know," she whispered.

Anna met Bryce for lunch at Scott's. Bryce stood as she approached the table.

"Thank you for meeting me." Bryce offered his hand. Anna ignored his gesture and pulled out the chair across from him. Ironically, they were at the same table where Anna had sat with Inman the prior evening. She sat.

On joining her, Bryce said, "I took the liberty of ordering a pot of tea. Edward said you liked that." She glimpsed the steam surrounding the teapot. If only Edward had attempted to fulfill other, less tangible, but no less meaningful, desires.

Bryce lifted his briefcase. "I've been meaning to call, but—"

"I see you've been speaking with Edward," she said. Bryce lowered the briefcase onto the linen covered table. "Then again, you are his attorney and the one person who works with him."

"In light of Edward's condition—" Bryce started once more.

"My husband's dying. It's taking a toll on all of us," Anna said. An air of strain overtook Bryce. He looked as if he might cry, or worse, that he lacked the words to state his cause. Anna's anger toward Bryce increased as he lowered his head.

She didn't know the meaning or root of her indignation. Bryce had been good and loyal to Edward. And he appeared to desire the same with Anna. She managed to say, "I appreciate you being there for Edward even when I couldn't."

Bryce's palm gave a slight tremble. The same tension that had overtaken him when Anna entered Edward's hospital room settled him once more. He opened his briefcase and removed a folder of documents. Anna sipped her tea.

Bryce laid the folder upon the linen covered table and then, with what seemed all that he could gather, said, "Edward has made you the owner and president of Manning Ventures."

Anna carefully lowered her cup onto its saucer. "Edward sold real estate. His company was called Manning Real Estate."

"Yes, but over the years, he invested much of his profits into what has now become three small, yet lucrative, conglomerates."

"Manning Ventures?" Anna tried absorbing the name.

"Startups that have subsidiaries in Angola, India, China, Saudi Arabia, and the Soviet Union. Most are related to Internet technology and the development of alternative forms of energy." Bryce went on. "They hold much potential for the future, particularly and in light of our recent economic oil crisis, I would suggest—"

"No, wait a minute." Anna raised her palm. Bryce's words, the full brunt of their meaning sank in. "You're saying that Edward's willed me his company, Manning Ventures, so that when he dies—"

"No. You're the owner and president right now." She stared at Bryce, the truth of his anxiety in earlier moments now eroding. "I filed the last forms yesterday. It'll take a week for the county and city clerk to record the change, but essentially you own Manning Ventures." Bryce spoke the words, as if having shed a weight.

"Well, the first thing I'm going to do is sell it. I know nothing about real estate."

"It's not that simple. As I said, these small conglomerates have nothing to do with the real estate company. In fact," Bryce pulled back his sleeve and read his watch, "Manning Real Estate has been sold. All that remains," his words slowed, "—is Manning Ventures. And you, Anna, are its major stockholder, and president."

"I don't want it. I don't want any of it." She shook her head then turned toward the window adjacent the table. She considered Inman from last evening, their argument, her leaving and then their lovemaking.

"The company is solid," Bryce reiterated, trying to make her understand. "There are some outstanding debts, which comes with any business. Yet, through the last eight years, the company held its own. It hasn't needed an infusion of cash from the real estate company."

"And you want a job." Anna turned back to Bryce. "Better yet to keep the one you have." She leaned into the table, and whispered, "How about *you* buy the company? I'll sell it to you. Make a loan you can live with." Anna wanted to be through with Edward Manning and his surprises.

"I would love to do that. But honestly, even with what I've learned from Edward, I have no skills at running this company." A sheen of tears slipped over Bryce's eyes and delivered a sad sparkle.

"And you think I do?"

Chapter 29

Anna hated double talk. And Henderson, as she sat in his office, was beginning to sound like Bryce. "Just, hear me out." Henderson begged.

"That's what Bryce said."

"Then perhaps you should." Henderson leaned across his desk. "Edward owes you."

"But not a company. I don't know what to do with it."

"Run it. At least don't sell it as a knee-jerk reaction. Take a look-see. Investigate what Bryce is telling you. The sale of Edward's real estate company provides more than enough for you to live on. In fact, once everything has settled, go to France." Henderson pointed to the sky beyond the window. "See Paris."

"Oh, but Bryce has to prepare me for a board meeting," Anna quipped. "Edward's dying." She sighed. "This is *Edward's* money. It's all he's worked for."

"That's right. Edward has cancer and won't live to see his third grandchild enter this world. But, you'll be here. The money will come in handy."

"How can you be so cold?"

"Few people come to grips with reality and their role in shaping it. Edward seems to have done that," Henderson said. "From the looks of it, he's going to leave this world in a better manner than he lived. I'm proud of him."

Tears threatened to overtake her. It had become like this since Edward had admitted he was scared, that life and all its uncertainties frightened him. Then Anna had slept with Inman. The emotions she had abandoned in her will to take care of her children had crawled to life.

Henderson came around his desk and lifted her hand. "Forgive me, Anna, but I'm not about to let you throw away what you've worked so hard for. Edward obviously agrees."

"I was a wife and mother, and of the latter, not a very good one."

"Life is dirty, Anna." Henderson's words took her back to that night Anna had Edward begged him to make love to her. *You're too good for me. I'm dirty and mean, like life,"* Edward had said. *"I won't soil you. I won't make you like me."* Hours earlier she had served him the filet mignon with pearl onions and asparagus with wild rice. Everything about Edward, his tone, the movement of his body, the slope of his shoulders had reflected his shame.

Despite his hatred for the physician to whom Violet had been a mistress, Edward had become like the physician. Anna had undergone a variation of what Violet Manning had endured. *They understand,* Wyntonia had said of others regarding Edward's long absences. Now Anna did. The house symbolized so much.

Anna said to her attorney, "Thank you for seeing me on such short notice." She stood and left Henderson before the tears started to fall.

During the drive home, Anna replayed her conversations with Bryce, and then Henderson. *Manning Ventures is a small conglomerate of companies with investments in the U.S., South*

America, Africa, and China, Bryce had said. Henderson then asserted, *Edward never involved you in any of his businesses. He spent more time in those countries than he did at home in your house.*

Anna crawled upon the bed and shut her eyes. She was at home and inside Theo's room. Moments later, there was a knock on the door.

"Who is it?" Anna called.

The door opened and Linda peeked inside. "It's me."

Anna sat up, smoothed back her hair, and made a feeble attempt at wiping her face. "Sorry, but I was tired."

"David said you met with Bryce." Linda lowered herself onto the bed.

"Yes." Anna nodded.

"How did that go? Are you alright?"

"Not well. And no, I'm not."

Linda chuckled.

"What's so funny?" Anna knitted her brows.

"For once you're telling the truth."

"When have I ever lied?"

Linda's smile dimmed.

"Let's just say that relaying the reality of a situation, particularly when it involves Dad, has not been a skill you've possessed." Anna sighed. Linda had verbalized Anna's struggle for the last thirty or more years. She lifted Linda's hand then explained what Bryce had said concerning Manning Ventures.

"I know nothing about running a company. What am I'm going to do?"

"Have you spoken to Inman?" Linda asked.

"What do you know about Inman?" Anna screwed her face.

"He seems to care for you."

"I love your father, but—"

"None of us have ever questioned that," Linda said. "Not even David."

"I doubt that." Anna's shoulders fell against a sinking feeling within.

Linda said, "You need to let yourself have some fun." She sounded like Theo.

"Your father's dying. And my children are unhappy. I don't mean you."

"You're so certain I'm doing fine?" Linda's smile returned.

"I am so happy that you've found happiness." Anna embraced her. "I thank God everyday for Brad and what he's given you." Anna whispered then, "And now with the baby . . ."

"You've given me a lot, too." Linda touched her stomach.

Anna placed her palm over Linda's hand to her stomach, then said, "I failed you in so many ways."

"That's in the past. And I certainly played my role."

"You were hurting," Anna said. "There was a time when I . . ." She began to cry.

"I wanted you happy," Linda said. "And no one wanted to talk about it. David was the worse."

"I guess that's why you treated him like your nemesis?"

"When it came to you and your happiness, he *was* my nemesis," Linda said.

"Would it be true to say that when it comes to David, you don't always see straight?"

"I can see why Heather won't sleep with him."

"Linda."

"David's charming. He's also bossy. And he can be passive aggressive."

"He's never been unfaithful," Anna asserted.

"That is true, unless you count self-absorption, being totally consumed with one's success, career, and status in the world as infidelities. What he needs is a taste of Millicent to set him straight." How different Linda sounded from Serine. "Then again, she's so much like David," Linda said of her sister-in-law, " . . . he might be overcome."

Anna laughed amid the echo of Linda's words. Change had arrived.

"You're right about David . . . " She sat still for a moment. "But somehow I feel as though I've failed you, Serine, and your brothers. If only I had been more truthful. But I couldn't have you hating your father. And there was no way I was about to fall into poverty by leaving him. He was a good provider. He never hit me."

"No one has a perfect marriage," Linda said.

"Some *are* better than others."

"And then there are those that are worse." Linda's round face warmed to another smile. "You never let us know the full truth about Dad until we could handle it. For that, I'll always be thankful."

"But my unhappiness . . . you said that—"

"I thought it was me or that it was something I had done wrong. I was angry," Linda said. "I wanted to fix you, make you smile."

"And you prefer that to me telling you the truth?" Anna was confused.

"I'm not saying I want my child to go through the same. But neither am I willing to tamper with history. I survived. That I was depressed in all that was going on makes sense. I know that now. Any child who sees their parent unhappy assumes some of the responsibility. My marriage to Brad has taught me a lot. Talking with his father has also helped."

Anna rubbed Linda's arm. "Things are working out for you two." She smiled.

"I don't know what I might have done had you actually told me about Dad's affairs when I was a child. It was one thing to sense something, and quite another for your mother to confirm your worst fears."

"You were sitting right there at the table when your father brought Gabrielle home to dinner. You watched the two of them, laughing and so excited about all of his plans. You called your father on it. But I pretended all was well."

"But you never affirmed what I suspected. My outburst during dinner, the pain I felt during adolescence was based on suspicion, albeit correct. You never said Dad was having an affair with Gabrielle or any other women. That gave me hope."

"It also confused and drove you crazy." Anna grew frightened.

199

Linda lifted her hand. "We're adults now. And I'm okay."

"And you love your father?"

"I love Dad for the father you let him be, not the man who left you alone. But most of all I love you for preserving the chance for me to do that." Linda smiled and this time reached out for Anna. The two embraced.

"What is Inman like?" Linda's intuition once again hit the mark.

Anna considered what it would be like to have Inman as part of her children's lives. Slowly, she began to tell about him.

Chapter 30

Hours after dinner that evening, and feeling certain Edward had fallen asleep, Anna called a meeting out on the patio. The sun, setting into a sky that moments earlier had poured blood-red-orange across the landscape of the heavens, edged toward indigo.

Anna considered how the transformation of day to night had arrived minutes earlier the previous evening. The days were growing shorter, daylight less plentiful. Change was taking place in the Manning family. Death would soon extinguish the light of Edward in their lives.

David, Theo, Linda, and Brad took their places around the table by the pool. Anna brushed aside thoughts of her time with Inman at his home atop Grizzly Peak, the two of them naked in his bed. She joined her children at the patio table.

"I met with Bryce this afternoon," she started. "He tells me that your father has given me his company, Manning Ventures."

"The real estate company?" Theo said.

"Not exactly."

"The company's now Manning Ventures," David interjected. "A collection of three, small companies."

Anna eyed Linda as she recalled their conversation from earlier that afternoon. *David can be a lot like Dad, bossy and stubborn.*

Anna turned her attention to David. "So you knew about this?"

Appearing somewhat anxious, he said, "Dad discussed a few things with me. Like his purchases."

"Well," Anna returned to her main point, "I've decided to keep the company. I'm not going to sell it as I'd first thought."

Linda smiled. Theo leaned back in his seat appearing, as on many times, as if possessed in thought.

David's interest was piqued. "Do you think that's prudent? Running a company takes—"

"*Acumen,*" Anna finished his sentence. David looked straight at her. Brad and Linda snickered while exchanging glances with Theo.

"Do you even know what you're doing?" David persisted.

"Not exactly," Anna said. "But Bryce assures me that the companies are strong and thriving. He also says that this is not a time to sell. With a recession looming, I'd never get what they're worth."

"At least you know that," David retorted. "Still, you can't do anything until Dad is—"

"I own the company right now," Anna again interrupted her elder son. All eyes around the table became alert, as if for the first time grasping the meaning of her words, *Your father's given me his company.* Theo's watchful composure clarified into a subtle show of glee.

Linda patted Brad's hand, their subdued smiles showing pleasure. Her thoughts again fresh, as when Henderson informed her of David's bogus suits, Anna said, "Is this why you sued Henderson and tried to have me declared insane?" All was coming clear.

Linda, Brad, and Theo turned to David in surprise. With his back to the pool, the moonlight shimmering on the surface of the water made David's figure silhouette-like.

"You actually did that?" Brad asked. "I remember what you said at dinner that first night after we arrived, but—"

"You're not in this." David shot Brad a glare of disgust.

"You knew what your father was going to do," Anna said to David. "He discussed this with you. You knew he was giving me the company."

"I can't believe you'd do such a thing." Linda displayed a contorted frown.

"Did Heather know you issued a suit against Mama and Henderson?" Theo asked.

Linda sighed once more then said, "You interned at Henderson's office. He invited you to join his practice." She began massaging her stomach. Anna grew anxious. It was happening again. The energy of Elena's diseased spirit was roaming among them.

David addressed Linda. "He was also Dad's friend and former attorney." He turned to Anna. "But that didn't seem to matter when you asked for a divorce."

"I asked Henderson to represent me because aside from your father's behavior in his private life, Henderson respected his accomplishments," Anna said.

"Dad's dying," David refused to listen. "The last year he's been fighting a cancer that's now eating him alive. And all you've done is fight him."

"I had no idea your father had cancer," Anna said.

"Would it have mattered? For Christ's sake, you're not even wearing his ring, never mind where you sleep."

Anna took in a breath as Theo, Linda, and Brad lowered their heads.

Anna finally said, "I am truly sorry that you father is dying. I would never wish this on him or anyone in a million years. But that does not change the fact that—"

"I was unfaithful to your mother," Edward spoke as he stepped from the kitchen onto the patio. David dashed to him. Edward lifted his cane and waved him back. He tried to smile on his way to the table. Carefully, he lowered himself onto the chair between David and Brad, sitting opposite to Anna. He propped his cane against the edge of the circular glass table. He placed his hands in his lap.

"I'm dying," Edward softly said to David, growing solemn and frustrated. "No amount of arguing is going to change that. And as for rings, I've worn one for over thirty years. The only meaning they hold is symbolized by our behavior."

The muscles in David's neck flexed as if he was attempting to swallow a rock covered in spurs. Again, Theo exchanged metered glances with Anna and Brad. David appeared about to cry.

Edward continued. "I don't need or want you arguing with your mother. Stop it." David remained silent and still, as if was steeling himself from the brunt of Edward's command. "Your mother's earned every bit of what the company's worth, and more of whatever it might bring her."

Theo, Linda and Brad lowered their heads. "I've not been the best husband," said Edward. It's a fact to everyone who knows me." Seething ever more deeply, David breathed in. Edward placed his palm over David's hand. "I need you to stand by your mother."

David jumped up and started toward the house.

"Is this because of Heather?" Linda called to him.

"I don't need you or anyone in this family peering into my business." David scowled.

"Son, we're not trying to hurt you," Edward said.

"I know what you're trying to do," David's voice cracked as he whipped around.

Theo reached over and grasped Anna's hand. She was feeling disoriented like she had when Grant arrived minutes after Matt, both wanting to see Serine. She rubbed her temples.

David stormed to Edward. "Why couldn't you have been better to her? Why did you have to go all those places and leave her here?"

The wounded seven-year-old boy in David emerged from the thirty-three-year-old man he had become. Like Theo,

David had also been sensitive to Anna's sadness in the wake of Edward's difficult-to-explain absences. Anna recalled him trying to comfort her as only a child and son could. They'd been sitting on her bed, and David had come in to check on her as Edward had instructed. Each time before he went away, he commanded David, "Take care of your mama."

David had stroked her cheek. *Mommy, don't you cry. I know you miss Daddy, but I'm here.* A second-grader, and missing two front teeth, his face, the color of maple syrup, had borne the seriousness of a man seven times his age. Anna pulled him close. *I love you,* she whispered and kissed the top of his head. David then said, *When I grow up I'm gonna get married. You can live with me. We'll take care of you. Me and my wife. We'll never let you cry.*

Anna wondered about Heather, and considered how much of David's misery was caused by his vow to save Anna, a promise he had made over two and a half decades earlier. How much of David's commitment to Anna was squeezing Heather out of his life? Or was it a vow to fixing his family of origin, a warped attempt to right what was broken within him that was distorting his vision of Heather, and her response to the recent loss of her father?

Theo said to Edward, "What can we do to help?"

Looking to David, Anna realized that she had accomplished the first task of the gathering.

"It's your mother I'm concerned about," Edward said as he eyed her. His words seemed surreal. Yet Anna felt them true and sincere. For the first time since marrying Edward Gordon Manning, Anna sensed the person behind the façade of accomplishment fueled by ambition, coming forth. It was frightening and heart rending.

Anna inspected her hands and considered her newly-imposed task regarding Manning Ventures. "I've only run a house and managed a family. That's quite another thing from guiding a company." She lifted her head.

"The two aren't that much different," Linda said. Brad nodded in agreement.

"Different tasks, but same set of skills," Theo chimed. "In fact, I think you bring a fresh sensibility to the company."

"Well, you would," David snipped.

"And who are you?" Theo said. "The voice of reason?"

"Perhaps in time, you and Mom'll recognize that," David said. "Until then, I'm also the executor of this estate." He turned to Edward. "If that's what you still want me to do."

"I do," Edward nodded.

"What will that include?" Anna said. "You've given me the company. And I was going to sell the house."

"I've given the house to the children," Edward said. Anna grew furious. "You never signed the divorce documents," Edward continued. "And if I'm correct, Henderson didn't file the deed. The house is still held in my name."

Anna's face and ears burned with indignation. She felt exposed. Edward had turned the clock back to when she first asked for the divorce.

"All I ever wanted from you was to sell this house and receive one-half the sale. That's all." She hit the glass surface of the table, and stood.

"You own the company," Edward said.

"I don't want your god-damned company. I want to sell this house and be done with all of it." She raised her hands. "Why do you have to be so doggone belligerent?" She blew out air. "You go off, live your life the way you want. Then when I—"

"I'm sorry," Edward said. "I love you." His words hit with sparkling clarity. Try as she might, Anna could not avoid his weakened gaze. With her son-in-law and three elder children looking on, she could not refuse Edward's words. Yet her anger and hurt welled.

"This will not change what you did," she said. "It doesn't take the hurt away." Anna touched her forefinger upon the table. "You have to live with the consequences of your actions."

"If living were only that simple," Edward said. "But you don't have to live with the consequences of my actions. I don't want you to."

"Then why fight me on the house? Why give it to David?" Again she threw up her hands and avoided what she knew to be hurt enveloping David. "You said that I'd earned—"

"The house is not just David's," Edward said. "It's the children's to do with as they like."

"I don't want your fucking company. I should have divorced you when I had the chance!"

"Then do it." Calmly Edward grasped his cane and pulled himself to his feet. "Henderson still has the papers. Sell the company." He started back toward the house. Within a few feet from the sliding glass doors, he slumped onto the patio. David, Brad, and Theo rushed to him. Linda followed. Awash with despair at what her life had become, Anna grew more anguished at what she had revealed of herself in front of her children.

Chapter 31

David left the next morning before dawn. Linda and Anna were eating a mid-morning breakfast on the patio, the very table where last evening sunset had moved to dusk before the darkness enshrouded them. And the blowout had taken place.

"David went in Dad's room and sat with him a couple of minutes right before leaving," Linda explained to Anna. "I looked in on them. He leaned down and kissed Dad's cheek and forehead. David seemed so hurt and lost." She shook her head. "He's got a lot of work to do with Heather."

"That much is clear. And of course there's the house." Anna lifted her hands as if to the heavens. "*This* house." She crossed her arms.

Linda reached over and patted Anna's hands, massaging her shoulders. "Let the house go. David needs something to lord over. Overseeing the sale of the house will give him something to do."

"You're going to sell it?"

"Why shouldn't we?" Linda asked. "Besides, I thought that's what you wanted." Once again Anna was hit with her ambivalence. "We could all use the money," Linda said. "Besides, who's going to live here?"

"But David's talking about moving back here to Oakland."

"Then, he can buy it from us."

"You'd make him do that?" Anna asked.

"I have a child on the way." Linda rubbed her stomach burgeoning ever so slightly with each passing day. The child Linda carried reflected the one clear hope of Anna's life, something she could look forward to, hold and love, without feeling guilty as she did when considering Inman.

"I'll give you and Brad money," Anna said.

"And we wouldn't take it." Again Linda reached over, and this time patted Anna's knee.

"I don't want you fighting David on my account."

"He needs to calm down," Linda said.

"There'll be time for that after your father's gone." Anna grasped her temples. "I can't believe I spoke to your father like that in front of all of you." She covered her face.

Linda embraced her. "This is family. And we're all adults." Linda brushed Anna's neck like Anna had done with her on so many occasions when she had been unable to hold a clear perspective on life, and accept the love Anna held for her.

Anna said, "My behavior last evening was atrocious."

"You were hurting and confused."

"That's what I used to say to you." Anna recalled how she had comforted Linda in the weeks and months after each of Linda's three attempts to end her life. "I was always afraid you'd succeed, and that we'd lose you," Anna said. "I don't know what I would have done." She began to cry.

Again Linda drew Anna into her chest. Anna let go of her emotions and wept like a child. When she was calmer, Linda cupped her palms around Anna's face. "You don't have to worry about that now. I'm okay. And so is my baby." A peaceful smile enveloped Linda's sienna face. "You were there when I couldn't be present for myself."

"You were that way because your father was unfaithful," Anna said. "And I was trying to act as if nothing was going on."

"You were there." Linda shook her shoulders. "That's all that matters. Even Dad says so." Anna looked down at the cement surface of the patio. "We counted on you, and you never let us down," Linda said. "And when Dad's gone, we won't let you down. Not me, Brad, or Theo. That includes David and Serine. You're stuck with us."

"That's what frightens me." A smile formed on Anna's lips despite her fears. With thanks and praise, she envisioned through her wash of tears, the young and beautiful woman her elder daughter had become. Again Linda pulled her close. Anna laid her head on Linda's shoulder and wept some more.

Chapter 32

Anna was on the patio when Theo came to her.

"Dad told us to leave," Theo said. "He doesn't want us to remember him this way. He also said he wants time with you."

"Time with me?" Anna laid her pen on the glass table and stared at it. She was making a list of things she needed to attend to in preparation for Edward's death. She also had yet to open the folder Bryce had given her detailing Manning Ventures and its assets. Theo touched her shoulder. She stroked his arm.

"Brad and Linda are packed and ready," Theo said. "They want to say goodbye."

Anna rose and went to them in the driveway where they waited. She hugged both Linda and Brad several times, not wanting to them to leave.

"Promise you'll call the minute you or Edward needed anything," Brad urged as he helped Linda into the car.

"I will."

After helping Linda into the car, Brad got into the driver's seat and they headed off. Anna continued waving until the sedan disappeared at the end of the block.

Minutes later she hugged Theo. He lingered longer than what Anna was comfortable with.

"You need to go." She kissed him.

"I love you, Mom." Theo embraced her then after placing his bags on the front seat of the rental car, he got into the driver's seat, and turned on the ignition. "I'm just a phone call away."

"I love you, too." Anna mouthed the words and stepped away from the sedan. Theo backed out of the driveway and started off. Again, she waved until she could no longer see the car.

Anna returned to the house and set about removing sheets from the beds. She was in the laundry room upstairs, removing shirts from the dryer, and folding them when Edward stepped inside.

"Seems like old times," he said.

"Are you hungry?"

"Time's out for that." Ignoring her question, he gave a half smile. "The kids are adults and gone."

Anna looked at Edward's dress shirts that she had neatly folded. "My mother used to starch and press my father's shirts every Saturday night," she said. "It's the one thing she seemed to freely give him. She said there was an art to it." Anna added, "Folding clothes calms me."

"And so does giving." Edward drew close then of the art on which Anna's mother had pontificated her ideal, he said. "I never was much for having you iron." Edward had always taken his shirts to the cleaners. "I always liked the way you packed them in the back, right-hand corner of my suitcase." He lifted a white shirt from the pile on the dryer. "You never let them get tattered."

"I got rid of them and bought you new ones." Anna stared at the shirt Edward was examining. She had bought it on a whim as a gift to welcome him home. As always, his arrival brought drama. He arrived home early only to leave again, so

214

Anna never presented him the shirt. She began to wear the shirt when he was away. The white shirt became her robe of mourning worn during his absence. Anna mused on the shirt as it had been when first purchased, pristine and white like the nightgown Elijah had bought for Elena a few days before she died. *Naïve and untainted*, Anna thought, just like she had been when agreeing to marry Edward.

Edward's eyes retreated against Anna, treading the emotional waters wrought by his absences too numerous to count.

"I wish we could have spent more time together and gotten to know each other better." His words startled Anna. "You're better than I could ever be," he said. "I've ruined your life."

"You give yourself too much credit." Anna slammed shut the door to the dryer, and lifted the pile of folded towels and shirts. She left the laundry room and headed for Theo's room. Edward followed.

"I'm not trying to be difficult," he said.

"Well you are."

"I'm dying. How much more difficult can I make it for you?"

She whipped around. "By saying the very thing I've fought against acknowledging throughout this entire marriage."

"I've been a bad husband, unfaithful more times and in more ways than I can count."

"I don't have to be reminded of that." Anna gritted her teeth. "You're the last person I need telling me what a big mistake I made in marrying you. Mama warned me. Elise warned me. I warned myself."

"Why didn't you listen?"

"Because I loved you," Anna said.

"Why?"

"And why are we talking about this now?"

"I've lived my life according to my own laws, the best I could make of those laid down before me. Now, a new set of rules has taken over," Edward said.

215

"Those rules, the ones you call new, have always been. You just chose to ignore them."

"I don't want to do that anymore. I can't." Edward's words shocked and surprised her yet again. "My life has been a lie. I want to set it straight. Now."

"And you think giving me your company does that?" Anna said. Edward's eyes blared red. A misty film overtook them. "I know nothing about running a company. David thinks I'm incapable of managing it, and believes I'm a horrible wife for wanting to divorce you. The way he speaks to me leaves little hope that he's any better with Heather as a husband than the one you were with me.

"Oh, and by the way, he's told me that he and Heather haven't slept together in a year. As for Theo, it seems he's married to a female replica of you. And we won't even go into Serine and the mess she's about to make of her life." A burning sensation swept across Anna's cheeks and engulfed her ears. "This is what the *truth*, or as you say, *lie*, of your life has wrought."

With his weakness apparent, even in the darkness surrounding the patio last night, she again refused to take in Edward's withered body covered in a brown and white striped bathrobe. She wanted to knock the ankle socks from his feet, push him to the floor, and scream into his face, "How could you do this to us?" The anger had returned. Yet, it could not satiate her need to know. She felt empty, culled, and hollowed out. Anna desired Edward and wanted to hold his soul, massage his body, and never let him go. She would take back what he had robbed her of, what death now sought to claim, and what he would fight in these last days to create between them, but . . .

"I'm doing the best I can," Edward said.

"Well it's not good enough." Anna began speaking the thoughts she had bottled inside for so long. "Where's the Edward Manning that could fly across the globe and carry out a deal that would make money for all concerned? Where's the Edward Manning with his goals and the tunnel vision of his one-track mind toward achieving them? Where's the Edward G.

216

Manning that I glimpsed only in between trips home? Where's the man your whores saw more than me?"

"He's right here," Edward said wearily. "This is what he's come to. This is what has become of me, the person I was, and have always been. They're one in the same."

"I don't believe that. The person I see before me is considerate. He acts with a rational mind. He's weak and afraid and says so. He does not lie or hold back. The person that you were never gave way to his feelings. The Edward Manning I know would never give away his company."

"That person died a year and half ago when his wife asked for a divorce."

"You're not about to tell me that I caused your cancer. I won't have it." Anna shook her head.

"My sickness was there long before you asked for the divorce," Edward said. "I won't have you blaming yourself. You're not the cause."

"Then why are you doing this to me? Why are you saying these things?" Anna placed her palm over her trembling lips.

"Stop defending." The energy of the old Edward flickered amid the tiredness of his amber eyes. "I was wrong. And I'm paying for it."

"Is that what you think?" Anna was shaking. "This is not what I wanted."

Edward drew near, and embraced her. Carefully he placed her head upon his shoulder. "I'm sorry," he whispered. Slowly he began to cry.

"Oh, my God," Anna whimpered. Her body shook more, stronger, harder. Edward was trembling too. She was overcome with grief in being vindicated. Edward was dying and like her, he was also scared. He was the person who had to go forward. Anna felt slivers of Edward's demise encroaching. Death was summoning him, not Anna, and yet she was dying too.

She dropped to the floor; Edward joined her. Tides of pity and confusion rolled through her, wave after horrible wave, a mix of emotions to which she could give no name. Anna wanted to both hold Edward and slap him.

"Forgive me," he whispered. "How much I would live my life differently, if I had the chance."

"Why didn't you do it this way the first time?" Anna whimpered. She searched his eyes. "I need to know. More than that company you've given me, I need to know to *why*."

"It wasn't anything you did."

"I gave you thirty-three years of my life. You weren't there even half the time, and in the other half, we couldn't connect," Anna said. Edward's eyes brimmed with pain and fury. *I'm lost and scared*, they seemed to say. "I loved you," she continued. "I need to know who that person was. Where's the person I married who then walked away from me?" Anna demanded. "I need to know so that if I see him in the next life, I'll not stop and listen."

"No, don't avoid me." Edward pleaded." I'll change, do what I couldn't in life. I'll make myself right in death. Give me one more chance, so that if we meet in the next life . . ."

"Oh Edward," Anna moaned, her face wet, she sobbing and Edward holding her close. He kissed her.

"Make love to me," Anna said.

"If only I could." But Edward was weak. She felt him slipping away. His gaze receded.

"Then let me love you."

Chapter 33

Anna and Edward went through the following days as if the argument and their love-making had resulted from Edward's return from a prolonged trip during which Anna, much aggrieve, had desired him. The thought that he would now leave only when death enforced its grip gave her pause. Each time they sat to eat, she reminded herself of this certainty amid uncertainty.

How would it be when the time came?

Anna had not been present when her mother died. She had stayed away from the hospital to protect the child she had been carrying, and, as Anna now realized, herself.

She had said to Edward, "I don't want to see my mother like this. She's dying."

"Then, don't go." Edward had said. He had not been present when his mother died of pneumonia while in a rehabilitation hospital for drug addicts.

"But I love my mother," Anna had said.

"And I loved mine." Edward had placed Violet in the rehab center during one of his extreme and futile efforts to save what had been lost before he was born. He lifted the bottle of beer to his lips as he sat at the kitchen table, and continued reading the newspaper.

Anna walked to him. "Don't you care that my mother is dying?" She sat at the table.

"The point is whether *you* care."

"I do."

"Then, go see her." Edward laid the newspaper aside.

"It's not that simple."

He fingered the bottle of beer, wet and sweating then clasped his hands. "What would you like me to do, short of taking away your mother's cancer?"

"Why do you have to always be this way?"

"And what way is that?" Edward's lips and shoulders went straight, betraying the virulent annoyance in his voice, tight and curt.

"Don't you care about me?"

"Yes, I do, Anna," Edward said. He raised his arms as if to encompass the house, *The House*, his gift to Anna and what Violet and he had lacked. "But if you expect me to be all broken up about your mother dying of cancer, I won't. She never liked me; she told you not to marry me.

Your mother accused me of having gotten you pregnant. No, I can't be sorry." He sighed, turned toward the sliding glass door and observed the pool where the midday sunlight was bouncing off the water's surface. "I'm not sad to see your mother dying. But I am glad that she's out of your life."

Anna slapped Edward. Realizing what she had done, Anna, then eight months pregnant, pushed herself up from the table. She was headed toward the steps when Edward gripped her shoulders. He turned her around. "I won't feel bad for what I've said."

"Have you no shame?" Anna's cheeks felt as if splashed with scalding water. "Is there nothing too low for you to stoop to?"

"This discussion is not about me."

"No. It's like everything in this house, and that goes on, and surrounds it," Anna yelled. "This whole marriage, *this house,* is about you."

Edward's face lost all signs of life. But for his amber eyes, energy seemed to escape him. "You won't blame me for your mother's illness."

"I'm not blaming you. In fact, I'm not holding you responsible for anything except that you've never been present in this marriage," Anna said.

"I'm in this marriage." Again Edward surveyed the kitchen.

"No, you're not. You're addicted to your work and those women, Stella, Esther, and Margaret." Anna had discovered a third letter. "You're hooked to them the way your mother was addicted to that medicine the doctor gave her."

The vibrant, ruddy hue in Edward's face died. His demeanor became hard as brick. The light in his amber eyes that had first attracted Anna faded. "What are you going to do, hit me?" she asked. "I spoke about your almighty mama."

A man could not make love to a mother. And heaven forbid that a mother display any amount of sexual vigor and desire toward him. With the birth of Linda looming, Anna feared her marriage would end and that Edward would leave her for one of the women with whom he'd been involved.

"You don't find me attractive," she broke the silence.

"Not when you're acting like this."

"You never found me attractive," Anna spat. "I was just willing and easy." And yet he had married, and given her a home for which most women would die. The envy of the wives of his colleagues, Anna stood caught in a web of misunderstandings and illusions built by Edward. Designed by an architect and built to Edward's specifications, the house had been transformed and maintained by Anna.

It had become a home. But with each child, the home became a tomb, a place where on returning from the hospital, she fell back into a routine of cooking, washing, and drying. There, in the house she found herself consumed with woman's work that sucked all hope and passion from her.

"I should have gone to Paris and worked. I should have never married you."

"And how far would you have gotten with that art degree? No." Edward corrected, "You had a *degree in art history.*" He sounded like Elena.

"A lot farther than I have with you."

"Toward what? Living in an apartment, alone, no children and with no one to care for you?"

"You're insane." Anna gave a facetious laugh. "I'm supposed to be thankful that you married and deposited me in this house." She threw her hand. "You're always off, God knows where, sleeping with whomever, and never loving me."

"Sex is not love," Edward said.

"That's a poor excuse."

"Don't confuse the two."

"You're using the oldest line in the book. And I'm a fool for having believed it all these years," Anna said.

"It's true. And you know it." She stared at him.

Edward fell still. He then turned and went outside.

Anna followed him. She felt dead inside, grappling for life.

"If my father wasn't a minister, and my mother dying, I would abort this child, set fire to this house, and leave."

Edward whipped around.

"This is all you care about," Anna said. Again she waved her hand this time like Edward, and as if to contain the whole of the house. "This house and the money you make to maintain it." She was crying. "That's all that matters."

Edward's lips trembled. "You know nothing about what it means to have nowhere to stay, no place to call home, and no one trying to give you one except a tired, beaten woman who had you when she was a child, and looked twice her age when she died."

"I'm not your mother," Anna said.

"No, goddamn it, you're not. And I promised to never have it that way. But you could easily slip to where she fell." He drew near.

222

"That would never happen." Anna broke in. "I'd kill myself and take the children with me before I'd fall to where you mother was. I'd never let David and Theo become like you."

"Then you'd be a better person than Violet. You'd do what she should've done a long time ago." Edward went back inside to the bedroom.

Chapter 34

Two weeks had came and went after Edward sent the children back to their homes. Anna and Edward remained in the house living as man and wife with Anna on the road to widowhood.

She set the plate of spinach, fettuccine, and baked chicken on the patio table in front of him. His eyes grew big. He said, "I don't think I can eat all of this."

"Eat what you can." She sat on the chair next to him.

"I can't eat anything," he said.

"You've lost your appetite?"

While Edward's appetite was never large; it had remained fairly stable in the weeks since he had left the hospital. Despite all, his weight had decreased.

"How long have you been feeling this way?"

"Just today," he said.

"It'll come back." Anna began to eat.

He looked to her. "I've never died before."

"Try living alone for thirty years. I found all kinds of ways to make myself eat." The heated words slipped from Anna's tongue, she speaking for all women betrayed by husbands in similar situations. "I'm sorry." She had reached a moment of peace when making love to Edward. The two weeks following had deposited her in limbo.

"You're hurting," Edward said. "And you're stuck here with me."

"It's my choice."

"Still, it's painful."

"For me or for you?" Anna said. Unlike those in her memory, his eyes were clear and soft as they had been two weeks earlier during their exchange of intimacy. Edward had laid in her arms after they had made love. He had cried.

They had not spoken of the experience during the ensuing days. Anna had let down her defenses and grown close to him. Edward now stood in a different light. Never had she thought he would be aware of her pain, or that he cared about her hurt.

Again, she silently reprimanded herself for the fearless honesty held within her words, cutting as if a sword, into their reconciliation and leaving both wounded. "I never knew you were so sensitive," she said. "That you held so much pain."

"It's been constant," Edward whispered then glanced toward the pool. "The pain."

"Were you seeing other women when we were dating and before we married?" Anna said.

Edward continued staring at the pool. "Why do you avoid me when I ask a question?" she asked.

"Perhaps for the same reason you turn away when I tell you the truth about what I feel. The women were easy. They took away the pain." He turned back to Anna. "They let me tell myself that it was *you* I hated, and not myself."

"Did you hate me?" Anna asked. Parts of her hated him.

"No, not really." He shook his head.

"Then, why make me the target of your anger?"

"I envied you, your ability to give. *You* were better than me—*stronger* . . . still are. It was easier to feel anger toward you than myself." Edward took in a breath. "Growing up was difficult. I've never liked who I was that much."

Anna shuddered at the thought of Edward's self-loathing, a trait she also held. She had perceived him as possessing confidence, the lack of which she despised in herself. Parts of her refused to hear Edward's words pointing to the *why* and *cause* of his actions. She grew warm in her shame.

"I thought marrying you would make me different," Edward said. "It only made me hate myself more."

"You had Manning Real Estate." Anna wanted to believe the truth of Edward's pain. "You worked so hard at making it grow."

"It was all for you and the children," Edward said.

"You didn't play around with those women for me and the children. We didn't need that."

"A company can't love you. It won't remember you when you're gone," Edward said. Anna sizzled with dread.

"What were you thinking when you were with those women? How much did you love their bodies? What did they give you?"

"Stella, Esther, and the others had nothing that you lacked. In fact it was the other way around."

"They must have had something. You preferred time with them to that with me."

"I wanted to escape." Edward clinched his jaw. He gritted his teeth.

"Escape what? Who? *Me*?" Anna pointed to her chest.

"*Myself.*" The irrefutable truth of Edward's wounded soul reared the head of the beast that had haunted him as a child, and now as a man dying. "They gave me peace. A fleeting, flitting moment of peace," Edward said.

Anna carried her own internal ghouls, another trait she shared with Edward. He had been so kind when they had made love two weeks ago, his hands, soft and caressing, not grasping and fighting as in the past. Anna grew angry with sadness at the pity she felt for him.

Edward twisted his face. "It was all that stood between me and the thoughts forever exploding inside my head," he said.

227

A gray sheen overtook his eyes. "They let me forget. They took me from who I was, where I had come from, and where I was going." He looked to Anna. "They gave me rest and let me forget what I'd never become in this lifetime." Edward choked up. Despite and because of her anger, Anna wanted to absorb his tears. She felt herself crumbling.

"They let me forget I'd never be like you . . ." Edward's voice cracked. Again he turned to the pool and slowly uttered, "The person I hated and loved most." A cloud of sadness descended and took hold of Anna's shoulders. "I could never be like her or as strong as her," Edward whispered.

He said, "I could never be like Mama. I could never measure up to *you*." He turned back to Anna. "You were stronger than me and her. I could never be like you. I envied that, what you were, who you are now, the person who took me in. Mama could have been so much more had she had a husband.

I tried to give you all the things she didn't have, a home, no need to work. I was determined to have you the way she should have been. But then when I was with you, I felt dirty."

Tears slid down Edward's cheek. "They gave me rest, the women, from all the things I hated about myself, what I wanted to change and couldn't. Stella, Esther, and the others let me think I was okay. With you, I stunk. I reeked of poverty. All the smells of that dingy apartment I grew up in came back to me when we made love." He wrinkled his nose against a frown.

"And what about now?" Anna said.

"I wish it would all end. But I have to stay here and face it with you. And—" Edward doubled over. He fell from his chair onto the patio.

Anna knelt by the pool, and took him into her arms. "Edward. What's happening?"

Spasms overtook his body. Beneath a sun that had nearly vanished into the sky of indigo, his eyes went shut.

228

Chapter 35

Anna called Dr. Grimes as soon as she had gotten Edward into bed.

"He seems fine now, but I was scared. I thought I had lost him. Do you think I needs to bring him into the hospital?"

"No. Unfortunately this is par for the course," Grimes said.

"But what if it happens again."

"The hospice worker will know what to do. Have her call me if she gets concerned. As for you, I'm always available. What I said about Edward, I meant it."

"Thanks." A lump formed in Anna's throat.

The hospice worker arrived within an hour. Anna sat downstairs at the kitchen table while the worker was upstairs making Edward comfortable. Anna set a cup of water inside the microwave to boil for tea. The phone rang.

"Mom, are you okay?" Linda asked after Anna answered.

"No, I'm not." Anna felt ashamed of her honesty and of her emotional retreat against Edward baring his soul. She told Linda about Edward's collapse.

"Do you need me and Brad to come back?"

"No. Hospice sent over a worker."

"How often will she be coming?"

"Every day."

"Is it that bad?" Brad had picked up the other phone. Anna was surprised to hear him. The porous web of relationships encasing and linking her family was growing ever more transparent. No hiding places and secrets remained.

"He's dying." Anna spoke the words as much to herself as to Brad and Linda. "But, I can manage. I'll call if his condition worsens." She clicked off, knowing that conditions would most definitely get worse.

~*~*~*~

Having arranged a meeting with Father Richard, Anna entered his study the next morning. Sitting upon the sofa across from him, she unloaded and shared the conversation she had with Edward before the collapse.

"So much envy," she said. "He hated me. And yet he said he loved me." How could I have made love to him? Anna berated herself. So stupid. So foolish. Just like Serine.

The priest explained, "A man can't make love to his mother. But he can hate her—or at least fool himself into thinking he hates her. Still, we can only hate what we once loved. In many ways, Edward, as a child, was also the husband his mother never had, protective, loving, and non-judgmental.

"He married you," said Father Richard, "and in a sense became the man he had wished for his mother, the father he had hoped to have. That little boy, who was never allowed a childhood, has now come *home*."

"Why did he leave me?" Anna was confused.

230

"One of the most respected psychiatrists in our department during my residency was a woman in her seventies," said Father Richard. "She was a wife, mother, and grandmother. She told us that despite what history and definition tell us, *eroticism*, in its most rudimentary form expresses the profound. Humans need to be held and nurtured. Only when encased in a body does the soul come alive, and grow aware of its vigor or consciousness.

Human touch. The feel of others. Their hands in ours, our fingers entwined with theirs, one body sleeping against the other. These actions let us know we are alive and that we matter. Intense sexual desire is but the wish to be loved, and cherished, most particularly by our parents."

Anna shuddered at the priest's words when considering her recent foray of intimacies with both Inman *and* Edward. "He was a little boy making love to all those women?"

"Edward was searching for his mother."

Anna considered how hard she had worked as a mother. So much giving and no receiving. And then how empty she had felt with Elena. *We all need a bit of affection. Someone to love. Someone.*

"Sex as an obsession, addiction, or a major focus in one's life evidences that a hole has been rent by the lack of love and nurturing. In an effort to heal, we seek the bodily nurturing we didn't receive as a child, a mother holding us close to her breast and feeding us, either from a bottle or—"

"Her breast," Anna said as she remembered, "Edward used to watch me breast-feed the children. He was always helpful, making sure I was comfortable and not interrupted. And then . . ." her thoughts retreated. Father Richard leaned forward, his movement brought Anna back. "He would watch me breast-feed them," Anna repeated. "It was as if he didn't understand. Edward appeared mesmerized by what I was doing." *I envied your ability to give.* "It was as if he was taken by what was going on between me and David, and then Theo."

"You gave to the children what he never got from his mother,"

"And what the company could never provide, nor Stella or Esther," Anna said. Again she recalled Edward's confession. *They were nothing compared to you. Fleeting moments without pain.* Anna murmured a lament. Edward had cried out for her during and then in his sleep after their lovemaking.

Anna said, "Edward had grown distant by the time Linda arrived, absorbed in work and his *affairs*. Yet he was empty. Life drained from his eyes while I breast fed Linda. He looked at me, intently." Anna screwed her face.

"Your children were full of your milk, your love and nurturing, what his mother had never possessed to give him." Father Richard leaned back in the burgundy recliner. He clasped his hands, interwove his fingers and set them on his stomach. "Edward wished for and yearned to receive what you gave David and Theo."

"He coveted what I gave them."

"And your ability to do so. But, he was not about to interrupt while you were giving it to them," the priest said. "He knew too well the pain of not having it."

"And so the women were his way of getting back at me?"

"Or perhaps his feeble attempt to get some of what you gave your children."

"You're saying Edward was torn between needing me to be there for his children, and yet envious of what I was giving them?"

"The more financially secure Edward became, allowing you to remain ensconced in the home as a wife and mother, the deeper he fell into realizing how much he'd never gotten during his childhood. What his mother could never give him due to her circumstances, not because of who she was." Father Richard then said, "This is why he never left or abandoned you."

"And why the house means so much to him." Anna then sighed. "It's why he didn't want me to sell it."

Father Richard joined her in the reverential silence that follows awareness.

"In all his sickness and hurt," Father Richard said, "Edward gave you what he most lacked, a *house* where you

232

could love his children, most particularly, his sons, and where you could feel safe, and hopefully loved."

"But I *needed* him. I still do." The truth of Anna's words sent a chill across her body. "That's what would have made me feel loved and safe." She had experienced that two weeks earlier when making love to Edward.

"Tell him," Father Richard said.

Aching in the wake of her self-revelation, Anna grew more frustrated. She looked to the priest.

His words resounded once more. "Tell Edward that you love and need him *before* he dies."

Chapter 36

The hospice worker, Bertrice, was with Edward when Anna returned home at noon. After making a cup of tea, Anna sat at the kitchen table. She thought of Theo while sipping her tea. She missed him cooking and moving about the kitchen, sharing tea with her, steam rising from the cups between her and him. Anna wished to speak with him now. No one had answered when she called his home last evening. This time she dialed his cell phone.

He answered. She told of his father's collapse.

"I'm leaving right now," Theo said.

"Don't." Remnants of her latest foray of berating Edward weighed heavily in Anna's head. And then there was the sexual reconciliation wherein their souls had touched. "Your father and I need some time."

Theo was silent, then "You know I'm here. Call anytime."

She blew a kiss through the phone.

Theo said, "I love you, Mom."

Anna had set the cordless back upon its charger when Bertrice entered the kitchen. Startled on hearing her footsteps, Anna jumped then turned around.

"I'm sorry," the hospice worker said

"No bother," Anna said then extended her hand toward the table, "Please, join me if you will."

"Edward's resting now," Bertrice said. She sat at the table.

"That's good," Anna said then added, "Thanks for coming so soon last evening." She offered Bertrice some tea.

"I'm fine. Bertrice waved her palm. Anna drank more of her tea, now lukewarm.

"I've had no experience at this. What I mean is that," Anna hesitated then rephrased her statement. "My mother died of a terminal condition. But my father took care of her." Regret engulfed Anna, "I abandoned my father; refused to see my mother in her last days."

Anna's thoughts drifted back to Reverend Elijah speaking of Elena. *Your mother had her way. She was difficult to understand.* Parishioners of Reverend Elijah's flock had struggled like Anna to make sense of Elena. *She wasn't always affectionate.*

"She was never affectionate," Anna muttered, deep in thought. *You could have used more love from her—a show of emotion,* Reverend Elijah concluded. *She meant well, your mother. She did the best she could.*

Anna said to Bertrice, "Papa hoped that one day I would see that Mama cared for me. He wanted me to forgive her." Anna had not. She took in the middle-aged Bertrice. The color of her chestnut face was like her Reverend Elijah's; Bertrice's salt and pepper hair resembled Elena's. "After Mama died," Anna said, "I wanted Papa to live with us—me, Edward, and the children. He refused."

"Death is difficult no matter how many times we've experienced it," Bertrice said. "Each case I take leaves me with a sense of loss. Every death asks me to become more than I think I can. We are all born once. For those who know of their impending death and receive advanced warnings, or a heads-up as my mother called it, there's a chance for a second birth, a re-birth."

Anna didn't want to hear any philosophical theories on how Edward's death could open up blocked passages in her, him, or their marriage. Hope had dissolved with Edward's confession and subsequent collapse. In her searching for a way out of the darkness of his encroaching death, she had given herself over to Edward. She had clawed her way through the depths of forgiveness. Amid Edward's hands trembling across her back Anna had infused his weak and ailing body with her passion.

Edward had then murmured, his fingers squeezing her breasts, "I don't deserve it, you taking me like this."

"*Shhhh*. You're the father of my children." Anna had received, and granted him her passion.

"I wanted to be so much more."

"*Shhhh*." For remembrance's sake, she had taken him unto her one last time. She now wondered, how in his condition could she have done such a thing. She had settled her body upon him, the door to her heart eking open. Her soul had given way. Edward had breathed more deeply, as if coming to life, the two of them liberated in their moment of coming together. Redemption intertwined with death. Anna had feared Edward might die while reaching climax.

Bertrice's words pulled Anna from her memory. "Death is difficult. We all make mistakes. We will all surely die."

Anna held her breath. Bertrice's words felt pointless. "I always thought I'd go first," Anna said. "That I was the weaker. I'd die of a broken heart."

"Broken by whom?"

"Edward," Anna whispered.

Bertrice appeared to ponder the idea. "He's a young man, relatively speaking. At fifty-six, he's is in what many might consider his prime."

"He worked hard. And played hard." Anna's breathing shallow.

Bertrice said, "If you could re-live your mother's death, how might you arrange things? What would you change?"

Anna absorbed Bertrice's question and then acquiescing to her mixture of bitterness, regret, and atonement, said, "I'd ask her why she was so closed, withdrawn, and unloving."

Bertrice placed her palm upon Anna's trembling hand. "Sounds like you might want to give *yourself* a chance at rebirth."

Anna wondered how many people, now deceased, had Bertrice's hands consoled. "How does it feel? Death—life slipping from a person's body?"

"Terrifying. And yet freeing. They've suffered so much, most of them, the terminally ill. They need rest, *relief.*"

Don't we all, thought Anna.

Bertrice's eyes sparkled, as if in the midst of Anna's torment, she was undergoing an epiphany, grasping a new reality. "As we live, so we die," the hospice worker said. "Many of the people I assist have held on to life so tightly, afraid it would slip away at any moment's notice. The harder we hold on, the more life snatches itself from our grips. Like people and love, life longs for freedom, to come and go as it pleases, and with us grateful and gracious of its presence."

"But what of all those who tell us to embrace life?" Anna said. Her thoughts shifted to Inman. He had filled her with such passion, enough for Anna to give Edward. Inman had fed her yearning to connect. Inman's very being exuded vibrancy and the will to live despite all losses. Basking in the rays of his perceptive attention, she had felt, seen, and valued.

Bertrice said of life, "Like the child who lives in each of us, we need to hold it with gentleness and kindness, not with fear and rage. We're the only person who can steal life from us. We do it by living in a way that robs our life of love and affection. Then again, sometimes our parents do that for us." Her brown eyes twinkled.

Poverty and Violet's struggle had stolen meaning and any semblance of love from Edward's life as a child. He took what remained and put it into his drive toward ambition.

Anna said, "My mother was not happy. She was withdrawn and absorbed into her world of knitting and crocheting, constantly reciting Biblical and religious aphorisms. I'll never know why, only that I couldn't make her happy." Anna bit back the claws of sadness. Her thoughts doubled around to Edward. "Some would say my husband lived life to the fullest," Anna said. "He built from scratch a successful real estate business, and gave us a lovely home. He did what he wanted, and in his way." She sucked air, and breathed out slowly. "Now life is having its way with him." The image of Bertrice's face ran blurry. Tears broke onto Anna's cheeks, the full meaning of her words revealed. Life was not only trying Edward and claiming its measure, but also issuing Anna the same charge.

Anna said, "Edward and my mother never liked one another." Years earlier she had said to Edward, *You're both the same—cold and unloving. I supposed that's why I married you.* Edward's reply now echoed in her head, *We would have been better off if my mother had done away with both me and herself.* Anna hated having left her father to care for her mother alone. And now, in her desire to offer penance by caring for Edward in his last days, the quake of impending death left her angry and frustrated.

The night she had laid in bed with him after dinner at Scott's Restaurant, Inman had said to Anna, *I want you in my life. I need you.* The thought of having been with another man while Edward was home and dying blistered Anna's conscience and soul, and then to have thrust herself on Edward two days later. Anna had needed to be with Inman. His passion, love, and words had fed her soul. Full and satiated, she had served Edward a full spread. Thanks to Inman, her cup had overflowed with goodness and mercy, all that Elena had lacked and withheld from Anna. While making love to Edward, Anna had envisioned herself living through and surviving what she thought she could not endure—Edward's constant infidelity. Despite everything, her reasoning had said Edward was not supposed to die, that he would outlive her, as she had foreseen her mother outliving her father. Strong and tenacious individuals

239

such as her mother and Edward had grit. Elena's fight had eloped when Elijah most needed her. Elena's will dissolved into the same fears and hopelessness that she had held throughout life. Anna accepted that she had survived and was very much alive, despite the slow rendering of Edward and his life unto death. It takes strength to give. Love moves mountains, dissolves walls, mends broken hearts. A change of heart is the ultimate of miracles.

Anna's mother and Edward were alike, but they were also like Anna. Edward had made that plain when he said, *I've always hated myself. As long as I can remember I've held no love for who I am, or what I've become. I was the soiled and dirty one; you were clean and pure. That's why I wanted and needed you.* It dawned upon Anna that perhaps Elena's anxieties and Edward's fears had exceeded her own, and those of her father. Again Anna recalled Inman's words, *I want you to be happy and free.*

She looked at her cup, the tea within now cold. She said to Bertrice, "My husband was a strong man. I've never seen him weak like this. It's frightening and sometimes repulsive. Yet, I've never felt so close or attracted to him."

"Death, like sex, is seductive. The French call it the *little death*, sex that is." Bertrice gave a sad smile. She had passed this way on many occasions, had witnessed families, who were entangled and grounded in their all too imperfect love, face sudden and impending illness. She had watched them push their warts from hidden crevices onto the surface of life for all to see. Despite her fear and frustration, Anna felt comforted that Bertrice had experience in these matters. All would not turn out as Anna wished. Yet as Bertrice had done time and again for others, she would see Edward through his transition from this life to what lay beyond.

"Your husband says he needs me to come every day," Bertrice addressed more practical matters. "That you'll be busy over the next few weeks with your company."

"My husband's illness is forcing me to rethink who I thought myself to be," Anna's chest tightened. One last challenge manifested by Edward left her afraid to move forward

240

concerning a matter where she held little choice. "Edward gave me his company, Manning Ventures," Anna said. Her voice felt tight, sounded foreign. "I have to prepare for a board meeting."

"How nice." Bertrice curved her lips up in a fashion that said she was not a death angel. Rather, she was a harbinger of *life* in the midst of death, a person who heralded transcendence when the abyss of uncertainty was all within its path. "Some say the greatest mystery lies in death," Bertrice said. "The Africans say it springs forth in life."

"We die as we live," Anna mused. She wanted to take a new path, and not clinch the reins of life too tightly lest they snap back and entrap her as she was beginning to feel with Edward's approaching demise. Anna wanted to be free. And for that, life demanded she let him go.

"I suppose we need to set up a schedule," Anna said to Bertrice, "and arrange times for you to come."

Chapter 37

Anna continued alongside Bryce down the corridor. Unsure of herself, she reiterated, "I still don't understand why Edward chose a hotel as the place for me to meet with stockholders and trustees of his company."

"Edward never held board meetings in the office," Bryce said. "We didn't have enough space, and he wasn't about to rent a suite of offices that included a boardroom. It's cheaper to book a hotel conference room when you need one. Neutral ground," Bryce said.

One more secret to the success of his company," Anna murmured.

Reaching the end of the corridor Bryce stopped at the door to the conference room. "Ready?"

"I feel like I'm trying to fake being an MBA," she said. Anna had spent the last two weeks cramming for the meeting. By day, Edward had sat in bed, bolstered by pillows and laid out the particulars of running of a company. At night and when Bertrice was seeing to Edward, Bryce arrived.

Sitting across from Anna at the kitchen table, he expanded upon the particulars to which Edward had introduced her. Anna's meetings with Bryce often ran past midnight and poured into the early morning of the following day.

During the afternoon, Edward provided pointers on what she had gleaned from Bryce the previous night. This continued for three weeks with Anna receiving from Edward and Bryce a crash course in business management.

Standing before the door to the hotel conference room Bryce said, "I've got a JD *and* a MBA, and you know more than I ever learned in graduate school." Anna frowned. "Edward Manning taught me everything I know about running a business. I've shared all of that with you."

Anna held the sinking feeling that Bryce and Edward had been up to something. She feared that unbeknownst to her Edward had crafted a master plan into which she had fallen prey. Inside the meeting room, she would crash face first, in front of the board members.

In truth, Bryce behaved as if he were a son doing all he could to grasp the essence of the man he had wished to be his father. Edward Manning, his mentor was failing in his last days.

Anna was about to ask Bryce what was really going on, when he smiled and said, "You're a wife and mother—two of the hardest jobs I know. You can do this." He took hold of the doorknob. "Take my cues. I'm with you." He opened the door.

Six men sat around the oblong table as Anna assumed her seat at the head against the wall. Bryce opened the meeting.

"Thank you for coming, gentlemen." He circulated leaflets containing a financial report of the previous quarter.

An empty chair toward the far end of the table caught Anna's attention. The men were leafing through their booklets when the gentleman on her left leaned in toward her and said, "That's Mrs. McGrath's seat." Anna recalled the six names Bryce had given her. He had provided no pictures to associate them with. Bryce had said nothing of a Mrs. McGrath.

"Is she usually late?" Anna said to the man.

"She'll be along."

At the lectern beside Anna, Bryce began speaking. "As you know, Edward Manning has decided, for personal reasons, to step down as president and CEO of Manning Ventures. To assume leadership in his stead he has chosen his wife, Anna Manning."

Bryce placed his hand upon Anna's shoulder. She forced a smile. "Though new to the business, in these last few weeks of acclimating her to the role, I have found Anna quite capable and enthusiastic," Bryce said. "I think you will, too. I ask you to welcome Anna to Manning Ventures."

Bryce lifted his hands and began clapping. The six men, their demeanors lodged somewhere between stern anxiety and outright anger, did not join him. Anna had never encountered faces bearing such hardened seriousness. Again, Bryce placed his hand upon her right shoulder. She stood.

"As Bryce stated, I'm Anna Manning." She touched her chest. "If I may, I'd like each of you to introduce yourselves and state your name."

"Everyone here knows each other," said a man at the other end. He was sitting next to the empty seat awaiting Mrs. McGrath's arrival.

"Yes, but I'd like to get to know you," Anna said.

"Elliott Thompson," Bryce whispered from behind her. Elliott's name flashed in Anna's mind. *Elliot will have a lot of questions.* Bryce had warned. So had Edward.

"This sounds like kindergarten," said the man across from Elliott.

Elliott interceded. "What I want to know is does the fact that you're assuming control of Manning Ventures mean you're no longer divorcing Edward? Has he given you the company to satisfy your demands for a divorce, or perhaps to pacify you?"

"Exactly what *is* going on?" Again, the man across from Elliott spoke.

"I am Edward's wife, Mr. Thompson. And no, I'm not divorcing him."

"Well, I guess you *do* know us," Thompson said with a dry smile. "So, why has he made you head of the company?"

Elliott Thompson was undeterred. "Has he given you the company to keep you married to him?"

Faced with her first challenge, Anna chose truth. "Edward is dying."

A moment of silence wandered the room as the men appeared to enter a struggle of grounding themselves in a reality they had not anticipated. A low residual of murmurs and mumblings rose and faded.

A new voice emerged from Anna's right. "How do you propose to run Manning Ventures since Edward will no longer be around to guide you or Bryce?" Before Anna could answer, a man sitting at the right center of the table leaned forward.

The man stretched his neck, looked beyond Anna to Bryce. Anna glanced back and saw that on his yellow legal pad Bryce had written the name *Pierce Dawson*.

She turned back to the men seated around the table and looking to her for answers. With his white hair, and butterscotch skin, Dawson could have passed for Anna's deceased father. "What's your specific concern, Mr. Dawson?"

"Money, of course, as it is with all of us," said the man across from Dawson. That was Claiborne Rochester. Not only did Rochester's dyed black hair betray him, but also his response about money and profits being the motive of their concerns.

They're all in it for the money, Bryce had stated. *For Claiborne Rochester, money is all that matters. No family, no children, no dog—just money.* Bryce had then added, *Rochester'll also be the first to pull out if he senses you're about to crumble.* Should Rochester leave, the others would surely follow.

The six men at the table along with the absent Mrs. McGrath comprised the seven major investors of what was now Manning Ventures. They were also the board of trustees.

Anna set about easing their concerns. "My plan for assuming leadership of Manning Ventures is to continue down the path Edward has laid. The company is running fine as is. I have no intentions of making any broad sweeping changes."

"Thank God for that," Pierce Dawson piped.

246

Rochester then chimed, "Yes, but what happens when the market turns down like it's trended these last few months? Or a competitor arises? Things happen every day. I want to know that you're watching the company, not home baking cookies for your grandchildren, worse yet, mourning the loss of a man that was," the man with jet black hair tilted his head, "— shall we say, less than faithful."

Elliott Thompson said, "How do we know you're not planning to raid the company and take what you feel Edward owed you." A round of mumbling resumed.

"Mr. Thompson, I assure you I have no intention or reason to steal from Manning Ventures or any of you." A chuckle escaped Anna in her nervousness. "As for Mr. Rochester's concerns, I can bake cookies, and watch the markets on my computer at the same time."

The grimness of the men's faces left little time for Anna to ponder the meanderings of Edward's mind when he signed the documents giving her Manning Ventures.

She burned with the thought that he had *done it again*, set her up for another disappointment, was perhaps back at home grinning at the thought of her standing before these men spearing her with questions to which she lacked answers, and grit to address head-on.

Anna could have kicked herself for not having filed the deed on the day she learned of Edward's illness. Bryce's words returned to her. *You're a mother. These men are like little boys who need food and time to play. Their favorite entrée and toy is money.*

Elliott Thompson said, "These are hard economic times." Frustrated, Claiborne Rochester pursed his lips in obvious agreement. Like David, the men were angry and hurt. Edward had been good to them. Now he was dying. Anna flexed her fingers and propped them in teepee fashion them upon the table.

"Yes, and despite all, the company has been doing well," she said. "Edward knows that good economic weather is not constant. He's worked hard to establish and maintain strong relationships with the companies and people with whom

Manning Ventures does business. I will continue nurturing these connections while cultivating new ones." The eyes around the table fastened their attention on to Anna's every word, she growing surprised at the ease with which she spoke. "My motto, as a mother has always been, '*If it ain't broke, then don't fix it.*'"

"But that's just the point, Mrs. Manning. You're a mother and a wife, with not a whit of experience running a company that's about to be incorporated." The man speaking sat to Anna's left and was across from Claiborne Rochester. His skin was stark white, with not a hint of pink. What little remained of his hair was blonde fading into white, as were his eyebrows and goatee. Must be Harrison Filbert. *Thoroughly white. And arrogant.* Bryce had said. *But it's all a bluff.* Anna breathed in and prayed she could apply what Bryce and Edward had taught her.

"Your concerns are justified, Mr. Filbert. But my aim is for Manning Ventures to continue making money. Anything less, I would have sold it to the highest bidder. And I will do just that if I fail to provide you a reasonable profit." The men around the table flinched. Just the response she was aiming for.

Anna continued. "Selling Manning Ventures would eliminate your roles as trustees and stockholders. You'd receive checks and your ownership dissolved upon cashing them. You most certainly wouldn't be sitting here now."

"And how am I to know that what the highest bidder would pay me is no less than what you'll produce, maybe even more?" Harrison Filbert would not let it go.

"You don't. But that's the risk we all take," Anna said. All eyes returned to her.

Hesitant to speak until now, the gentleman on Anna's right said, "You have a point, Mrs. Manning." The gnarled fingers of his dark hands stood knotted upon his cane.
"Please, call me Anna." Instincts said the man speaking was Chester McGee. That meant the man to her left, the one who had mentioned the absent Mrs. McGrath, was Ephraim Hennessey. Hennessey was also the company's largest investor.

Chester McGee said, "We all would agree that what you've said sounds good—fine and dandy some might say." The low rumble in McGee's voice sounded as if he were about to start a sermon. "But, the fact remains that you are not a businessperson. You have no experience in running even a corner store."

And neither is running a home for over thirty years child's play, Anna wanted to scream against the lump expanding in her throat. McGee's poor paraphrasing of what she had said left little doubt of his archaic and patriarchal views of women. His tone bordered on misogyny.

"Chester has a point." Ephraim Hennessey spoke. "What's your plan for taking Manning Ventures into the future, the nuts and bolts of *mothering* the connections Edward's made, and *raising* new ones, as you say?"

Anna was about to explain her plans for guiding Manning Ventures forward when the door to the back of the room opened.

"Well, she's here," Hennessey smiled with expectant relief. Pierce Dawson, whose chair was only steps from the door, turned around. The remaining four men pulled their eyes from Anna and directed their attention to the door. The mood around the table went from joyful reception to surprise and dismay when without his cane, Inman entered the conference room. He had not used the cane during their recent times together. Only now did she realize he had not been using the cane—he seemed different now—leaving Anna to realize that Inman had fully recovered from the car accident.

He strode to the end of the table, and sat in the chair that had been awaiting Mrs. McGrath. Anna gave a low groan. A second stretched into what felt like ten minutes. And then Inman turned to face her. Anna would not look at him.

Pierce Dawson leaned toward Inman. "So where's McGrath?"

Inman said to everyone, "She's asked me to take over the management of her investments." Again he tried to connect his gaze with Anna's. Again she refused him.

"And who the hell are you?" said Elliott Thompson, who appeared livid.

"Inman Hayes."

Anna forced herself to breathe. Had he known when agreeing to represent Helena McGrath on the board that Manning Ventures was Edward's company—the Edward Manning to whom she was married? Anna quaked at the thought that she had slept with Inman while he bore the knowledge that he would be sitting on the board of her company.

Chapter 38

In intricate but clear fashion, Anna listed the steps she would take to ensure the continued success of Manning Ventures.

"Financial markets and world consumers demand personal availability and a clear understanding of their needs along with user-friendly methods of ascertaining the services we have to offer. Edward established and maintained contacts over the years by traveling and meeting individually with potential customers.

He strengthened those connections through phone calls and the use of the Internet. I will be doing the same. Recent improvements of chat sites and video mailing allow me to talk to various customers across the globe on a weekly basis. Bryce and I agree," She glanced back at him, smiling. He flashed a thumbs up. "We want to use the same technology to attract our smaller customers as well."

In a low tone, Ephraim Hennessey responded as if speaking for the totality of the men around the table. "This sounds nice. Much of it I don't even know about. Can't begin to understand how it works. Internet, chat sites. It's all beyond me. You've laid it out well." Hennessey gave a sweep of his hand. "But as Chet," otherwise known as, Chester McGee, "—pointed out, you haven't run as much as a corner store, and not even a lemonade stand with your kids."

It was as if Hennessey had not heard a word Anna had said. They viewed not the plan as problematic, rather the person delivering it, a *woman*. I should have sent Bryce to address the men, and never shown my face, Anna bemoaned to herself.

She simmered as Inman, silent and still, watched the men nodding their heads amid the brewing din of murmurs circulating the table.

Again, she was about to speak when with a curious and solemn air Inman said, "Running a home takes a lot of ingenuity and perseverance. It's a 24/7 job. And rarely do you have an adequate budget."

"What did you say?" Pierce Dawson appeared stunned.

"Forgive me," Claiborne Rochester broke in, "Mr. Hayes, is it? No one's knocking the gifted ability of raising children, and keeping a home afloat. Most of us here owe our successes, how few or ample, to the women in our lives." Again heads nodded in agreement. "But as you so aptly put it, their importance is in the running of a home, not a business."

"There's a lot of money involved here," Dawson chimed.

To which Inman argued, "The person who knows what to do with a little money will know how to manage a lot of money."

Across from Dawson, and to the other side of Inman, Elliott Thompson's demeanor shifted from confusion to what seemed carefully managed rage.

Harrison Filbert declared, "You can't be implying that the running of a home is more than mere housekeeping. That being a wife and mother entitles or engenders one with the capabilities of managing a company."

"Have you not listened to what she said?" Inman demanded. "Or did you simply dismiss the messenger because of her gender?" Like the six other men, he sounded incensed,

252

indignant, but for a very different reason. "Have you ever run a home?" Inman said. Filbert leaned back as if struck, his eyes blaring with consternation. "Better yet, have you made a grocery list week after week? Do you know how much a pound of butter costs?"

"I fail to see the point," Ephraim Hennessey said then turned to Anna. "Anna, we are all quite certain that Edward Manning provided generously for his family."

Hennessey was old enough to be her father. And albeit she had invited him and the others to address her as *Anna*, she wanted to reprimand Ephraim Hennessey's condescending tone as he spoke her Christian name. His patronizing air reflected blatant disrespect for her place in the company.

"It's not like she's starving," interjected Thompson as if Anna were not present. Everyone laughed except for Inman and Thompson.

"My point exactly," Inman said. He stood. Though calm, he spoke with firm conviction. "If a man like Edward Manning would leave his wife the company he spent his life building, then it means she must have managed his home and raised his children, amid his frequent absences, in a way of which he approved."

The men fell quiet and attentive. "All of you have benefitted generously from Edward Manning's guidance of this company." Inman knitted his brows. "You trusted him with your money and it paid off. His decisions were sound. What makes you doubt his present decision to place his wife in charge of the company? Are you jealous that he didn't put one of you there?" A low rumble rose from among the men. "Or are you afraid that this woman might best you? Is that clouding your judgment? Something is."

"I don't like this." Elliott Thompson stood and joined Inman. "We've had two major changes slammed upon us. One came a week ago with Manning's letter stating that his wife now owns the company, and then . . ." He looked over at Inman. "Today, Helena sends you to take her place on the board."

Inman smiled as if prepared for the entanglement. His attack had turned the tide. "What troubles you about my

253

presence?" Inman said to Thompson. "That Mrs. McGrath as chosen not to attend board meetings, or that she chose *me* to represent her?"

"Both." Elliott Thompson stared at Inman. "We were doing fine until Manning decided to up and die, and give his company away in the process."

"My husband didn't choose to die." Anna's throat burned.

"I'm sure he didn't." Thompson turned to her. "But we all know he hasn't shown much respect for you either. All the women he's had. Is this his way of trying to buy his way into heaven, repent for his wayward lifestyle?"

"That's enough." Inman threw Thompson a hardened stare. Anna wanted to drop into the chair and bury her face in her hands, better yet, leave the room. She felt Bryce's warm hand settled upon her shoulder.

Inman said, "This is about business, not our personal lives."

"And who made you head of this board?" Thompson's indignation swelled upon his dark, chiseled face.

Ephraim Hennessey's voice emerged from the noise and emotion encircling the table. "Money and emotions are tightly interwoven. And where Edward Manning's concerned, we all have questions about both."

Thompson added, "Manning's decision to give Anna the company has more to do with his own guilt than his concern for our investments."

"What if it has to do with both?" Inman again.

Anna swallowed hard and took in a deep breath. Bryce's hand shifted to her back. She forced herself to remain standing.

"We're not some priests." Thompson's words were bitter.

Anna had rather not run Manning Ventures if she would have to face Elliott Thompson on a regular basis. She was frightened.

Inman's voice pierced the noise of confusion. "If you're more concerned with Edward Manning's personal life than remaining committed to a company that has brought you sizable profits in a down market, and looks to do the same in the future, then perhaps you'd better sell your shares. Pull out. Now."

Anna lost her breath.

"And whose side are you on?" Harrison Filbert, nearly white as a ghost, looked from Inman to Anna, and then back to Inman.

"The same one as everyone here including Mrs. Manning," Inman said. Anna grew ever more anxious. She had never heard Inman refer to her as Mrs. Manning. Why is he telling the men to pull out? Anna thought. Manning Ventures needs their monies.

Inman sidestepped Filbert's question. "I've examined the quarterly statements as Helena asked of me. Manning Ventures has a lot of potential."

"But I'm not hearing money," Claiborne Rochester noted.

"And potential does not make money, nor guarantee it," Ephraim Hennessey chimed once more, making plain his investment in the argument.

"No, it doesn't, Ephraim." Inman spoke with condescension as had Hennessey when addressing Anna. He seemed to know all their names, appeared quite comfortable in confronting the men. The sinking feeling that had abated earlier threatened to overtake Anna once more. "Potential says a whole lot to investors who are looking to get in on the bottom floor," Inman ended.

With both hands gripping the curved handle of his cane, Chester McGee leaned forward. "And what are you suggesting?"

"He's threatening us!" Thompson shouted.

"I'm telling you what you'd already know had your accountants read the proxies and spreadsheets Edward's provided." Inman was stern. Anna grew dizzy. Bryce helped her sit down. Inman said, "All of you have depended on Edward Manning to invest your money *and* honestly inform you of what he's doing." He surveyed the faces around the table. "Unlike most investors, he's done just that. And you've turned a profit."

"Now that he's no longer the president and CEO, you're worried that you're going to be treated, I should say, mistreated, and lied to, like investors and trustees at most other companies. Edward Manning's been your brother, your keeper, and your papa. That's all over. You know it. I know it." All eyes remained focused upon Inman.

Mesmerized with how he had taken command of the situation, Anna felt a sense of awe and fear. She had never seen this side of him. While she knew Inman had worked as an investment counselor, they had talked little of his job. His display of strength in the meeting juxtaposed to the reality of Edward dying at home mortified her.

Awash in shame for having made love to Inman, she recalled how his body had enlivened hers, and to the point of enabling her to give back, and reclaim, ever how temporary, what she had once felt and held for Edward. Inman's warmth had spread throughout her. It had delivered a sense of peace and protection.

That sense of safety had returned when she was intimate with Edward some nights later. It had expanded and opened her heart when watching Edward sob.

Inman landed another blow to the trustees. "How many of you have discussed these changes in the company with your attorneys?" All heads fell except for Harrison Filbert. He looked to Filbert. "What about you, Harrison?"

"My lawyer advised me to sell."

"And why is that?"

"He said that any man who would give his company to his wife under any circumstances held a questionable mental state." Filbert's voice was low and quivered.

Inman placed both palms upon the table and leaned toward Filbert at the center. "Under any circumstances?"

"He didn't like the fact that," Filbert's voice reeked with shame, "Mrs. Manning has only been a stay-at-home wife and mother.

"And I'm sure that as soon as you sell your stock, your lawyer will run out and buy shares in Manning Ventures." Inman launched his jab. "That is if he hasn't already lined up someone to purchase it from you, someone you don't recognize as representing him."

His eyes wide with anger and frustration, Harrison Filbert whipped his head around to Inman. Goosebumps spread across Anna's back. The men grew still. Inman then lifted the large manila envelope on the table, walked to Bryce, and handed it to him. "I'll be in touch," he said to Bryce.

Making no final attempt to engage her attention, Inman turned. Anna felt about to implode and shatter.

Chapter 39

Anna stared out the window. During the ride home, Bryce was driving, his hands clinching the steering wheel.

"You did well," he consoled. "Those men are a tough bunch." She continued looking beyond the passenger window. "Anna, did you hear me?"

Bryce brought the sedan to a halt at the stoplight. She turned to him, said, "I don't know about this."

"It's never been easy. And it won't now, not with all that's happening."

"And what *is* happening?" Anna said.

Bryce's shoulders slumped. The light turned green. He drove through the intersection. Three stoplights beyond he said, "Edward could only offer promises when he was seeking investors years ago. He had to prove himself. He did, and has continued to do so, time and time again.

These men have come to trust, and lean upon him. They depend on Edward Manning to make them money. Now they' re worried about losing what they've come to expect." Bryce turned his attention back to the street.

Again the light turned green. He drove through the four-way. "If it means anything, these men aren't your average investors." He said, "The money they entrusted to Edward was their life savings. Even Harrison Filbert's."

"Maybe they're right." Anna still doubted herself. "I have no experience in running a company or turning a profit. Why *should* they trust me? All I have been *is* a housewife. What can I do except help them keep what they have, at the least, not lose their money?"

"Are you asking me or yourself?" Bryce said, still driving. "You've also been a mother. And as for your experience, expertise, or *acumen* . . . " Memories of Serine having used the word took Anna back to the day both Matt and Grant had arrived to her home.

"Hayes is right," Bryce said. "Being a mother and running a home is great preparation for overseeing a company. One need only look at your children as evidence."

Taken with his words, Anna turned to Bryce.

"Edward's proud of who they've become and what they have done with their lives," Bryce said. "He credits it all to you. For all it's worth, these geezers came to check you out, see what you were made of. They would have pulled out and sold their shares long before the meeting today had they truly been afraid of you losing their money."

A comrade in age with David, Bryce seemed far more seasoned in deciphering the truth of men's hearts when words and actions opposed one another. It was obvious how he had earned Edward's trust.

Anna turned back to the passenger window. What had Edward been trying to say in giving her Manning Ventures before he died rather than allowing her to inherit it upon his death? That he had been trying to avert chaos within the company seemed unlikely in light of what had taken place during the meeting. Perhaps Thompson was right, that Edward was trying to reach heaven.

Bryce brought the car to a stop in the driveway. Anna got out before he could come around and open her door.

"I can see myself inside," she said then headed toward the front door.

Upstairs, Anna met Bertrice coming down the hall from Edward's room. Bertrice's hands stood upon her hips, small and curvaceous like Elena's.

"So how was the meeting?" she asked.

"It went well," Anna lied and took in a breath. She was in no mood for niceties. Though Bertrice presented a version of Elena that Anna had many times wished for, the hospice worker's presence also evidenced that Edward was dying.

Anna longed for Inman, wanted to call him, but . . .

Bertrice smiled then said, "I'm sure Edward will want to hear all about it."

Unaccustomed to Edward being the weaker one, Anna was hesitant. "Did you have anything else to say or tell me?" she said to Bertrice.

"I was wondering the same of you."

Anna hated Bertrice's presence that she had come to depend on. And then there was Bertrice's intuition. She read people. That Bertrice stayed overnight seeing to Edward provided Anna freedom from Edward. And yet Anna felt guilty in her avoidance of Edward's dying, and his needs that arose in his failure to thrive.

Anna had consoled herself when preparing for the board meeting that she was not ignoring Edward, rather focusing her efforts on what would remain after he was gone—*That's it!* The startling thought gained and brought order in Anna's mind. Manning Ventures was not simply Edward's mark on the world, or evidence that he had traveled this way. It would also live after he died.

But with my lack of experience why me to see over it? Again Anna felt as though she was a pawn in a sick game crafted by Edward. She grew angry. How narcissistic. His work and his position at the helm of his company always came first. Then, again, why not? Anna had occupied second place for the nearly thirty-four years of their marriage. First it was the women. Now it was the company. She stormed past Bertrice, and without knocking, entered the bedroom where Edward lay half asleep.

"I need to know—" Anna started. Edward turned from facing the wall. Lost underneath the covers, his body appeared to have shrunk to half his normal weight. His eyes, forever reflecting energy, lolled with weariness. Anna's throat ran dry. Unable to speak, she turned back toward the door, was about to leave when she glimpsed the cover of *Tricycle* magazine. It was lying upon his Edward's chest. He had fallen asleep while reading.

He had also been reading it the day of the fiasco, when both Matt then Grant arrived to console Serine. Then as now, a middle-aged white woman with a shaven head—the Buddhist nun on the cover—called out to her.

Resisting the summons to compassion, Anna recalled how Edward had read the magazine throughout Serine and Grant's argument on the other side of the pool. He had clung to the magazine in the days and weeks since, as if it were an object transitioning him to a beyond that no one had truly lived, and returned to speak of.

Again Anna resisted the furious desire to grab the magazine and throw it at Edward. Then, as now, the Buddhist nun on the cover called Anna to calm down. Her anger subsided in deference to mercy.

Anna had never considered Edward to hold spiritual inclinations. Yet, death brought changes. The serenity of the nun's face on the cover soothed Anna. Edward's death had yet to arrive, but Anna was already undergoing the pain of transformation. Against her desire to ask why he continued reading this magazine, what words upon the pages between the covers drew and held his attention, she instead asked, "Why did you send me in there?"

Edward forced his way to sit up, let the magazine slide down to his thighs, and revealed more of his withered body. Dark splotches dotted his skin that held a vibrant, red undertone beneath the clear shade of walnut. "I wanted you to see what you'll need to do once I'm gone."

"You think handing me Manning Ventures can make up for all the years you left me here alone?"

"What did they say?" Edward rescued her from her moment of despair. He swung his feet to touch the floor. Squared and sitting up, he reached for his bathrobe.

"You knew they'd attack me, take what little dignity I still had, rip me to shreds."

"Men don't like change, particularly when it involves their money." Edward slipped his right arm, then his left into his robe.

"And what about McGrath?" Anna demanded. Edward's eyes widened. "Mrs. McGrath sent someone to represent her," Anna said. "Inman Hayes. It seems women are the same as men. They too can keep people on a need-to-know basis."

"I would agree." Edward lowered his head, and stared at his bathrobe's hem hanging by his leg. A wave of heat swept over Anna. Only the fear of hurrying his death stilled her hands from hitting his face.

She was afraid of losing him. *Yes, that was it.*

The realization gripped her as a sheath of rage enwrapped, and entrapped her. Why did she have to be so sentimental and committed? Why did she have to take her promises so seriously? Elena's words called.

When the time comes, I don't want to be alone. The words had translated to Anna as, *I want you near so I can inflict more pain.* It is hard to lose those you love, even more so when they have not been what you needed and wanted, or hoped and longed for them to be. Anna's mother had not died alone. Reverend Elijah, Anna's father, had been present.

Anna said to Edward, "I want to sell the company."

"There's nothing I can do to stop you," Edward said. Darkness mixed with an essence of surrender filled his eyes. "It's all I have."

Anna knelt and took his face into her hands. She pinched his sagging cheeks as if he were her long lost pet that had disappeared when a puppy, and now fully matured, had returned faithful and protective. The bones of his flesh were lost in death.

"All I ever wanted was you," she whispered. "Not the company, not this house. I love the children, but . . . I needed you."

Edward placed his forefinger to Anna's lips then enfolded her into his arms.

The two wept.

Chapter 40

The phone rang later that night. "I need to see you." It was Bryce.

"What's wrong?" Anna asked.

"Thompson and Dawson are pulling out. They're offering us first dibs on buying their shares before taking them public. I'd like to keep their shares in house, but—"

"Do we have the money to pay them without taking the company under?"

"You learn fast," Bryce said. "It would be a stretch, well worth it, and then, I opened the envelope Hayes gave me." Anna recalled what she now considered Inman's swagger when he walked past her to Bryce, handing him the large envelope. He had not glanced her way, had left without trying to connect with her one last time.

She had yet to call Inman and apologize, then explain why she had ignored him. He had not called her.

Bryce's voice came through the phone. "No sooner than I hung up from speaking with Thompson and Dawson's attorney, Inman Hayes called."

"Don't tell me he's had a change of heart, too."

"Quite the opposite. Mrs. McGrath wants to buy more shares in the company," Bryce said. That's what the folder in the envelope was about."

"Would that be wise?"

"Ordinarily I'd advise against it," Bryce said. "But I'm expecting that on hearing the news about Thompson and Dawson, Harrison Filbert will go with them, if he hasn't already made plans. We'll know by the morning."

"How many shares are up for sale with Thompson and Dawson leaving?"

"Eight percent in the company as a whole," Bryce said. Anna owned fifty-one percent. "Of the investors, it's thirty percent."

Bryce explained. "And with the shares being valued over ten-thousand dollars each, we're talking about . . . let's see," His voice slowed. Anna imagined him punching numbers into his calculator. "Thompson alone owned almost two hundred of the shares of the company. Pierce Dawson owned approximately one hundred shares."

"I could sell some of my shares to pay Dawson" Anna said.

"That would flood the market and instigate signs of a takeover," Bryce said. Anna broke into a sweat. She was glad not have to deal with Thompson, Dawson, and perhaps Filbert. Yet the possibility of the man with whom she had slept with over the last year also overseeing twenty percent of the shares in Manning Ventures felt dangerous, too.

Bryce continued, "Hayes says Mrs. McGrath is prepared to buy however many shares become available due to the company's new ownership."

"Do they know three hundred, perhaps more, are available?"

"His attendance at the board meeting was my first time seeing him," Bryce said.

Had Helena McGrath anticipated this might happen, or perhaps Inman? Is that why she asked him to represent her? Worse yet, Anna said, "Is Helena McGrath using Inman to

266

orchestrate some sort of takeover?" Anna left Bryce little time to answer. "In fact, what sort of person is she?"

"That's easy." Bryce chuckled. His humor dissipated. "Despite being a sturdy eighty-year-old, she's quite smart. Reminds me a lot of you. Her husband, not unlike Edward, started out small then got pretty big."

"He was in real estate?"

"No. Boxes."

"Boxes?"

"Meet me for breakfast in the morning," Bryce said. "I'll explain."

Chapter 41

Anna met Bryce for breakfast the following morning at the Amory Village Egg Shoppe down from the house, during which time he explained of Helena McGrath's husband.

"Canning McGrath owned a small store for over fifty years," Bryce began. He buttered his bagel, took a bite and swallowed.

"But what about the boxes?" Anna asked. "How can someone make a small fortune selling boxes?"

"Canning sold boxes on the side, ones he designed and put together. No one ever thought much of Canning McGrath or the boxes he made. What no one also knew was that he owned the patent to his boxes."

Bryce took another bite of his bagel, again swallowed and drank some coffee. "The boxes were well designed, came in all sizes, were extremely cheap. The companies that purchased them assumed the freight and shipping charges. Canning McGrath would have loved the Internet."

"He died?"

"About fifteen years ago. His key to selling the boxes was direct relationships between user and maker. No middlemen. Just sellers to buyers. Using the Yellow Pages, he searched out what companies might be interested in purchasing his boxes, called them and wrote letters."

Bryce said, "He never asked more than a worthy profit. The companies he contacted were small and rarely known, all in the U.S. Many of them sold products to third-world countries and were pleased with what he provided. Everybody got what they wanted."

"In that way, he was like Edward," Anna said.

"Yeah." Both Bryce and Anna knew that many third-world countries were not so third-world anymore. Several of them had burgeoning middle-class populations.

"Canning McGrath was the first person to invest in Manning Ventures, Edward's prime interest outside of real estate," Bryce said. "He wanted to leave something for you." Edward's right hand man, and now Anna's, paused in the echo of his words. The weight of their meaning grew heavy in the silence. Anna looked upon her hand to which she had not yet returned her wedding band.

Bryce continued. "Edward had been looking to get into something beyond selling properties. Canning gave him the boxes."

"How so?" Anna said.

"Edward had been playing with one of Canning's boxes at the outset of one of his trips to Brazil. The plane had yet to take off. Edward busied himself with inspecting the box while the plane sat on the tarmac. When the passenger beside him asked to see it, Edward handed it over. The man spent the remainder of the flight studying the way it was put together.

When deplaning at the end of the flight, he told Edward he could use a box like that, but he needed it to be two-inches by three-inches in size. He also needed 10,000 of them each month starting immediately. Edward called Canning, but there was no way Canning could come up with that many boxes that size that soon. Neither could he produce that many on a consistent basis. Through one of his contacts in Hong Kong, Edward found a company that could make the boxes at a price that would allow McGrath a sizeable profit. Things ran smoothly since Canning owned the patent, not that the Chinese cared.

All this happened before the British released Hong Kong to China. Anyway, the boxes were made and delivered to the man Edward had met on the plane. He was from Argentina. When Edward delivered Canning his first check, Canning gave him half and said, 'Take the rest and make it grow, like you did with my boxes.'"

"So Edward started Manning Ventures. The whole purpose of the company has been to bring together needs, those of consumers and business people, and ideas to fill those needs.

Some of the money's in stocks as you see. But many of the small startups Edward seeded came with profitable ideas much like Canning McGrath's boxes, simple inventions that met the needs of consumers and businesses around the world. Edward felt like he was getting a lot more than he was giving."

It warmed Anna's heart that Edward had achieved success fueled by such idealistic standards. Manning Ventures sold everything from toothbrushes to tutorials on how to use various Internet sites.

Customers ranged from foreign governments to independent schools across the globe to various philanthropic organizations seeking to improve the quality of life of those they served.

Bryce said, "Throughout his travels, Edward became increasingly aware that foreign countries and consumers did not often benefit from the products they imported from the U.S.

Most times they paid much more than the product was worth. Purchasing and overseeing the sale of foreign properties put him in contact with many of the countries' wealthiest and poorest citizens along with government officials, a nice mix for developing entrepreneurial ideas and doing business.

When he was out inspecting a raw piece of property near a village or small town, Edward would often see a little boy playing and tinkering with something. Or maybe he'd discover a device an old woman had made to help her carry water or to cook with. 'It's amazing what many people develop to survive,' he'd say. 'They're small inventions that others could benefit from.'"

A bittersweet taste filled Anna's mouth in considering all that Edward, the little boy and his mother, Violet, had done in their efforts to survive. And what that survival had made him see even beyond his success.

"The knowledge he held as an American citizen guided him in counseling those who welcomed his ideas on how to make money," Bryce said of his mentor.

"As a liaison, he bargained for individuals with inventions that U.S. companies wanted to purchase. Edward mediated sales between various governments purchasing U.S. products. The American companies, mostly small, welcomed the opportunity to sell their products around the world."

"They were like Canning McGrath," Anna said.

"A win-win situation for all." Bryce smiled. "Canning invested a little of what he made from the boxes into each new venture Edward founded. That, along with Canning's grocery store, gave him plenty to live on. Edward always felt he owed him."

"But it was Edward who helped him sell the boxes."

"And it was Canning McGrath who first urged Edward to investigate the buying and selling of foreign properties. Much like he perceived the Internet would change the way commerce was transacted, Canning also foresaw the expansion of the global market. He told Edward, 'The man who only does business in America is hamstrung.'"

Anna said, "How did Edward meet Canning?"

"Canning McGrath purchased the first property Edward ever sold. It was right here in Oakland. He'd come to Edward in search of a small warehouse to tinker with his ideas about making boxes. It had been sort of a hobby McGrath did on the side after a long day in the store."

Bryce explained. "He needed some place to work and store the boxes. The two became friends while Edward searched for and then managed the sale of the building Canning purchased. They maintained contact after McGrath acquired the property."

"Edward never mentioned Canning McGrath or his wife, Helena," Anna said. "Not even when he was prepping me for the board meeting. He focused on Pierce Dawson, Elliott Thompson, Harrison Filbert, Claiborne Rochester, and the others. From your description, Canning McGrath is the closest to being what I would consider a father to Edward." Anna wondered if McGrath knew of Edward's dalliances, or that he even had a family.

"McGrath made a fortune selling his boxes," Bryce said. Bryce shook his head in continued amazement.

A burst of energy flooded through Anna. "You check on Inman, I mean Mr. Hayes," she said. "Find out where he's worked. What do colleagues and clients who've used his consulting services think of him?"

Throughout their relationship Anna had hesitated delving into Inman's professional life. There were things she wanted to know about Inman, aspects of his professional life that she'd avoided treading into. Like how he'd been able to afford a year away from work after his accident.

He had been broken up pretty badly and had needed time to recover. He'd said nothing about having to sue the other driver. Nor did he seem worried about accumulating unpaid bills.

She instructed Bryce, "While you're doing that, I'm going to talk to Mrs. McGrath. Do you think she'll see me?"

"Certainly, if I make the call."

"Do it. And don't share any of this with Edward." Anna would confront in-person any ideas Helena McGrath had about overtaking Manning Ventures.

A newfound strength in having addressed her first battle rose within Anna. Still she regretted how she had reacted to Edward. She was also still angry and hurt and would most likely remain so long after his death.

The image of the Buddhist nun donning a burgundy robe, and her head shaven, appeared before Anna. The flames of anger burning upon Anna's words from night fall of last evening, now slowed into a cloud of steam swelling with compassion. *All I've ever wanted was to be with you, and share your life.* She could not deny that some part of her relished the challenges of running a company.

Manning Ventures was not some toy or a monopoly game. It was a way for her to make some money and to gain her freedom, something she had never possessed with Edward nor prior to their marriage. As his wife, Anna had received a house, wherein she had created a home, one wherein Edward had resided between business trips, and then sometimes only for a day or so.

It would take time for Anna to become accustomed to accepting and acknowledging that Edward, in facing terminal illness, had given his company over to her *before* he died. For that reason, she needed to stop Inman from carrying out what appeared to be a deliberate takeover of Manning Ventures.

Back at home, Anna considered Bryce's words as she started up the stairs. *Edward has a way of seeing into the future. If he wants you at the helm, the company needs you.* Bertrice had gone for the evening and Edward was sleeping. On reaching the landing, she headed for Theo's bedroom where she had remained despite her recent intimacies with Edward.

Anna laid down and recalled Bertrice's questioning stare from earlier that morning. Anna had been on her way out to meet Bryce for breakfast when she encountered Bertrice in the hallway outside of Edward's room. Had Bertrice's look held what Anna had expected or needed to see?

Anna turned over on the bed, placed her arm under her pillow, and chided herself for not having looked in on Edward before lying down. It was only ten-o-clock, not the dead of the night. Moments slid by. Anna forced herself to get up. While slipping back into her night robe, her cell phone rang. She clicked it on and placed it to her ear.

"Hello." It was Inman. "I've been waiting for your call."

"I've been waiting for yours." Anna lowered herself back upon the bed.

Chapter 42

The next morning around eleven, Anna arrived at Helena McGrath's house located in West Berkeley. The spry and chipper old woman invited Anna inside then led her through the house and out to her garden.

"Indian summer's given my roses longer than usual to bloom." Helena McGrath slipped her fingers back into her gloves and lifted her pruning shears. She focused her attention on the buds she was cutting. A basket of pink and orange roses lay at her feet. "At some point, I've got to till the ground and prepare for next season."

The octogenarian peered over her silver-rimmed glasses and stared at Anna. Had Anna's mother lived, she would most likely have been Mrs. McGrath's age. For a moment Anna felt as if her mother had come alive, and that Helena McGrath was harboring the "now transformed" spirit of Anna's mother.

"Thank you for seeing me," Anna said to Helena McGrath. The two had foregone introductions and pleasantries in Helena's haste of welcoming her inside and returning to her garden.

"It's my pleasure." The old woman resumed cutting her roses. She laid another orange bud on the stack of what seemed a dozen or so in the basket. "I've worked for years to grow these Ecuadorians. And now they're . . ."

She turned to Anna. "But you didn't come for a lecture on flowers." Again she looked over her glasses and inspected Anna. "What can I do for you?" asked Mrs. McGrath. "Or perhaps I should I say, what would you like for me to explain?"

Anna was torn. She could ask why Helena had chosen Inman to represent her on the board, and what were her intentions in offering to purchase more stock. *More specifically Anna could ask if Mrs. McGrath had anticipated Dawson and Thompson pulling out?*

If so, had her desires to purchase more stock influenced Inman's performance during the meeting? Then there was the nature of Canning McGrath's relationship with Edward. Yet with McGrath now dead for over a decade, Anna wondered whether that was an appropriate subject to raise with his widow.

The weight of these matters swirling in Anna's mind jettisoned her thoughts back to last night's conversation with Inman. Anna said nothing to Inman about having spoken with Bryce, and certainly not about having ordered Bryce to research Inman's professional reputation.

Anna's conversation with Inman had been short, Inman instructing Anna to speak with Helena McGrath since she had been the one to hire him.

"But why did you take the job," Anna had insisted on knowing.

"Because she asked me. It's what I do." Inman then confessed, "Helena McGrath is my aunt. She was my mother's sister, my only living relative beyond Dancia."

That Inman had chosen family over friendship softened the blow. Yet, he remained committed to his position. "Believe

276

me, I never knew that Manning Ventures was Edward's company."

Confused and frustrated, Anna said, "I wished you had at least called and given me forewarning." Hurt and anger had mangled Anna's hearing.

"I didn't know it was your company," Inman repeated.

"You've never heard the name *Manning* as in *Edward* Manning."

"Of course I knew the name. I just never put the two together. You said he was in real estate. And you never told me that Edward had given you the company, that he had even formed one. Why didn't you call me?" Inman said.

Anna hadn't spoken with Inman since their night at Scott's and their time afterwards. Three weeks had passed, nearly a month, since lying in Inman's bed, her body satiated in warm, and yet tranquil, passion.

Her mind had absorbed so much during the last twenty-one days, wherein Edward, who despite growing weaker by what sometimes seemed the hour, had prepped her for the board meeting followed by the late night sessions with Bryce downstairs in the kitchen.

Anna recalled her intimacies with Edward, the reconciliation of their hearts and souls.

"Forgive me," she said, "But my husband is dying."

"So now he's your husband?"

"Like Mrs. McGrath is your aunt," Anna retorted.

"Seems like we've both been duped." Inman's closing words toiled their way through Anna's mind.

Anna watched Helena carefully snip buds from her Ecuadorian rose bushes and lay them in the basket by her feet. They were the last ones that would sprout this season. Anna concluded others would return with Edward long gone.

She said, "Why did you choose Inman Hayes to represent you on the board of Manning Ventures?"

"It's my prerogative." Helena made a snip. "I also felt my holdings needed looking into." Once more she gazed over the rim of her glasses. "All I have is invested in your husband's company. It'll be Inman's when I die." From all appearances Helena McGrath might outlive them all.

"The company's mine now," Anna said.

"I have no problem with that." The old woman said. "In fact, I've been thinking for some time Manning Ventures needed new blood."

And just what did she mean by that? Anna folded her arms.

The old woman said, "I like your husband, I mean your former husband. Or have you divorced yet?" She cut another stem bringing with it a beautifully formed pink rose.

"No." Anna was torn between her frustration in the other trustees and board members and Helena's prying into her private life. Yet as her parents had taught, she honored the elderly, of which the trustees were, of which Helena was the most senior.

"I hear he's dying," said Mrs. McGrath. The presence of what felt like the spirit of Anna's mother in Helena McGrath intensified.

"He is."

"How long does he have?"

"Three to six months, or less." Anna's will to battle with the old woman left. Tears encroached upon her eyes. She wiped them.

"You'll need help with your company," Helena said. Diligently attending her rose bushes, she was yet to look back.

"I have Bryce."

"Bryce is loyal. But he's young."

"So what do you suggest? Have Inman Hayes take over running the company?"

"That wouldn't be such a bad idea. But he's my nephew." Helena McGrath turned to Anna from her rose bushes. "And that would present a conflict of interest." Helena stood straight. Laying aside the clippers, she let her arms hang. "Let's have some tea, shall we?"

Minutes later and at Helena's kitchen table, Anna gathered herself. Helena returned the teapot to the stove and sat beside her at the kitchen table.

"I never liked the way Edward ran around," said Helena.

278

Anna observed the basket of buds at the center of the table. Helena McGrath poured tea, gave Anna a cup.

"Canning always urged him to stop his philandering, warned Edward he would come to no good engaging in it." Mrs. McGrath poured her cup of tea. "Then again, some men suffer so."

The shock of how much the investors knew of Edward's life grew thick and heavy. Then again, black folks were always in the know. It's how they survived. Anna chastised herself for being such an idiot.

Helena sipped from her cup then returned it to its saucer. "You're not like most wives of today, particularly not the black ones."

"How is that? I'm more *stupid*?"

"You bided your time." Helena gave a knowing smile.

"I never wanted Edward to die."

"No. You wanted *him*. And when it became obvious that might never happen, you set out to create a new life for yourself. And you did it with no fuss."

"What was I supposed to do?" On considering how much Helena McGrath knew about her, Anna reminded herself that Canning had been Edward's mentor.

"You have a lot of alternatives," Helena said. "Your children are grown. All doing well, I hear."

"That's debatable." Anna lamented David and Theo's marriages stitched together by a thread unraveling. And then there was Serine who couldn't make up her mind about who she loved, or whether she was even capable of affection and commitment.

"They've completed college, graduate school, I'm told", Helena said. "Some are married."

An image of Linda and Brad rose in Anna's mind. Her heart slowed. "My eldest daughter is expecting her first child, my third grandchild."

"That's a blessing," Helena said.

Anna settled deeper into herself. "How much has Inman told you about me?"

"Enough to know that you're not eager to rush into another marriage."

"And is he?" A rush of relief filled Anna. Although she still felt exposed.

"I'm not going to lie." The old woman returned her cup to the table then interwove her fingers. "My nephew loves you. I should also say he had no idea that the company I held stock in was Edward Manning's, or what do we call it now? *Manning Ventures*. Only after I asked him to look over the proxies and spreadsheets, did I add that I also wanted him to represent me on the board. He didn't learn about the meeting until the night before."

"So why did you do this? Why did you set me up?" Anna said.

"Why do you presume that I'm trying to take over your company, that I set you up? Inman could say the same of me concerning him."

"Has he?" Anna said.

"Not to me. You might want to speak to him about that. His mother was my elder sister," said Helena McGrath. Anna wondered how much she could or should trust this woman. Helena said, "You'll probably be seeing him before me." Again she brought the cup to her thin lips and sipped her tea, then added, "He's pretty angry with me right now."

Helena placed her cup of tea in the saucer, set both palms upon the table then pushed her slight body to stand. No more than five feet and perhaps a few inches in height, the woman wore a housedress that Anna wanted to wash.

Anna detected an air of sadness as she observed the old woman wiping down her range. Perhaps Helena McGrath posed no problems.

Anna lifted her purse. "Thank you for seeing me." She walked to Mrs. McGrath and extended her hand.

Helena smiled on accepting it. "I hate when people presume to know everything and don't seek evidence of their fears. I'm glad we talked."

She led Anna to the door. It was a small house, a few rooms that sat at the end of the block on a street in Berkeley not too far from San Pablo Avenue. Few would recognize it as the home of the owner of over one hundred million dollars. Anna felt ashamed of her prejudices.

Anna stepped outside and turned back to Helena standing in the doorway, one hand holding open the screen door. The other steadied her small frame against the entryway. Helena reiterated her appreciation of the visit. "I'm glad you took the time to come by. It gets pretty lonely around here. I miss my husband."

"I'm told that his boxes were unique and well-designed," Anna said.

"They were a hobby that Edward was instrumental in transforming into a successful business. Sales from those boxes keep me afloat in Canning's absence." Helena McGrath was doing more than remaining afloat. Yet Anna sensed that she had been speaking about matters that lay beyond money.

The demure little woman lifted her hand and added, "Canning's boxes are to me what Manning Ventures is to you," then pointed to Anna. "Perhaps we can do for each other what our husbands accomplished between themselves."

Anna frowned at the perplexity so obvious in the old woman's statement. From the pocket of her housedress Helena lifted a small rosebud and presented it to Anna. "I never liked all those women with whom Edward was involved. But then Canning would always remind me how well Edward saw to you and the children."

Anna shuddered in contemplation of how many discussions of her and Edward's marriage Helena and Canning McGrath had carried out.

"Thank you." Tears filled her eyes on accepting the orange-pink bud.

Helena said, "Canning always said that men hurt just like women. 'We men don't know how to heal. We're not like the women we bring pain to. Nowhere as strong.' Those were his words. Since Canning's death, I've come to see that Edward was hurting." Anna took a long, stiff swallow.

Helena said, "It's hard watching your mother struggle day-in and day-out. Violet was trying to make ends meet and never able to catch her breath."

Anna was about to ask about how she knew Violet when Helena McGrath said, "Canning found hope in his boxes. The money they brought was just extra. It was what he wished to have given his mother."

Again she looked to the bud now appearing more orange than pink. More tears came.

Chapter 43

Anna left Helena McGrath's house and started to Bryce's office in downtown Oakland. The Ecuadorian rosebud lay on the front passenger seat. As she exited onto Highway 24, her cell phone rang.

It was Bertrice. "You need to come home."

Anna dialed Bryce. "Bertrice called," she explained. "Said I needed to come home. It's Edward."

"Okay. Let me know what's up," Bryce said, then added, "If I don't hear from you in a half hour, I'll be over."

Anna turned the car around, and headed home.

Anna met Bertrice midway up the stairs. The look on Bertrice's face pulled at Anna. Bertrice said, "He's moaning and calling for you."

"Can't you give him something? I won't have him in pain and suffering."

Anna didn't want to see Edward, not like this. She needed time to sort things out. Life was crowding in. Manning

283

Ventures. Inman. Helena McGrath. Anna's discovery of Canning McGrath's relationship with Edward. Though twenty years apart in ages, Canning and Edward had shared similar childhoods, perhaps even a penchant for extramarital relations. And then, there was Helena McGrath, Inman's aunt.

Bertrice said of Edward. "I've given him the morphine. It's *you* he now needs."

Anna bit her lip, angry that Edward couldn't have asked for her in the years prior. She made her way up the steps, pushed open the door to the bedroom, and walked to Edward asleep upon bed. He lay curled like a baby in a crib. The Ecuadorian rosebud Anna had received from Helena McGrath was in the pocket of Anna's sweater. Beside it was Anna's wedding band that she had kept in her pocket ever since visiting her father's gravestone.

Like all other changes and transformation wrought by life, the dying of her husband went against everything in Anna; it defied the laws of physics stabilizing her mind. Edward, and people like him, by Anna's estimation were to have outlived those like her.

Anna had felt the same about her mother compared to her father. Elena had been stern and strong; Elijah, deeply emotional and feeling—weak, in Anna's estimation, frail, and unable to cope and succeed—like herself.

Anna and her father had been uncertain and fearful, and not quite sure of life or themselves. They had felt uncertain of their power and ability to survive the world, and weather storms and losses.

Despite being a man who distributed the word of God, Reverend Elijah Chason had made plain the doubts he held. It was the one thing Anna's mother had hated about him. One Sunday after church she had pressured Anna's father concerning his fierce questioning of life.

She said, "If you don't trust the Lord, you can't expect the congregation to trust you." Earlier that morning Elijah had spoken, during his sermon, of the venomous gray areas that plagued life and living.

"I never said I didn't trust God," Elijah defended. "I'm just not going to lie about the questions I hold."

All three had sat eating dinner, the Reverend Elijah at one end of the oval, dark pine table; Elena at the other and facing him. Anna sat in the middle, an empty chair across from her. Fifteen years old and finding a narrow way through high school, Anna yearned for Elena's counsel to guide and comfort her.

Elena said to Elijah, "Your questions show a lack of faith, and raise doubts about you."

"In what, my ability to be perfect? Or that I have needs, and don't lie about them?" Elijah slammed his hand upon the table, causing Anna to jump. "I'm human, Elena."

Anna had and would never again witness her father so disturbed. Her mother did not veer her attention from him. "I'm just saying—"

"You don't have to say it. I know what you mean." Elijah confessed. A watery film of redness filled the white encircling his large brown irises. "You doubt me," said Anna's father. "You don't love me as a man. But you cannot accuse me of lacking faith in God." Elijah's words carried vehement strength. "I've preached too hard and long in doing the thing I love, ministering. You will not take that from me. No." He threw down his fork.

"What are you saying?" Elena egged on.

"I'm saying that I'm not God. Not your god, not the church's god, no one's god. I don't have all the answers. Neither can I get them, not all of them. I will preach the word, as best I know it. I will tell the truth about my own struggles. Perhaps that will comfort my flock."

His brown raging eyes appeared to settle. The redness cleared, but not the mist. Whatever had stirred them never truly died.

During her mother's last days over a decade later, Anna sensed her father struggling and tormented by what had driven him to speak with such anger and hurt. By then, Anna had lost what little roots of faith her mother had planted.

She had yet to join the Catholic Church, her mother's religion. The question remained and fueled Anna's doubt. *Had Elijah been unfaithful to Elena? And if so, why? Had he, like Anna, longed for a show of affection, a sign from Elena that he mattered?* In his yearning, had Anna's father sought and received comfort elsewhere?

Anna lifted Edward's hand. Guilt for having refused to come when her mother asked to see her one last time descended upon her like a white sheet of despair. Anna felt dingy and blackened by her refusal.

Parts of Anna craved to abandon Edward like she had her plans for selling the house and moving to France. She had stopped the divorce proceedings, turned her life upside down, and taken him in. But had she halted everything only for him?

Edward opened his eyes. Slowly, he tried to smile. Failing, he licked his lips then in a low rasp uttered, "I'm sorry for abandoning you all these years." Anna lowered her head as he fought to speak through the clouds of death settling around them. "I'm sorry . . . truly . . . please . . . forgive . . . "

"I forgive you," Anna whispered.

Edward murmured, "I was the one who lost out."

Anna's chest grew full; the pain within threatened to overwhelm her. She clinched her jaw against a low moan that managed to slip through.

"You have to go on," Edward said.

"How the hell am I supposed to do that? I hardly know you. Thirty goddamned years and I don't know you. We were supposed to spend a lifetime together."

"You know me better than you think," Edward uttered. A sad smile overtook his face as if it were a death mask.

"You were supposed to tell me who you are, we were supposed to learn about each other. You cheated. You quit."

"This is who I am," Edward said. He raised a weakened finger and lowered it upon his chest. His eyes were like those of Elena when searching the Reverend Elijah's face concerning the doubt and faith he had preached. *I'm not your god. I can't be.*

Anna held tightly to Edward's hand. "This marriage was supposed to set me free." Anna sobbed. "I'm not your mother. I worshipped you in the beginning." She considered the women, Edward's women, tried seeing their faces. *How many were there?* She would never know.

She placed her other palm underneath his, and sandwiched his hand between hers. Her head dangled; a stream of tears descended first upon her hand holding Edward's, then onto her lap. Their trail obliterated Anna's vision of the carpet where her feet rested. Edward's night shoes lay beside them.

Why all the women? And why is God is taking him now that the approach of illness has delivered him to me? Helena McGrath's words returned from hours earlier. *He was hurting and searching. The women had been but way stations in the trek to find his mother, and then his way back to you.*

Anna crawled onto the bed and took Edward's frail and withered body into her arms. She brushed his head. *What were those women like?* She failed at wiping the thought from her head.

They were *her* obsession, or rather what Anna imagined that she lacked, what had driven Edward to them. Anna had proven herself faithful. She had not abandoned Edward as she had her mother. The circle of thoughts would not let her go.

"Moments," Edward said in more certain terms. His breath growing more shallow ebbed and flowed. "They were but moments, just moments. Stella . . . Esther . . . Gabrielle . . . all moments in time." He breathed in as if it were his last. Now fifteen minutes into the morphine Bertrice had given him, Edward struggled to make each breath. "I love you . . . "

Weeping, Anna laid her head upon his chest. "You cannot die." Her will was no match for the universe's divinations. "If you felt that way then why did you leave me so many times?"

Edward said, "You thought I was your mother." Anna cringed at his awareness of her truth.

Edward's eyelids fluttered as he strained to keep them open. "The house was all I had," he rasped. "My mother never had one. I wanted . . . needed one as a child . . . a home."

"I only wanted you, not the house," Anna sobbed against the pain of cradling his dying body in her arms. The conversation was traveling in circles, leading to oblivion. Anna would emerge changed, but not where she desired.

Edward lifted his eyelids. The brightness and sparkle never strayed from her gaze. He connected one last time. Edward with Anna then drifted off to sleep. Anna sobbed, not knowing if he would ever open them again.

Some moments later, Edward parted his lips. He fought to speak. "They were never you. Only moments in time. You . . . you . . . you were . . . an eternity." His words though slurred, settled upon Anna's ears and heart with an uneasy clarity.

Anna pulled the Ecuadorian rosebud, now pink, from her sweater pocket. She brought it to her lips, then laid it upon Edward's chest. She kissed Edward's forehead. Though warm, he remained silent and still.

Chapter 44

Anna's call to Bryce was brief. "Edward has died." She again spoke those words to David, Theo, Linda, Serine, and then Father Richard.

Hours later, she sat at the kitchen table. The rosebud from Helena McGrath's garden lay before her with Anna's wedding band beside it. And next to that the *Tricycle* magazine to which Edward seemed to have grown attached during the last few weeks.

Images of him reading as if mesmerized by the words upon its pages streamed before her. He had been reading it upon Anna's return from a weekday morning Mass after which she had met with Father Richard. Edward had put it aside when she confronted him about Stella and Esther.

He had returned to reading the magazine, had continued to do so when Serine and Grant had argued on the other side of the pool. Anna had last caught him reading it when, following the horror of the board meeting, she had burst into the bedroom.

In the dim glow of the kitchen light, she stared at the Buddhist nun on the cover. *Forgiveness* was the theme of the issue. She peeled back the cover of the magazine and thumbed through the pages until reaching one with the right corner folded back. The dog-eared page held several underlined sentences.

Penitence and the Art of Forgiveness, read the title at the top of the page. There was a picture of the Buddhist nun beside the title of the article that she had penned. In this second image she wore an orange robe, lighter in fabric than the burgundy one she donned on the cover of the magazine.

With Edward's body now in the mortuary, Anna began reading

We are all seeking forgiveness or penitence for something. We have all been treated wrongly. We have all acted incorrectly at some time or another. Anna scrolled down, noting the passages wherein sentences were underlined, words that had apparently moved Edward. *Salvation is granted to those who acknowledge their regret, and to those who possess the strength to show mercy.* Her eyes moved across the page.

Misdeeds demand something of both the wrongdoer and the person who has been hurt, a change of heart. That is the grandest miracle. It is what both must undergo, the wrongdoer and the one mistreated. Each is hurting.

Out of regret and sorrow for her or his hurtful actions, the wrongdoer must ask forgiveness. Likewise, the person who has endured suffering on account of the wrongdoer's actions is called to display mercy.

Should either one default on their responsibilities: the wrongdoer fail to acknowledge and apologize for her or his actions, or the oppressed one refuse to show mercy in the face of the wrongdoer's penitence, both are lost . . .

Our salvation rests in the hands and hearts of each other. It is rooted in our ability to change the rhythms of our hearts. None of us are safe until all of us are rescued.

The gold wedding band on the table drew Anna's attention. She brought it to her lips and tenderly kissed it. The Ecuadorian rosebud took on a shade of orange, not unlike that of the second robe worn by the Buddhist nun. Closing the magazine, she clutched it to her chest.

"*Oh, Edward*," Anna said. And she wept.

Chapter 45

The funeral took place four days after Edward died. *Good Friday*, Anna silently termed it as she stood before the grave site amid the crowd of two hundred or more surrounding her and the children. Edward had died on a Monday, the day for the graceful child.

He exited this life on earth, while lying in Anna's arms, she having granted him a peace and tranquility that while not encompassing all understanding, had certainly touched her heart and soul.

Born on a Saturday Edward G. Manning had worked hard throughout his life. That quality formed the essence of his identity, and the common denominator that drew those who came to bid him farewell. It stood as the most positive quality for which people would remember him.

The face of the Buddhist nun on the cover of the magazine loomed large in Anna's mind as Father Richard spoke. Anna closed her eyes and recalled words the nun had penned, sentences that Edward had underlined. *None of us are secure until all of us are saved.*

It offered a maternal perspective—loving one's children and wanting the best for them despite their misdeeds and shortcomings. It represented unconditional love at its greatest, something with which Anna's mother seemed unacquainted.

Always obedient, Anna had grown up feeling as if she was under the spotlight of her mother's eyes. She had never pushed the envelope and tested Elena's affection. As with Edward, Anna had never known the depths for which either her mother or her husband had valued her until death drew near.

Anna slipped her hand inside the left pocket of her black jacket and felt the Ecuadorian rosebud now limp. She fingered her gold wedding band. Unlike Edward, it remained strong and sturdy. David tightened his grip on Anna's right hand. Theo patted her left shoulder. Tears filled her eyes. Again Anna stroked the rosebud in her left pocket.

Father Richard spoke of Edward Manning, the family man.

"Edward Manning was many things to many people. Some of those things weren't what we always liked or wanted. Others were more than we expected. He surprised many of us in the end." The crowd released a round of laughter, evidencing their agreement, and startling Anna. "Despite what thoughts or opinions we held, all of us respected Edward Manning's work ethic."

Anna had wanted to make the services private. Bryce had advised otherwise. Among the mourners, several rows back, stood Pierce Dawson, Elliott Thompson, and Harrison Filbert, who had sold their shares in Manning Ventures.

Claiborne Rochester, Ephraim Hennessey, and Chester McGee, who had remained shareholders and trustees stood in the line behind Anna and her children. Helena McGrath was absent. Inman had left a message on Anna's cell phone, *I'm sorry about Edward. You're in my prayers.*

Father Richard continued as he unfolded a piece of paper. "I spoke with Edward Manning before he died. Here, I have words that he wrote and asked me to read."

The priest approached David. David squeezed Anna's right hand. "To my eldest, David, I wish you and Heather all the happiness in the world." David's lip trembled.

Anna felt herself sinking as if the ground was opening up to consume her. To the right of David, Heather drew Josh and Emily close to her. She wiped their faces and then her cheeks.

David's attention never wavered as the priest continued. "You have been all a father could want and hope for in a first-born child and elder son."

Father Richard turned to Heather and read, "It pains me that I didn't get to tell you this in person. Heather, I know I didn't often say it, but I love you. *Truly*. Take care of David. Kiss Josh and Emily for me. I'll say hello to your father, if I'm blessed to see him." Heather lowered her head and nodded in agreement. She then burst into tears. David, stoic and reserved, maintained his grip on Anna's hand.

The priest proceeded past Anna to Theo at her left. "To my second son," he started. Anna would not look at Millicent standing beside Theo. For all intents and purposes Edward's death had certified Anna's conviction that if given the chance she would encourage Theo to divorce the woman. Theo deserved better. Anna had wanted more for him.

Father Richard read Edward's words upon the paper. "You stood apart from your elder brother, but you never fought him." He said to Theo, "You looked up to David. But you were your own man. You respected your brother. For that I respect you. I love you. And I love Millicent."

The priest turned to Millicent. Eagerly she lifted her head. "And to Millicent—" She wiped her face as if to receive a blessing. "You remind me of myself when I was just starting out. Certain things can't be rushed. Sometimes we must let life come to us. And if we can't do that . . . well," Father Richard squinted in an effort to make out Edward's writing.

Anna glanced at the casket containing Edward's body above the earthly hole into which it would be lowered. *What might Edward have been thinking when writing the words the priest now read?* Had he felt tired, overcome, and sad?

Anna did not hear Edward's words that Father Richard had continued reading, rather the ones that remained in her heart. *I was scared . . . afraid . . . moments in time. That's all they were. Moments, barely seconds, if any. You. You. You are an eternity.*

A second round of laughter from the mourners startled Anna once more. She saw little humor in the situation. The voices settled. Father Richard stepped beyond Millicent to Serine. Bryce placed his hand upon Serine's shoulder. Anna gave thanks for Bryce's presence.

"Serine. You're our baby, the youngest part of me and your mother. You hold the brightness I held toward life when starting out, the glory I sought in taking risks despite my fears.

You are the best of what I offered, what old age and worrisome experience can never jade." The irony of Edward's use choice of words, *. . . what I offered . . . old age . . . worrisome experience . . . ,* filled Anna's chest. Serine was truly her father's daughter. What spark of youth or hopefulness had remained for him to put these farewells together and then ask Father Richard to read them?

The priest's eyes took on a kindly glow as he read Edward's last words to Serine. "Don't be afraid." Anna imagined Father Richard's experience of transferring Edward's words to the youngest of the bereaved children was the closest the priest would ever get to being a parent. "Never fear, I am with you. Right now. *Always.*"

Serine was a lost child. Lacking the capacity to embrace that loss, she was unable to let it inform her of where to allow life to take her next. Grant and Matthew in the line behind her seemed ready to accompany Serine wherever she chose to journey.

Choosing with whom to travel would be Serine's challenge, a task Anna no longer faced in her own life. With Edward dead, and Inman but a shadow of the person she thought him to be, Anna would make her trek into the future alone.

Against lips unable to remain sturdy and stiff, Serine began to cry. Edward through and through, Anna mused as she observed Bryce place his arm around Serine's shoulders. Again she gave thanks for Bryce. Father Richard patted Serine's hand. He then grasped Bryce, Millicent, and Theo's, and did the same.

Walking past Anna, the priest handed Linda the remaining pages of Edward's letter. Linda accepted the words her father had penned and held them to her chest. It struck Anna that Father Richard had yet to read Edwards' words to Linda.

With Father Richard and Brad on either side, Linda came to Anna. Anna's stomach began to churn. Linda removed the letters from her chest. Slowly she began to read from the one on top. Anna's lips trembled and her breathing slowed as Linda read Edward's words to Anna.

"I won't start out with my dear wife. That's too dramatic. Besides, it obscures the true nature of our relationship." Every urge to have Linda stop reading rose and died. David and Theo drew close and tightened their hold on Anna's arms. I don't want to hear this! I don't want to hear this, Anna wanted to silence Linda. I don't . . . want . . . to . . . More tears flowed.

"Anna, you mean everything to me. I didn't show it. Believe me, I've suffered for that. What I don't want is for you to ache now that I'm gone. Do not blame yourself for my shortcomings." Linda's voice began to crack. Brad rubbed her back. She breathed in. Edward's words with Linda as the medium spilled forth.

"Some of us are so afraid and fearful. We're wrapped up in terror and never realize what's gripping us. Caught up in doing whatever it is we think will take away the pain, we never recognize how we're hurting those we love, and those who love us. We are running from the beast.

"This battle becomes our all-consuming affair to escape the demons within the ones who wear our face and stare back at us each morning, neither recognizing the other, both terrified. Yet what frightens us most is that if we take one moment and let ourselves love, better yet, *be* loved, and receive the affection people like you offer, we will disintegrate. But in the end, love tames the beast, turns it into our friend. The two become one.

We see ourselves for who we really are. I was the beast,

Anna. You endured me. In the end your love helped me meet death. For that I thank you."

After what seemed a lifetime, Linda folded the letter and handed it to Father Richard. Brad then lifted a black case. Linda opened it and lifted out a bow, and then, *her* violin, the one Edward had brought her from Strasbourg when she was fourteen.

Linda placed the wooden instrument under her chin, and tuned it. Slowly, and with her stomach exhibiting a motherly bulge, she played "Lo, A Rose 'Ere Bloometh."

The sad and lilting melody filled the air and erased all traces of laughter from moments earlier leaving only the sound of the violin strings followed by the silence separating the notes. It was in those spaces, as she again fingered the Ecuadorian rose within her left pocket that Anna heard sighs and sniffles.

Memories edged upon her chest and consciousness. She wrapped her fingers around the petals that had opened and bloomed in the hours following Edward's transition. Anna's muted sobs poured forth.

Chapter 46

Edward's death and all that came with it was surreal. Within eight weeks, he arose and relived his life only to die again, this time his bodily presence extinguished from the earth. Anna considered the graveside ceremony and the reading of Edward's letter bearing messages to each of them, a spectacle. And yet Edward's words had stirred her heart. She could not cease crying.

With anger as her defense she said to Linda in a subtle, yet biting tone, "It was just like your father to create a scene."

Anna sat across from Linda and Brad. All three rode in the limousine taking them back to the house where attendees of the graveside services would gather one last time.

"His life was filled with drama," Anna continued. "It ended with more of the same. And now his funeral and these letters. Those letters," she repeated.

"And he didn't even address one to *you*," she again spoke to Linda. Anna's elder daughter lowered her gaze as Brad raised his eyebrow, something he rarely did, and almost never in response to anything Anna said or did.

After a momentary silence, Linda said, "Mine was the first he wrote. It would have been the only one, but I encouraged him to write others."

On reaching the house, Anna wanted to rush inside, lock herself in the upstairs bathroom and expel her insides. Beneath the surface of her annoyance and anger, she wished to die. She could not, *would not*, say that. It would mean telling the truth.

She missed Edward. But how do you grieve the loss of what you never possessed, or mourn someone you barely knew? Things would never be the way they were during those last days with Edward, how she had wished them for their entire marriage.

Anna had expected that her love for Edward to fade with his passing. Perhaps she was grieving the loss of her own expectation.

Linda's words from weeks back haunted Anna as she greeted guests at the repast. *For one time, you're telling the truth.* She felt dishonest in seeing to the comforts and needs of her guests while she, the bereaved, failed and ignored her own desire for comfort.

Seeing to others in deferment of herself had been her life. After greeting everyone and encouraging them to eat, she headed for the stairs.

She would lie down then perhaps the people would be gone and Anna could set out on the trek of living life without Edward. No sooner that she had reached the first step she heard, "Mrs. Manning."

Anna turned back and saw Grant. He approached her and extended his hand. "My condolences," he said.

"Thank you for coming," Anna said. She felt awkward that Serine had not invited Grant to stand with the family at the gravesite.

Grant had instead stood with Matt, the two of them behind Serine in the line ahead, and next to Bryce all too eager to comfort and support. Anna would have to do something about that.

Grant said, "I've told Serine to take as much time as she needs. We can spare her for a couple of weeks."

"Thank you. That's very kind of you." Anna could barely speak the words. The shame of how Serine had misled both Grant and Matt still churned within her stomach, and wrenched Anna's emotions.

"I thought it was the least I could do since she came clean with me."

"Oh?" Anna said.

"She returned my ring. She said that the idea of marrying frightened her and that she would not make a good wife in light of how her father had behaved toward you."

Anna took a hard swallow. "It seems Serine realizes that she needs some time to think, and grow up."

"That may be the case." Grant glanced down at his feet and then pocketed his hands splaying the sides of the jacket to his black suit. The matching vest bestowed an air befitting that of a judge, which Anna imagined him someday working as. "Serine needs to know that she's not a bad person."

"That's kind of hard considering what she did with you and Matt."

Again Grant glanced at his shoes, shiny and black like his suit. "It was ridiculous of me to imagine Serine marrying me and becoming mother to a five-year-old."

Once more Anna took a long swallow. She then breathed in. Serine had said nothing of Grant having a child. "My daughter's mother and I divorced last year. I love Serine. But I also have to admit, the idea of having a wife made it easier for me to demand part custody."

Sadness overtook Grant's chestnut face with a red undertone. For a moment he looked like Edward. "A child needs two parents," Grant said. "I was determined to give her that. Only problem was I never pushed Serine to tell me how she truly felt."

"Has she told you now?"

"She didn't have to. Returning my ring was probably the hardest thing she's done in a while. She did it two days before her father died."

Anna lowered her head. Grant drew near, lowered his voice. "I'm only telling you this because I don't want you blaming her for everything that happened. I know about Matt. I didn't like it. But . . . " He turned away. His hands were still pocketed. "Don't let her isolate herself. I've told her she can return to work whenever she's ready."

"How long will it take for you to accept what's happened and to see her back at work, not as your fiancée, but as one of your assistants?" Anna said.

"She won't be working with me as closely anymore. I've transferred her to another division. We both thought that was best." Grant appeared about to cry.

At that, Anna reached out and embraced Grant. Moments passed, Anna sensing the spirit of his deceased mother close by and watching as he lowered his head upon Anna's shoulder.

"Take care," she whispered in Grant's ear. "You're a good person." She released him and he left.

Anna went upstairs with all that Grant had shared heavy upon her heart. Closing the door, she walked across the room, memories of Serine's argument with Grant by the pool tugging her to the window.

She gazed onto the pool below still of full of water. She would have to drain it. Noting that task, she gazed left and there stood Serine with Matt.

They occupied the same spot, as Serine had with Grant, at the far steps from the patio chair where Edward had reclined while reading the magazine with the Buddhist nun on the cover.

Tears filled Anna's eyes as Serine, with shoulders slumped stood speaking with Matt. Even from a story away, Anna could see Matt's eyes intensely following Serine's every word.

After a few moments Serine embraced Matt. He kissed her cheek and then left. As he walked away Serine gripped her shoulders as if cold. She then slumped to her knees.

Serine was still clutching her shoulders when Bryce approached and tried helping her up. She pushed him away, gently but firmly. Anna screwed her face, felt the impulse to run down and scold Serine. Grant's words then seeped into her mind. *Serine needs to know that she's not a horrible person, that you love her.*

Anna was meditating on Grant's missive when a knock arose at the door. Anna turned and Millicent entered.

"Is everything alright?" The younger of Anna's daughters-in-law inquired.

"I'm fine, just tired, thank you." Anna was hoping the words of appreciation would signal a dismissal. Instead Millicent remained.

"I want you to know, Mother Manning, that I really appreciate what Father Manning wrote."

Anna hated those names, *Mother Manning, Father Manning.* So ancient. And to be coming from a person who had yet to give her a grandchild, who for all intents and purposes, in Anna's mind, did not care for her son and saw him only as an accoutrement and appendage. Anna turned around and simply stared.

"I'm sure it's going to be difficult for you," Millicent continued, apparently unaware of Anna's brimming anger. The girl was pushy and brazen. "I wish I could have come and helped." Millicent lowered her head. "It's been hard these last few months."

Anna's body became what felt like a large welt of flames. "Perhaps you mean the entire five years of your marriage." Anna would not succumb to the pain of losing Edward coupled with her feelings of having misjudged and failed Serine. Millicent, in whom Anna had envisioned Edward's worst traits, became Anna's target. "You don't love my son."

Millicent's soft dark eyes ran dry of life, and lent a whisper of vulnerability against her ebony skin. "That's not true," she said.

Those words only fueled Anna's anger. "You don't think Theo is ambitious enough. Tell the truth."

"Theo has his goals."

"They're just not as important as yours or time with your father?" Anna retorted. Millicent arched her back as if to regain composure in the defiant way that had crossed Anna the first time she had met Millicent. "Don't let your father-in-law's posthumous dramatics in those notes fool you into thinking that I don't see what's happening. You've never meant my son well. He's been your lap dog, a punching bag to empty your frustrations on through this sham of a marriage. He gets the anger your father deserves."

"I'm going to assume that you're hurt by the death of Father Manning," Millicent said. "And that you've lost all reasoning. Especially in light of all that it took for you to accept him back."

"You have no idea what you're talking about."

"I know all too well what your marriage and Theo's life was like growing up in this house with his father away all the time," Millicent stammered. "Edward's dilly dallying with everyone about town and across the globe."

"Shut your mouth."

"Never. Neither will I let you stand here and insult me about my marriage that I've worked hard at trying to make succeed."

"Oh, you mean like those late night meetings with your father that stretch into the morning?" Anna said. "Thelonius is no foreigner to having his own trysts."

"You know nothing about my father."

"I know everything I need to. He is everything and more than Edward was."

"My father may have made mistakes, but at least he found a way to apologize *before* death came knocking at his door," Millicent said.

"I won't have you stand here in my house and speak of Edward, no, *Father Manning*, as you so like to call him."

"I'll speak of him as I see fit," said Millicent. "Don't stick your nose into things you know nothing about."

"Get out," Anna yelled.

"Perhaps I will, and take Theo with me."

The door opened. Theo entered.

"There you are. Some of the guests were asking about you," he said to Anna on approaching her. "Should I tell them you're resting?"

Anna calmed her anger. Perhaps Theo would think she was upset about Edward, her loss, *their loss*. She eyed Millicent, her head down and observing the carpet. Theo popped back to Millicent as if he had recalled something. Ushering her toward Anna he said, "Have you told, Mom."

What could it be now? Anna wondered.

Millicent shook her head, no.

"Well if you won't then—" Theo gleamed. "Mom, Millicent is pregnant. We're going to have a child, same as Linda and Brad."

Millicent's head shot up. "Linda's pregnant?"

"I didn't tell you, but she's seven months," Theo said, and then turning back to Anna added, "Millicent is five months."

"I thought our son would be born into his own space." Millicent said with a frown.

"Think of it this way, he'll have a cousin who can be like a brother." Theo patted her hand and smiled.

There she goes again, focused on self, and wanting her own space. The girl knows nothing of sharing. On closer inspection, Anna realized a bulge forming within Millicent's thin frame. She smiled as best she could.

"I'm happy for you," Anna said. She leaned over and kissed then hugged Theo. To Millicent she said, "This must be a surprise."

"Actually not." Millicent's dark eyes, having regained some of their fierceness, sparkled. She looked to Theo standing between her and Anna, "We've been working to conceive for the last three years." Millicent's voice grew soft and dry. "I underwent fertility treatments this past year."

"We we're hoping for twins." Theo gleamed.

An ache absorbed Anna's heart. Theo had said nothing of their struggle, nor of Millicent's pregnancy. She would have been around three and half months when Theo was home visiting Edward that last time.

Perhaps this was also part of the reason he needed to speak with Anna each week, plunge his energies into caring for her, and expunge himself of worry about Millicent and her

305

inability to conceive. *Yet what of all the talk and concern over Millicent's time with Thelonius?*

Anna inspected her younger son's eyes, shining and on the verge of tears. How afraid he must have been. Had Thelonius become the target of Theo's frustration?

She turned to Millicent. "I'm to have two grandchildren born this year. What a blessing."

Dazed and shocked, Anna returned to the first floor of the house. Overwhelmed by the news of Millicent's pregnancy, Anna could not deny the warm smile that had lit up her daughter-in-law's eyes, and that spread over her face when Theo appeared.

The gesture told Anna all she needed. The two were in love.

Maneuvering through the crowd of mourners, she felt light headed and disoriented. Gripped in thought, she nearly walked head-on into Heather.

"Oh!" Anna gripped her elder daughter-in-law's arms and steadied her, the two having almost collided. "Forgive me. I was so caught up," she said.

"Are you all right?" Heather asked.

"No, I'm not. But, then again, I just buried my husband."

"It was a stupid question," Heather conceded. "How could I—"

"The same way I was about to ask you the same." Anna laughed. Heather joined her. The two were quite knowledgeable that seeing to the needs of others was their favorite pastime. That's what Anna had always liked about Heather.

Where Edward had envisioned so much of himself in Millicent, Anna had experienced the same with Heather. Edward had cared little for David marrying a white woman. Though disappointed, Anna had been open to getting to know Heather.

"Want to talk?" Heather asked.

"Sure." Anna trudged back upstairs to Theo's room, Heather accompanying her. "I don't know what's come over me," she said, and then slumped onto the bed.

"There's no need to apologize," Heather sat beside her. "I was doing the same thing when Papa died." Anna liked the way Heather referred to her father as Papa. It reminded Anna of Reverend Elijah. "It's hard to keep your head straight when you're hurting," Heather said. "Especially if you're accustomed to taking care of others."

Feeling Heather about to cry, Anna connected with the despair hanging in her hazel eyes that held hints of green. Only a few weeks into grieving the death of her father, the rawness of Heather's loss remained fresh.

"I thought I had let Edward go," Anna whimpered. "And then to learn he was dying. I don't know how I'm going to get through this," she said.

Anna felt herself drifting. Snippets of scenes from the last three months eased before her then dove into and under the waves of memories. "I was on the verge of selling the house and then . . ." She met her daughter-in-law's misty gaze.

Heather said, "I've decided to keep Papa's house."

Anna considered David's words about Heather, and their marriage. *There's another man. Her father's neighbor, Rob. I think she wants to divorce me. Heather and I haven't made love in a year.*

Her body recalled the warmth of Edward's breath and hands in their last time of intimacies. Though weak and dying he had been kind and soft, Anna ministering to him, he breathing life and redemption into their marriage.

Now sobbing, Anna said, "Why did I ever stop my plans and take him back in?"

"Because you love him."

"But if I loved him, why am I so angry?"

"Because you miss him." Heather's eyes were soft and kind. She embraced Anna. "He's with my father," she whispered. "I'm sure of that. They're taking care of each other." She embraced Anna, adding, "We only get angry about the people and things we care for." She patted Anna's shoulders. Anna sank into her daughter-in-law's chest and wailed.

307

Chapter 47

A saddened sense of foreboding enveloped Anna as David's words hit her. "Heather and I are divorcing." It was the morning after the funeral, Saturday. Anna had been cleaning Edward's things from the room where he had died five days earlier when David entered with the news. "I'm filing papers as soon as I get back to Detroit."

She looked to the bed she had shared with Edward for three decades until asking for the divorce fifteen months earlier.

"And what about Heather," Anna said.

"She has her father's house in Santa Rosa."

Again Anna's attention settled upon the bed. *Moments in time. That's all they were. You were an eternity.* Anna's fingers trembled and grew cold in remembrance of caressing Edward, his chest rising and falling, life slipping from him, he easing from her.

"I'll be handling the divorce," David said in a matter-of-fact manner that tore at the seams of Anna's heart. "I'm not about to hire some shyster who'll walk away with what little I've saved."

She turned to him. The anger at his dispassion pulsated through her body. "You mean what you've amassed."

Like his father, David had an eye for making money. His clients in and around Detroit owned some of the wealthiest estates, another reason

Anna had grown concerned when he'd expressed strong interest in moving back to Oakland. He would be giving up a lot.

"Are you sure this is the best way to handle it, you representing yourself, and Heather," Anna said.

"There won't be a fight. She's not stupid."

"What you're saying is that you've told her your plans, and she's going along for the ride."

David arched his eyebrows as if some part of Edward had come alive in him, the part Anna had dueled and wished to remain buried. "I'm also asking for full custody of Josh and Emily," David added.

"On what grounds?"

"Josh and Emily are black. I won't have that hillbilly, Rob, raising them."

"I can't believe Heather agreed to give up her children, not without a fight. Have you told her?"

"She'll find out soon enough, when she reads the divorce papers."

"That you're drawing up. And like the ones you filed trying to declare me insane. There's an awful lot of conflict of interest here."

"Stay out of it, Mama. You may be running Manning Ventures, but that doesn't give you grounds to control my life. Heather and I can do this quietly—"

"Have you asked Heather about Rob? Maybe you've misunderstood his eagerness to help Heather with her father."

"I'm no fool. I know what I know."

"David. Please." Anna sighed. "Don't do this. It will destroy Josh and Emily. Sit down and talk to her. Tell Heather your concerns. Or at least let me."

"If you do, then warn her not to fight me."

"What if I encourage her to keep the children? She's a good mother." Anna recalled the words in Edward's letter to Heather. *Like with many things, I regret not having told you how much of a good wife you've been to David. You're an excellent mother to Josh and Emily. Forgive me. I love you.*

"Don't play me, Mama. I'll shut her down, call in every favor I have to keep my kids." A hard worker like his father, David was known to pull his own weight, and that of others if it served him well.

That quality, and the fact that he had been a faithful husband, coupled with the powerful people he knew would present a formidable force.

"Don't do this," Anna pleaded once more. "Heather's loving, trusting, and kind. You're worldly, knowledgeable, and confident like your father. Heather's like me—"

"If only she were like you." The consternation on David's face thickened. "On second thought, maybe she is, the two of you one and the same. You wanted to be rid of Dad; Heather wants me out of her life. Unlike *you*, she didn't have the balls to ask for a divorce, something I learned from *you*."

"Shut your mouth." Anna slapped David. A second slid by, Anna's palms growing warm with frustration.

"I'll take that as evidence of the truth," David's voice remained low and firm. Edward's child through and through.

Anna said. "Leave my house."

"This house belongs to Serine, Linda, Theo, and me," David reminded. "And *I'm* the executor."

"Don't think for a minute that I won't have you removed. After that stunt you pulled with Henderson, attempting to sue him, he'd be too glad to—"

"Don't try it, Mama." David leaned forward. "I'll fight you the same as I'm ready to take on Heather." Anna sensed David's soul harboring a hate-filled passion fueled by the same anger Elena had held. The fear of losing Heather coupled with the hurt of Edward's quick death had driven David to the edge.

"Don't do this." Anna warned in a more calm fashion.

"Or what will you do?" David's words sounded as if having risen from a smoldering pit of venom.

"I'll fight you every way I can." Anna then recalled what Heather had said about Edward. *He's in the beyond with my father. I'm sure of that.* Anna said, "I'll stand behind her."

Could David be right, and Heather have been unfaithful? Anna had grown certain, during the hours following Edward's burial, that her father, Elijah, had sought affection outside his marriage to Anna's mother. His determination to remain with Elena until she died evidenced not only love, but also his need to atone.

David stared at her. "I'm not your son." He turned and left.

~*~*~*~

Elise came later that afternoon and took Josh and Emily to Fairyland, after which they would have lunch and remain at her house for the day. On seeing them out to Elise's car, Anna went upstairs and asked Heather to join her in the kitchen for tea.

"Despite what you may think, David is more like me than he is his father." Anna said as she lowered herself onto the chair. Heather's shoulders slumped, as if Anna's words, a confession of sorts, had bestowed an invisible weight upon them. "Has he been unfaithful?" Anna asked.

Tears filled Heather's eyes and dropped onto the lap of her black dress. She shook her head *no*. Heather had sunken deeper into her state of mourning during the twenty-four hours since Anna had cried upon her shoulders. "I didn't ask for the divorce," said Heather.

"I know. He doesn't mean what he's saying. David's wrong. And I'm not going to allow him to—" Anna stopped short fearing that if she exposed David's plan to take the children, Heather would grow more upset. "I'm not going to let David leave this marriage."

Heather's hazel eyes darkened against the momentary flicker of brightness. "He's accusing me of having an affair. With Rob of all people." She gave a sad, facetious chuckle.

"Have you been unfaithful?"

"No. And certainly not with Rob. He's gay. Rob and my father were lovers." Heather breathed in. "I didn't tell David because he would have gone ballistic and refused to let the children come with me."

Anna's shock met with relief. "I'll have to speak to David about that. Anna returned to her first question, rephrased it. "Has *David* been faithful?" She needed to hear it a second time.

"Yes, always. I've never suspected or felt the presence of another woman in his life. Then again, if you count work as a second spouse . . ." Anna leaned back in her chair and sighed. "David's a good man," Heather defended him. "He works hard, provides well for me and the children. It's just that he's so—"

"Distant," Anna said.

Again Heather's eyes brightened with the recognition of being understood.

"David is like me *and* his father when it comes to work. Despite everything, we remained committed to carrying out our roles in the family. David would never leave you or anyone unless he feels unappreciated and devalued, or that the work he's put his heart into has become futile." Anna tilted her head. "Which is why I don't understand that he's so eager to leave Detroit and his clients. They love his work."

"His clients may like him," Heather said, "but he doesn't always like what he sees in them. Or what they do. All the bickering over who gets what when someone dies. Heather explained. "The threats mothers and fathers make as to who they'll keep in their will, and who they'll take out unless the children do as they say. The manipulation and animosity among family members sickens David. It depresses him. And then with you divorcing Papa Edward—" Heather lowered her head. Anna sighed in realizing that David's bogus efforts at suing Henderson and having her declared insane lay rooted in the pain

313

of a little boy afraid of losing his parents, the bedrock of his internal home.

Heather said, "I was the one who suggested we needed to move back home to California. Then Papa got sick. And with Papa Edward dying . . ."

"David needs you," Anna said. "This fight with you is fueled by his anger toward me." She spoke with Heather as an equal, told her of Inman, explained how they had met, five months after she asked for the divorce, and how they'd spent much time together before.

"Edward finally agreed to the divorce and my wanting to sell the house. I knew something was wrong," Anna said. "I brought him home to die."

Anna grew hot and wet when recalling her recent intimacies with Inman. That Edward had been home and dying left her to wonder what kind of woman, person, she had become. *Not* much different from Edward, the fifty-five year-old widow, mother, and grandmother concluded.

"We met at Scott's Restaurant down at the Embarcadero. After a tense meal . . ." Guilt and shame had pulled from every corner and crevice. Yet Anna had given way to her needs. With Inman leading the way in his car ahead, she had driven back to, " . . . his house in the Berkeley Hills." Anna had been there many times prior, but the streets that night had deposited her in unknown territory. She continued to explain. "I didn't make it home until late, 3 a.m. David waited up. Of course I said nothing of where I'd been, or with whom. Days earlier, Inman had come here to see how I was doing. I'd introduced him as a friend. But David knew."

Facets of herself to which she had never been aware sprouted within Anna each time Inman penetrated her defenses. "Without that night I doubt whether I could have stood before the trustees of Manning Ventures, and made clear my decision to run the company. But then Inman entered the meeting of Manning Ventures. He took on the men. He's been a good friend." Her words drifted off. "It's *me* David's angry with," Anna said to Heather. "I was unfaithful."

314

"But Papa Edward was dying. You and he had been in the middle of divorcing."

"I wanted the divorce, not Edward." Anna then said, "Your marriage to David is not the same as mine was with Edward. What stood between us has never penetrated you and David. You and David are tired and weary. Your fathers were sick this last year. Now they've died. David's also wounded from his father's *and my* past mistakes. As for you," Anna brushed Heather's cheek, "You never knew your mother. Neither you nor David are anything like me and Edward." Anna smiled against tears threatening to spill. "You're better."

Heather reached for the box of tissues at the center of the table.

"Don't let the strains of life tear you apart," Anna said. "Josh and Emily need both you and David. And they need the two of you loving and *in* love with each other."

Heather sniffled then dabbed the tissue underneath her eyes. "I love David more than anything in the world." She wiped her cheeks. "He, Josh, and Emily are all I have. But he doesn't want me."

Anna grasped Heather's arms then said, "He wants and needs you now more than ever. That's what's hurting him so. He's vulnerable. None of us likes to feel week, especially men. David's wounded. But he's not beyond saving. He's not a rabid dog gone mad. His father came home to me. David will find his way back to you. You've let me see that."

"I don't want to lose him," Heather sobbed.

"You haven't, and you won't." Anna rephrased Heather's words from the previous day. "People get angry and upset because they care, because the object of their frustration matters." Her daughter-in-law gave a crumpled smiled. "Let me work on David." Anna caressed Heather's arms. "And as for you thinking that your family consists of only David and the children, you have me."

Anna embraced her daughter-in-law, hoping she was returning at least half the solace and calm Heather had granted the previous afternoon.

Chapter 48

Anna had barely turned over in bed when her cell phone rang. It was Inman. "I hope I didn't wake you."

"I need to get up, but—" Lifting her head from the pillow, Anna glimpsed the clock. Its red numbers flashed seven o'clock Sunday morning. Anna lowered her head and sank back into her pillow.

The times when she used to meet Inman at the gym by seven-thirty to work out seemed distant and relegated to a place Anna had little desire to go. Still, like memories of Edward, they haunted her.

"I'm so tired," she moaned. Her conversations and efforts with David and Heather to keep their marriage from falling apart had drained her.

"David and his wife are on the verge of a divorce. And Serine . . . she needs me and I haven't been there for her." Anna missed Inman and the easy way she could speak to him and be

317

herself in his presence. With Edward gone and Inman now representing Mrs. McGrath on the board, Anna was unsure how much she should share with him.

"It sounds like you've been busy, beyond the funeral."

Anna sat up with a start. Her mind flitted back to her visit with Helena McGrath. She had left the old woman's house with the intentions of calling Inman. Anna had been on her way to Bryce's office to hear what he had learned about Inman when Bertrice called saying Edward was dying.

"I don't think it's good for us to be talking," Anna said. Immediately, she felt sorry for her brash tone. Softly, she said, "I've been meaning to call, but . . ." Her heart sank at the thought of David and Heather's troubles even more so now that she had started to share them with Inman.

"I'd like to see you." The familiar softness of his voice pushed past Anna's resistance. "I want to explain why I agreed to represent Mrs. McGrath on the board."

"It was obvious. She's your aunt."

"She told me you visited her."

"She's a nice woman."

"She can also be nosy and pushy." Inman's tone was sharp. "I've found someone else who can do her bidding."

"Is that what you call it?"

"I had no idea that Manning Ventures was your husband's company when she asked me to represent her at the meeting." Inman's explanation seemed simple enough.

"You wouldn't even look at me when you gave Bryce the envelope; you seemed so invested in strengthening your aunt's stake in the company."

"I tried to connect with you throughout the meeting," Inman defended. "Neither did I want the others to think it was a setup."

"Was it? I can't help but wonder whether it is," Anna said. "Particularly when you essentially told Thompson, Dawson, and Filbert to quit the company and sell their shares. Then when they do, your aunt is conveniently ready to buy them."

"Manning Ventures is better off without them," Inman said. "And so are you."

"That may be, but—"

"I know how this may seem." He gave a deep sigh. "A lot's gone on. And with Edward's death. Can we meet and talk about it?"

"Edward's death has no consequence on how I feel about your place on the board."

"It's not me on the board. It's my Aunt Helena," Inman repeated. "Either way, I've found someone else to represent her. I've also spoken with Claiborne Rochester, Ephraim Hennessey , and Chester McGee."

"You did *what*? And who gave you permission to do that?" The three remaining stockholders and trustees had attended Edward's funeral. During the repast at the house, Rochester, Hennessey, and McGee, had spoken with Anna and assured her that they would do all in their power to keep Manning Ventures afloat.

Inman said, "I told them Manning Ventures was rock solid. I also said I wouldn't be remaining on the board as Aunt Helena's representative."

"Did you tell them why?"

"I said it was for personal reasons," Inman said.

In an effort to plaster on an unaffected front, Anna remained silent. Inman then said, "You mean more to me . . . our relationship is worth far more than representing my Aunt Helena. I would do nothing to hurt Edward's company."

"You mean Manning Ventures, which is *my* company." Anna was angry. Yet she could not discount that beyond Dancia, Helena McGrath was Inman's only living relative. "I'm sorry but—"

Inman interrupted. "Despite what you may think, Edward's death and your ownership of the company doesn't have to change things for us, especially *if* I leave the board."

"It colors everything. So much has happened in the last two months." Anna contemplated her life without Edward. Inman could not replace him. She and Inman had slept together more times than she could count. But the night at his house after

319

eating at Scott's had been different. Anna recalled the way he had taken her unto him, his body warming against hers. Edward's touch had never spoken to her like that, not even when they had reconciled.

Anna pinched the bridge of her nose, and closed her eyes. How am I, a widow, mother, and grandmother, supposed to integrate and interweave what Inman has given me with Edward's gift of Manning Ventures?

"I love you," Inman said. He sounded so much like Grant when speaking of Serine. Anna then considered Grant's five-year-old daughter, his desire to create the perfect family. Things had not been as they appeared.

"Call me old fashioned," Inman continued. "But you're the only person I've been with since my wife left me and Dancia." Now twenty-two, Inman's daughter had been seven when her mother left Inman and her.

Anna breathed in. "I've enjoyed being with you."

"*Enjoyed*? I'm not suggesting we hurry and get married. But what about France? You made plans." He had offered to accompany her. They would live there either as man and wife or as lovers. Inman had proposed marriage before Anna had learned of Edward's cancer.

"I can't up and sell the house," Anna said. "Edward's bequeathed it to the children."

"But you have the company. Surely, money is not the issue. I'll do whatever you want or need."

With Edward dead, Inman off the board as Mrs. McGrath's representative, and Thompson, Dawson, and Filbert gone, there was no one to fight, not even the olive branch Edward had offered in giving her Manning Ventures.

"I'm free," she said. "And I'd like to stay that way."

"I've never wanted to enslave you."

"Most men don't set out to. But many of us women are still shackled."

"Only you can remove the chains."

"I need time," Anna said.

"I can wait." Yet, Inman sounded desperate, unlike himself.

Anna made no promises. "I'll call you."

~*~*~*~

Bryce called later that day. Careful to ask how she was doing, and then of Serine, he then said, "When can we meet to talk about the company?"

"How about tomorrow at noon?" Anna was not ready to visit Edward's office. "Where would you like to meet?"

"Would Scott's be okay?" Bryce's tone held urgency. "I'll be finishing up some business at the Embarcadero around 11:30."

Anna was hesitant. Bryce had been Edward's one employee. Could she trust him to accept the totality of who she was? And what kind of business had he at the Embarcadero? Still, he had been honest about Edward's decision not to tell Anna about Mrs. McGrath being a board member and trustee, and *why*.

Anna needed to tell Bryce about her relationship with Inman; she needed for him to hear it from her and no one else. She couldn't run the company without Bryce and she wanted him to remain loyal to her as he had to Edward. Should Bryce falter due to judgments concerning her relationship with Inman, there was David. But that was a last resort.

Then again, what would David do, never mind Serine, upon learning about her and Inman? By that time, Inman and her relationship would be a thing of the past. Still, with David licking his own wounds and Heather hurting, Anna did not want to risk having to turn to David. Until now, she had found safety in knowing that Edward Manning was out there somewhere. Despite his propensity toward philandering, he had not let anyone attack his family. She ached to tell Inman her woes and fears.

Anna returned to her conversation with Bryce. "Scott's tomorrow at noon. I'll be there."

~*~*~*~

321

Scott's was quiet for lunch on Monday. Life without Edward was taking on a melody and rhythm of its own. Seated at the table by the window, Anna observed the yachts docked on the other side of the harbor.

She contemplated her last moments with Edward. He had felt so light in her arms. His body had shrunken to a mere feather of what he had once been not that long ago.

Illness had brought him back for death to whisk him from her. That had been the theme of their life, Edward's eternal leaving and Anna perpetually mourning his absence and yearning for his return.

Edward had uttered, *I was scared, Anna.* She would hold onto those words. Anna too was afraid. Edward's words had carried an unblemished truth. They had revealed the real Edward Manning and exposed him for the child he had remained throughout life, a son yearning for his mother. He had wanted her to have been more able and strong. In the wake of what his mother lacked, Edward had become the man he wished for her to have.

Except for his propensity for maintaining relationships with women beyond his marriage, he had been successful. Edward had given Anna all the material things any man, or son could wish for his wife and mother.

Anna's decision to accept ownership of Manning Ventures—Edward's peace offering, his penance and alms— was her act of forgiveness for the truth that stained their marriage. It was Anna's way of saving his soul, and *hers. None are saved until all are secure.* Edward Manning had loved his company.

It had been his life's work. He had put his heart and soul into it. From its profits, he had yielded the one thing he had never experienced as child: a house and home, safe from poverty and threat. Anna would handle it with care.

Through the restaurant window, Anna watched a yacht leave the marina and set sail for San Francisco Bay. The man and woman aboard walked to the aft of the vessel. Grasping and accepting the other's hand, the man and woman looked out upon the water.

Anna could not see how young or old they were. Through the eyes of wishful thinking she saw herself and Edward. On hearing Bryce approach and call her name, she turned to greet him. Beside him stood Inman.

"I left my car in the garage and was on my way up the steps when I ran into him," Bryce explained his chancing upon Inman. "This seemed to be as good a time as any to talk about Ms. McGrath's offer to purchase the stocks, so I invited Inman to join us."

Both men took a seat. Bryce sat in the chair beside Anna and placed his briefcase on the table. Opening it, he withdrew two documents. "You'll want to look over this." He handed one to Anna then another to Inman.

"It would seem that Thompson, Dawson and Filbert are determined to sell," Anna said in a lamenting voice. She turned to Bryce in avoidance of Inman across the table.

"Seems that way," Bryce murmured in continuance of the charade, albeit for different reasons. Bryce seemed hesitant in appearing too eager or thankful of Mrs. McGrath's most timely offer.

Furious at the hand of cards fate had delivered her, Anna turned back to the window on her left. The trail left by the vessel on the water had all but disappeared.

Unlike earth overturned by the wheels of a car, the water over which the yacht had traveled seemed bereft of memories. It lacked any evidence that the vessel had passed that way. Things were settling in the wake of Edward's passing.

At times, Anna felt that her life held the same qualities as the water. Had Edward really been in her life? Had they had a marriage? Manning Ventures evidenced that they had.

No longer able to continue the charade, Anna looked across at Inman. He lifted his head from reading the documents.

"What had you and Helena McGrath planned to do with my company had I not gone to see her?" Anna asked.

From the side of her right eye, Anna could see Bryce squirming. Obviously, Inman hadn't told Bryce that he had left the board.

Inman met her gaze, his eyes saying, *We discussed this earlier.* He said, "I want nothing but to support you. And now that I'm off the board—"

"Support me?" Anna said. "It seems more like a takeover. I can't believe it was a coincidence that Thompson, Dawson and Filbert pulled out just after you showed up as Mrs. McGrath's representative. You practically dared them to sell and leave. In fact, I think you went to Harrison Filbert with a proposal to buy him out *before* the meeting."

"Anna—" Inman started.

"Don't *Anna* me." She snatched a breath. "Leaving Bryce with this bogus packet and wanting to buy more shares should they become available. It was all drama. Just one more movement in your plan to take over Manning Ventures."

"I can't believe you think that I—" Inman knitted his brows, ones Anna had once loved to stroke.

Bryce touched Anna's hand. "I think we might want to reconsider—"

"Manning Ventures doesn't need your help." Anna said surprised at her own words. Her cell phone rang. Any other time she would have ignored it, but—

"Hello."

"Where are you?" It was Linda.

"I'm downtown at Scott's for lunch."

"You need to meet us as the hospital. Millicent's bleeding. Theo's afraid she might lose the baby."

"I'm on my way." Anna clicked off. She stood.

Bryce and Inman joined her.

"It's Millicent. She may be having a miscarriage."

"Let me drive you." Inman offered. The care in his voice spread across his face.

"My car's in the garage," she said.

"Please." Inman seemed in genuine anguish to accompany her.

Anna turned to Bryce who was wearing a sense of surprise and wonder concerning the familiarity peppering Anna and Inman's way with each other.

"Give me a call when everything's settled." Bryce said. He closed his briefcase. "Tell Serine I'll call her this evening."

"Thanks." Anna reached over and kissed his cheek, all the while hoping that Serine would take his call and not push him away as she had at the pool during the repast.

Outside the restaurant she turned to Inman.

"Why are you doing this?"

"I want to," he said. Again his eyes shone with sincerity, but this time with intense worry and fright. Recalling that Inman's loft that served as an office two blocks away, Anna wondered what business had brought Bryce down to the Embarcadero.

Chapter 49

Linda, Brad, Serine, David, and Heather were in the waiting area outside the emergency room when Anna entered with Inman.

"How is she?" Anna asked of Millicent upon reaching Linda.

"The emergency room physician's examining her," Linda said.

"Theo's with her," Brad added.

Anna caught David eyeing Inman.

"This is Inman Hayes," she said to David. "You remember." Inman moved to extend his hand, but David's hand remained at his side. Anna introduced him to Heather.

"Please to meet you," Inman said.

"Same here." Heather smiled and shook his hand.

Anna turned to Linda and Brad. As with David, Anna recalled how Linda, Brad, and Theo had met Inman when he had visited the house a month before Edward died.

"Nice to see you again," Linda said. She and Brad shook his hand.

Anna eyed Serine and said, "Inman, this is my daughter, Serine," and to Serine, "This is Inman Hayes."

Like David on that initial meeting at the house, Serine cautiously extended her hand all the while staring at Inman as if trying to remember from where she had last seen him, that he was a criminal whose true identity she was attempting to recall from either a crime scene photo, or mug shot.

Anna said to everyone, "Inman's aunt, Helena McGrath, holds stock in your father's . . . , I mean Manning Ventures. She's on the board of trustees."

Serine spoke to Anna. "Bryce said you three were having a meeting.

He wanted to know if there was anything he could do," Serine said. "I'm calling him after everything's settled here."

David drew near Inman and said, "Are you always so friendly with the owners of companies whose board members you represent?"

Serine shifted from Anna, and again, as if an eagle zeroing in on its prey, sharpened her inspection of Inman.

"I try to help where I can," Inman said to David.

Fearful of where David's questioning might lead, Anna rushed to Theo as he entered the waiting area. The others followed.

"They're admitting her," Theo explained as the others gathered around him and Anna. "She'll be in Room 312."

"How is she?" Anna asked.

"She still has the baby." Anna touched his arm and gave a light smiled. "She wants to see you," Theo said.

"Me?"

"Yes."

Anna proceeded with Theo to the third floor; the others were right behind them. On reaching the doorway, Anna and Theo entered the private room to find the bed empty. Linda, Brad, David, Heather, and Serine followed them inside. Inman remained in the corridor.

328

"Where are they?" A worried look had consumed Theo's face. He started for the door when a nurse exited the bathroom.

"The orderlies are bringing her up," she assured him.

Anna felt David's heated and interrogating stare upon her back as she moved to the window. Though Bryce was first on her list of those due an explanation, she would at some point have to tell David who Inman actually was.

Voices rose in the hallway. Everyone was headed toward the doorway when Anna heard Millicent's voice.

"Oh my God! Papa Inman! I can't believe you're here." Millicent lay on a gurney. The orderlies standing beside her were waiting for everyone to step aside so they could push her into the room. "I can't believe this."

She grasped Inman's hand, and said, "My godfather is here." She looked to Theo then to Anna, and back again up at Inman. "I've known him since . . . I can't remember when."

"Your godfather?" Anna turned to David on her left and met his simmering stare.

"You'll have to call Daddy," Millicent said to Inman, "Tell him I'm okay, and that he won't need to come." Millicent turned back to the rest of the family. "Inman's like a second father to me," she said.

"So we meet again," Theo said to Inman, "As almost relatives." Theo extended his palm. The worry of possible miscarriage appeared to have momentarily lifted.

With an anxious smile, Inman shook Theo's hand.

Everyone stepped aside and the orderlies pushed the gurney carrying Millicent into the hospital room. Linda, Brad, and Heather entered into a dialogue of their own as Theo and Inman moved to see about Millicent.

Serine drew close to David. His focus unchanged, he remained intent upon Anna.

"I suppose we're to be happy," he said. "Millicent certainly is. A stroke of luck that her godfather's here."

"At least for Millicent." Serine pouted. She joined Heather and Linda speaking with Millicent, who was now lying upon the hospital bed.

David observed Inman, who was by the window. His arms folded, he speaking with Theo and Brad.

David said to Anna, "Care to tell me who this man really is? Or do I have to find out for myself?"

Anna sent him a heated stare. "I thought you were no longer my son."

Chapter 50

Millicent was released from the hospital and sent to the Manning home with strict orders to adhere to stay in bed. "You have a weak placenta," Dr. Amy Hilliard had said. "You can't travel for at least three weeks. Once you arrive back in Chicago, I'm sure your obstetrician will prescribe same as me, complete bed rest."

Theo waited on Millicent hand and foot while Inman remained constant at her bedside. The two of them discussed topics that ranged from the Genesis of her life to the Revelation of his life since she had last seen him.

Inman and Millicent had not seen one another since a few months before Millicent's marriage. This differed greatly from what Millicent had told Theo, that she had not seen Inman since adolescence.

Inman had exited her life during her teenage years. But the two had kept in touch by phone, letters, and e-mail. Millicent had wanted the mysterious godfather, Inman, to meet and grant approval of Theo as her life mate.

But something stopped Inman from returning to Chicago. The mysterious godfather had not made his appearance at the wedding. In fact, Millicent had never shared with Theo her wish for him and Inman to meet.

Though having met Inman prior to Edward's death, Theo had not learned that Inman was the mysterious godfather, whose name Millicent resisted divulging and about whom her parents detested speaking.

Neither until four days ago when Millicent found Inman waiting in the hallway outside her hospital room did Theo learn and witness the depth of her bond with the mysterious and until then unknown godfather.

Two days after Millicent's release from Berkeley General Hospital, Anna met with Bryce and revealed all she had learned about Inman and his role as godfather to Millicent, who continually referred to him as *Papa Inman*.

Bryce said, "I did some checking and he seems above board. Concerning Manning Ventures he's come through on everything he promised regarding his work for Mrs. McGrath as one of the trustees." Inman had relinquished his seat on the board.

But Anna remained yet convinced. "She's his aunt. Did he tell you that?"

"He mentioned it. But that didn't seem to have any effect on Dawson, Filbert, and Thompson's asking price for the shares."

"Why would it?"

"They tried to get higher than market value, more than we would have asked had Manning Ventures been selling the shares." Bryce explained, "Inman was about to pay it, but I told him to hold off. I didn't think it was right. That they were asking for a higher price further substantiated what Inman asserted. They had no problems with the company itself, rather who was running it."

"Did Inman pay what they asked?"

"He called me. Filbert was trying to bully Inman. I called Filbert and he backed down. Mrs. McGrath purchased Dawson, Thompson, and Filbert's shares at fair market price. I facilitated the sale with Inman only as spectator." Bryce's ability to work smoothly with Inman unnerved her.

Anna then asked, "Has he or Mrs. McGrath convinced you to represent her on the board?"

"That would be Victoria Thompson. Inman was ahead of me on that." Bryce averted Anna's doubts of his loyalty. "I was going to insist they choose a woman."

Bryce's words indicated his awareness of Anna's fears. "If Inman or Mrs. McGrath had asked me to represent her, I would have told them what I'm telling you. That it would present a conflict of interest. And my interest is in working with you."

Bryce's demeanor and tone softened, the transition from hard line bargainer to confidante both shook and awed Anna. Bryce said, "Understandably, you have questions about Inman. So did I."

"Who answered them?"

"Colleagues at the companies he's worked with, past and current clients he's represented since going out on his own. They all say he's great," said Bryce.

"*Great* can mean a lot of things to many people. Just what were their words, particularly those of past clients?" Anna had lost count of how many times she had thought of how Millicent had risen from her despair of nearly miscarrying to gleefully embracing *Papa* Inman.

"I initially spoke with people who are no longer his clients. All of them lamented how they had not taken his advice. They had thought they could do better. Some wanted a lower consulting fee. Inman Hayes doesn't come cheap," Bryce said.

"They lost their money." Anna's heart sank. Could Inman be that honest, and she unable to see it? "What was even more interesting was what they said when I told him of the work he'd done for us."

"He was representing his aunt," Anna retorted.

"That's not the way they saw it," Bryce said explained. "When I described how Inman had stood up for you in the board meeting, both his past and former clients were shocked." Anna was too as she listened. "They knew. Or rather they had heard rumors."

"What rumors?" Anna said.

Bryce leaned in. "I never said anything, but when Edward was sick . . . " Bryce paused. "When it became apparent he wasn't going to make it, and that he wasn't going to sell the company, I grew concerned that someone would get wind of what he was going to do, give you the company. I was afraid someone would instigate a takeover."

Anna's heart pounded.

"The world of business is like the Serengeti, Anna. Eat or be eaten. Edward knew that." Bryce said. "He also had debts to pay. He wanted to make things right before he died. Right with you." Anna met Bryce's gaze. "I agreed to stay on and help you. But I'm no Edward Manning."

Bryce's sorrow over losing Edward stirred her emotions. Anna felt ashamed that she had ignored Bryce's hurt, still gaping and raw. "Like you, I've been worried about a takeover," said Bryce.

He continued. "All the people I spoke to about Inman were not only shocked at how helpful he had been, they also expressed awe at his silence about the company. He said nothing concerning his representation of Helena McGrath on the board. I didn't know Mrs. McGrath was Inman's aunt at the time.

None of those with whom I spoke seemed to either. Which explains why his current clients were surprised they hadn't received a call. Many of them were waiting for Inman to inform them of a newly formed company with value and startups that held great potential. Manning Ventures was a company without strong and knowledgeable leadership."

"A company ripe for takeover by eager investors." Anna shivered.

"Inman Hayes did want Dawson, Thompson and Filbert to sell their shares in Manning Ventures. But not because he wanted to maneuver a takeover for his aunt, or anyone. And believe me he could have started one. *Easily,*" said Bryce.

He looked at Anna and said, "What puzzles me is why he would do all of this. We're certainly better off without Dawson, Filbert, and Thompson. But why would Hayes clear them out and then stop working as Helena McGrath's representative? He hasn't prepared Manning Ventures for a takeover by outsiders. Mrs. McGrath's got too much of her husband's work and money invested in the company. From what I can see Inman cares about her. They seemed to be on the outs right now."

Feeling sheepish, Anna sank further into shame. She was not ready to tell Bryce of her relationship with Inman. Bryce said, "Do you have any idea what's going on between them— Inman and Mrs. McGrath? You spoke with Mrs. McGrath, right before Edward died. Did she say anything?"

"We talked about the company, that I was eager to make no changes." Anna omitted Helena McGrath's admission that Inman had thought her nosy and that he was annoyed she had not told him that Edward, then Anna Manning owned Manning Ventures. "She's his only living relative," Anna said of Helena McGrath. "Other than his daughter."

"That would be Dancia," Bryce said. He glanced at the sheet of notes he'd made on Inman. "Over the years several corporations have offered him the chance of being CEO. Inman turned them all down. One guy I spoke with speculated it had to do with his daughter. He worked with Inman at the firm in San Francisco where Inman started out. This guy knew Inman when he was married.

"He was there when Inman's wife died. The man took the call. Inman's wife had left him and Dancia two years earlier. He said Inman took it hard, his wife dying. After that, Inman made Dancia's care his sole purpose. He went out on his own so he could be more available to her.

Trouble is he didn't count on so many clients following him. Turned out good for Inman. He could call his own hours and price. But he never went beyond consulting for what many

335

in our field would have killed to have. He's got talent, expertise, experience, and the contacts."

Moments of silence passed. Anna was astonished at what Bryce had uncovered about Inman in the face of her questions, and all she had missed. Inman had suffered a lot. And yet he had retained the ability to give. He had also renewed within Anna the ability to believe in herself. She recalled how he had entered the board meeting and spoken up for her. Yet questions remained concerning his relationship with Millicent, the texture of which was as visible and viable to Anna as Inman's arms enfolding her when they had made love.

She said to Bryce, "We're missing something. And it's right before our eyes."

"I don't know what it could be," said Bryce. He shook his head as if in doubt of Anna's intuition. "Everyone I spoke with described Inman as personable, trustworthy, eager to serve, all the things you never hear about in *our* line of work."

Anna smiled in response to Bryce's use of the word *our*. That he had included her, underscored his commitment to working with her, even if it were rooted in his relationship with Edward.

"They also said he was no pushover," Bryce added.

"And that's what bothers me."

Inman knew the ins and outs of what constituted a financially solid company and what kind of person was needed to keep it that way.

But his acumen at assessing whether a person possessed the qualities befitting a loyal and loving mate needed honing. Anna had her doubts about Inman's wife, Marilyn. Having been at the receiving end of betrayal, Anna had concluded Marilyn to have been hewn out of the stock from which people like Edward emerged.

Those like Edward, Thelonius, and the class of people to which Anna had concluded Millicent belonged. Despite the certainty of her judgments, circumstances of the last three days had caused Anna to reassess her ability—or lack thereof—in sizing people up.

Anna had grown confused. Still facts remained. Inman's wife had abandoned him and their daughter, Dancia, to be with another man. Yet when learning of her death, he had felt even more sorrowful. With that, Anna identified only too painfully.

She said to Bryce, "Find me every scrap of information you may have missed about Inman Hayes. There's more here than meets the eye."

Bryce screwed his face, appeared truly bewildered.

"Call it mother wit, or the intuition of a betrayed wife. I'm not comfortable." It would be foolish to pretend that Bryce had no knowledge of what kind of man Edward had been. Not if Bryce's relationship with Anna was to grow into full maturity. "I need to know everything about Inman Hayes. *Everything*."

"I'm on it," Bryce appeared energized by Anna's honest skepticism.

She reached out and touched his hand. As if proud of having pleased her, he smiled. Anna then realized why Edward had placed so much trust, or rather how Bryce had earned such deep respect, from Edward—no small feat. Perhaps Serine might come to see that, too.

Chapter 51

Anna drove home, her mind meandering back to the afternoon of Theo and Millicent's wedding in Chicago. Edward, as best man for Theo, had trekked back and forth between a room off the church narthex where Millicent, her family, and bridesmaids had gathered.

Anna had been sitting on the right front pew when Edward, returning from one of his trips, had slumped onto the seat and said, "Millicent's a wreck."

"What's changed from last night? You said she was all smiles and beaming." Feigning jet lag, Anna had not attended the rehearsal dinner.

Edward sighed. "That was before she found out her godfather isn't going to make it."

"Her godfather?" Anna was mortified. The look on Edward's face had said Millicent wasn't far from calling off the ceremony. Millicent wanted to marry Theo. He was a good catch, everything Thelonius Regarde was not, and never could be.

"I'm going to see if I can help." Edward left again.

Edward could have a calming effect on Millicent, another thing that frustrated Anna about Millicent's entrance into their lives. The daughter-in-law Anna least cared for served as a walking mirror reflecting all that lay unclaimed, lost, and hidden not only in Anna and Edward's marriage, but also in Anna.

Anna had closed her eyes and prayed that the wedding would take place. She also asked for protection over Theo, and that despite becoming the husband of Millicent Regarde, divine powers would prevent her from transforming him into some variation of her father, or Edward.

On Edward's last return, he was smiling, something he rarely did. With one hand grasping the pew in front of them and the other to the one in back, he bent down and whispered, "It's happening." His smile brightened. He left one last time to serve as best man in their younger son's wedding.

Anna never asked Edward what words, if any, he had spoken to Millicent. Nor had she asked Millicent what her father-in-law had said and how or if his words had transformed her mood. Questions lingered. During the ensuing five years of Theo and Millicent's marriage, the closeness between father-in-law and daughter-in-law evidenced something having taken place.

Guided on the arm of her father, Thelonius Vincente Regarde, Millicent proceeded down the center aisle of Trueblood African Baptist Church of Chicago and toward the altar where Theo waited with joyous expectation brightening his face.

Edward stood behind him. His hand lay upon Theo's shoulder. It had been a momentous image, one reflecting the joy and ecstasy upon Millicent's face despite the absence of her godfather, what Anna had wished to experience with Edward.

Anna turned the corner and drove onto the street where she lived in the house that Edward had built. Now in the wake of his death last week Anna once again pondered why five years earlier Inman had not attended the wedding. Millicent clearly loved him. Despite her misgivings of Inman concerning his role as representative for Helena McGrath, Anna also recognized that Inman cared deeply for his goddaughter.

This became Anna's obsession. She wanted to understand Inman's connection to Millicent. She also needed to piece together why he had so easily relinquished his role of representing his aunt on the board of Manning Ventures.

Could he have been telling the truth when stating why he had taken the role in the first place? *I had no idea when she asked me.* Amid ample opportunities to benefit himself, and others, Inman had done nothing to hurt the company. His love for Millicent, clear and evident, pulsated to the same depth as Edward at the wedding five years earlier when trying to calm Millicent's disappointment and hurt in the face of her godfather's absence.

In light of his affection for Millicent, Anna found it particularly odd that Inman had not made it a priority to attend Millicent's wedding. It seemed so strange now as Anna considered how close she and Inman had come to meeting each other. Had she possessed the ability to foresee future events, Anna would have sworn Inman had avoided the wedding to prevent her from learning of his connection to Millicent whom Anna did not like.

Anna entered the kitchen and found Theo preparing tea. He poured two cups, and with Anna following, walked to the table and settled down for what she knew would be a discussion of Millicent and Inman.

"It's like they've rediscovered each other," Theo said.

Relieved that Millicent and the baby were holding their own, Anna gave thanks and tried listening without judgment. She prayed that the recent scare of miscarriage was hopefully on its way to becoming a disposed memory. Theo would be crushed should the worst happen.

"I can't believe she never told me how much he meant to her," Theo said. "Yet again, her parents always get nervous and hush-hush when she mentions the word *godfather*."

"I suppose that's why she never told you Inman's name," Anna said mulling over her tea.

"Yeah, but I'm her husband. And we don't live with her parents." None of the recent events seemed to explain the reunification of Millicent's relationship with her father. Rather, they stood in stark contrast to what Theo had described.

The connection binding the affairs of Theo and Millicent's wedding to the surprises that arose from their recent dilemmas bore an exceptional oddity. "I don't understand it," Theo said.

Anna's mind flipped back to the reception following Millicent and Theo's wedding. Unaware of Anna's identity, certain guests had spoken of how the wedding had come close to not taking place. *Millicent insisted the godfather give her away*, one had said.

Another had whispered that Thelonius had *been obscenely offended by Millicent's behavior.* So much so that *he,* not Millicent, *had threatened to call off the wedding, and not pay the vendors,* who, in Anna's mind, had lacked the good sense to require payment up front.

Theo sipped his tea and said, "I like Inman. He's good for Millicent, better than Thelonius could ever be."

Like Edward, who had written the letters that Father Richard and Linda read at the gravesite, Thelonius Regarde wanted to be at the center of events even when those not celebrating the milestones of his life nor feting him, or his achievements. For them it mattered little or none that some of those occasions commemorated the joy and happiness for others, even their children.

Feigning her acquaintance and intimate knowledge of Inman, Anna said, "I wonder where Inman has been all this time?

"Right here in Oakland with you." Theo looked to her. "He told Millicent and me that the two of you have been dating." Anna slowly sat her cup upon the table. She had hoped not to have her life further exposed, rather to gain more information about Inman from Theo as yielded by Millicent. "Why didn't you tell us?" Theo said.

"I didn't think it was the correct time, particularly with your father—"

"Daddy's dead. And you need to get on with your life." Having momentarily abandoned his concerns, Theo aimed his attention upon Anna, and her happiness.

"I have the company, Manning Ventures." Anna held her breath wondering what else Inman had told Millicent, such as his now-defunct position on the board. In Anna's worry, Helena McGrath's words came to mind. *I'm Inman's only living relative besides Dancia. After us there's no one.* Anna wondered what, if anything, Helena knew of Millicent.

"Mama?" Theo reclaimed Anna's attention. "You have my permission to fall in love again, or perhaps for the first time, and with the right man." Anna's heart sank at the seriousness with which her second-born spoke. The solemnity upon his face touched her heart and soul.

Unlike David when a seven-years-old, Theo, one year younger had, upon finding her lying on the bed and crying, consoled Anna with words bolstering her inner strength. Theo had not promised to care for Anna when became a man.

"It'll be better one day, Mommy," he had said. He had instead patted Anna's hand then kissed her cheek. "One day you'll learn to smile. I'll teach you." The little boy had then wiped her face and smiled as only a child, naive of life's torture and pain, could.

Presently, Theo touched her hand. Mustering all her energies Anna held back tears.

Chapter 52

Anna was shaken from having been upended and exposed. She pulled her hand from Theo's grip and trudged upstairs. At the top of the landing, she walked to what had been her and Edward's bedroom. David and Heather had slept in there for two days following the funeral.

In the aftermath of Millicent's near miscarriage, they gave it to Millicent and Theo. Inman and Millicent were presently inside. The door was closed. Anna imagined them expanding on and illuminating the events of their lives briefly touched upon in e-mails, and short phone calls during the last five years.

She went to Theo's room and closed the door. From the window, she saw Theo sitting by the pool. The cell phone to his ear, he was most likely giving Dr. Hilliard the daily report on Millicent as he had promised the obstetrician.

Encumbered to the milieu of questions pounding within her head, Anna lay down on Theo's bed. *Who was the real Inman Hayes?* Why had he not visited Millicent since her marriage to Theo? *And why had he missed Millicent's wedding?* Why had Thelonius been so angry that Millicent had wanted Inman to give her away, so much so that he had threatened to call off the wedding? *Why all the secrecy around Inman's relationship with Millicent?*

According to Theo, both Millicent and her parents, Thelonius and Henrietta, had committed themselves to silence on the matter. In spite of that loyalty, Millicent now in Oakland, appeared quite comfortable in being and talking with Inman.

Anna's thoughts doubled back to her conversation with Theo. *I want you to have some fun. And from what I can see, Inman is willing and eager to provide it.* What had Theo seen? Clearly not what David nor Serine had perceived. Perhaps if Anna were to become more like David . . . She pushed away the thought.

A loud voice resounded from the hallway outside.

"I want you out of here!"

What the hell? Anna sat up and rushed to the door. She joined Linda out on the landing.

"You need to leave. This is not your home," David said. "I'm not about to let you come in here and set up shop." He held up his fist as he yelled at Inman.

"I mean you no harm. I'm only here to see to Millicent," Inman said calmly.

"And at our invitation," Theo interceded. He sided with Inman. Millicent slid between the two men.

"Calm down. Let it go," Heather urged David. She pulled at his shoulder.

"Let what go?" Anna said as she walked toward David.

"This is my father's house," David said. "It always will be despite your trying to sell it."

"No one's selling anything," Anna said.

"You certainly tried. And with him here there's no telling—" David pointed his finger at Inman. "He put it in your head to go to France."

Anna shot Inman a questioning look.

"He was telling me how much he loved you," Millicent said. Her mocha face was penitent and fearful. "David overheard us speaking."

"Is this true?" Serine drew near. Anna turned to her. Serine then said, "Have you been dating this man, even while Daddy was dying?"

Anna glanced at Serine, and then Inman. She took in the faces of her children. Linda holding her stomach. Brad beside her. David with Heather rubbing his shoulder. Theo who wanted Anna happy. And Serine casting a stare of judgment with the heaviest of sentences. Anna settled her gaze back upon David.

"Yes, I've been dating Inman for five months," she said. "We've slept together."

"I don't believe you," David said.

Serine began to cry.

"This is all a lie." David said to Anna. "It isn't true. Take it back."

"Don't talk to her that way." Inman stepped forward.

David again cocked his fist.

"David, please," Heather said. Serine rushed to David, but not in time to prevent him from hitting Inman. Inman pushed back. He was about to punch David when Millicent slumped over. Theo broke her fall, then said. "She's bleeding."

Anna and Inman rushed to Millicent.

Chapter 53

At the hospital Dr. Amy Hilliard explained, "Millicent's having a reaction to the baby's blood."

"Why is this happening? What's causing it?" Theo asked.

"Your baby and Millicent share the same blood type. But your baby is *Rh* positive. Millicent is *Rh* negative," Dr. Amy said.

"But shouldn't the obstetrician in Chicago have known about this," said Theo. "Why didn't he pick it up during the testing?"

"I don't know. But Millicent lacks another antigen that the baby's blood possesses, most likely inherited from you," Dr. Hilliard said.

You mean in addition to the *Rh* antigen?" Theo said. Anna empathized with his anxiety and anger in trying to understand. He and Millicent had tried so hard to conceive.

"Yes. Your baby is bleeding because your wife has formed

antibodies to two qualities on your baby's blood cells," said the obstetrician.

"But isn't that going to hurt the baby? And to think I caused this." Theo gripped his head.

Inman grew noticeably anxious as Anna tried to calm Theo.

"This is not your fault, Theo. We can stop the bleeding. And we can give the baby a transfusion."

"I want the baby to have my blood," Theo said. "Can I do that?"

"As long as it matches the baby's," said Amy. "We'll type your blood and see. But I'm worried about Millicent. She's lost a lot of blood also. There's been a tear in the placenta. I can't quite figure out why."

"Can she have some of my blood?"

"Most likely not. Millicent has a rare blood type. As I said, she's *Rh* negative. Only five percent of African Americans are *Rh* negative. In addition to that, she lacks another antigen that most people have. It's hard to find blood that lacks these two antigens."

"There has to be someone out there who can donate blood that she can use," Inman said. He approached Dr. Hilliard.

"I've alerted the Alameda-Contra Costa County Blood Bank," the obstetrician explained. "I've also called blood banks in San Francisco and in L.A. If they have blood that matches, we can fly it up here," Dr. Hilliard then said, "Does Millicent have any brothers or sisters?"

Inman and Theo shook their heads.

"What about her parents?"

"They're in Chicago," Theo said.

"They need to get here as soon as possible so we can test them," said Dr. Amy.

Theo flipped open his cell phone and started dialing as he stepped away.

"What are you going to do while we wait for Henrietta and Thelonius to arrive?" Inman asked the obstetrician.

"Hope the bleeding stops, or that she can receive blood from one of her parents."

350

Desperation overtook Inman. Anna drew in a breath.

"It's that rare, this blood type that Millicent has?" Inman said. He appeared bewildered and fearful.

"Yes. Ninety-eight percent of the human population carries the *Rh* antigen that Millicent not only lacks, but also carries an antibody for. And then she lacks another antigen common to most people."

"Does she have antibodies to that?" Inman said.

"Yes. That's why her immune system is attacking the baby's blood cells." Dr. Hilliard explained, "Millicent was most likely exposed to both these antigens when her mother was pregnant with her. Do you know if Millicent's mother experienced any bleeding while carrying Millicent?"

"She did," Inman said then as his voice trailed off he added, "You think Millicent has her father's blood type?"

"That's my hunch. And I hope he can get here fast," said Dr. Hilliard.

Inman lowered his head. His eyes receded as if coming into recognition of what he wanted to forget. Anna was all too aware of the look in Inman's eyes. She had seen it in Edward's throughout their marriage, and then weeks before he died, it had swirled within layers of shame dosed with regret and sorrow.

Years of Edward's unfaithfulness, and lies wrapped in a package of cautious truth had taught her much. It was all coming clear. The secrecy. Inman's absence from Millicent and Theo's wedding. Thelonius' anger toward Millicent wanting Inman to give her away.

Inman lifted his head. To Dr. Hilliard he said, "It won't take long for her parents to arrive. One of them is already here. I'm Millicent's biological father."

Chapter 54

During the amniocentesis preceding the intrauterine transfusion of Theo's blood to the baby, Dr. Hilliard discovered a second fetus inside Millicent. Millicent and Theo were due to have twins in four months.

That Millicent was carrying not one, but two babies who were both *Rh* positive, had placed an additional amount of stress on Millicent's uterus, causing it to attempt to separate from the placenta. Millicent would need complete bed rest through the end of her pregnancy.

While Theo had donated blood to be given to the babies, Inman simultaneously gave blood that Millicent was to receive. Anna arrived on the fifth floor of Berkeley General on the morning after Millicent and the babies received their first transfusions. She was half way down the corridor, headed for Millicent's room when Inman called to her.

"Dr. Hilliard is examining her," he said as he approached.

"Where's Theo?"

"He went downstairs for a cup of coffee. I was in the waiting room here." He glanced back at the room from where he had come.

"I guess I'll go down the cafeteria and find him." Anna moved to leave. She had remained quiet and cordial during the last three days, as had Inman. The two of them were focused on Millicent, the babies, and Theo.

"Can we talk?" Inman asked. Anna turned back. "I don't know about you, but this hospital food is driving me crazy," Inman said. "I hear there's a nice restaurant across the street. They say it serves fast."

Like Inman, Anna had spent the last forty-eight hours subsisting on the food served in the Berkeley General cafeteria.

"That would be nice."

A half hour later while seated at a table inside the Mediterranean restaurant across from the hospital, Inman nursed a cup of water in an attempt to replenish his body with fluids as the nurse had directed. The two placed their orders. Inman then provided an update on Millicent's progress since last evening.

"Dr. Hilliard thinks we're out of the woods." His use of the word *we* indicated how the babies Millicent was carrying indelibly bound Anna to Inman. Appearing more relaxed, but not fully relieved, he drank more of his water. "I want to tell you how I became Millicent's father."

A weight seemed to fall from Inman's shoulders as Anna drew still and listened. "Like most of us in the middle of setting up our business, Thelonius was self-absorbed and working as hard as he possibly could," Inman started. "I was interning for Thelonius one summer while finishing up my MBA program. When I met Henrietta she was doing all she could to absorb the strains set upon her marriage. She was lonely. I was also hurting from a fiancée who kept putting me off. It was not Marilyn.

"My fiancée ultimately returned my engagement ring. Everything she hated about me Henrietta seemed to love. Henrietta made herself available to listen. I didn't have to hide my feelings. We were young, she was thirty and I was twenty-eight. It wasn't something I'd planned, falling in love, and sleeping with another man's wife." Inman sighed.

"When she told me she was pregnant, the seasoned side of Henrietta emerged. I also saw how immature and unprepared I was for being a father. Thelonius was ten years older than me and bound for places in the Chicago real estate world that I dared not even dream about. He would overreact when or if he learned Henrietta was carrying my child. I wanted the best for them."

"So you didn't tell him," Anna said.

"I was no match for Thelonius socially or financially. And Henrietta deserved better. We agreed, Henrietta and I, that she should raise the baby as Thelonius' child. I wanted the best for her and my child." Anna's heart sank when considering how low Inman must have felt about himself to draw such a conclusion. "We never imagined the kind of trouble Henrietta would have while carrying Millicent. Henrietta's placenta began to tear just about the same time in her pregnancy as in Millicent's."

"Five months," Anna said.

"That's when the doctors learned that the baby—Millicent—was *Rh* negative. Henrietta was *Rh* positive. The doctor said that normally this kind of thing didn't show up until the baby was born, or when child was older, maybe never. But, the bleeding from the tear in Henrietta's placenta exposed Millicent to a large amount of Henrietta's blood. Millicent made antibodies real fast."

"So what did they do?"

"Thelonius wanted to give blood. The doctors assumed that he was *Rh* negative. The tests showed he was *Rh* positive like Henrietta. There's only a twenty-five percent chance of *Rh* positive parents having a child that's *Rh* negative. But it was enough to make Thelonius nervous." Inman closed his eyes then opened them. "They gave Henrietta *Rh* negative blood to replenish the blood she had lost. It shouldn't have harmed the baby. But as sooner as she received the transfusion, everything went crazy. Henrietta almost lost Millicent."

"She rejected the *Rh* negative blood?" Anna said.

"Not really." Inman shook his head. "The doctors explained that it looked like Millicent lacked not only the *Rh* antigen, but also an *E*-antigen or a *Kell* antigen. Most people have them like Dr. Hilliard explained."

Anna listened.

"I'm Rh negative," Inman said. "My blood cells also lack the Kell and E antigens." He clinched his jaw. "Thelonius started freaking out and demanding answers. Why did *his* baby have this weird blood type that prevented the baby from receiving Henrietta's and his blood?" Just like Thelonious. Anna thought. The fact that Inman had taken the time to learn about this condition and could explain the intricacies of what had been happening with Millicent as a fetus underscored that he was indeed her biological father. He obviously loved her.

"Thelonious was really confused," Inman said.

"What did they tell him?"

Inman's face took on a demeanor of having been worn, and beaten. "From the moment Henrietta found out she was pregnant, we pretty much knew I was the father. When the doctors said Thelonious was *Rh* positive like Henrietta and that Millicent was *Rh* negative, we knew for certain."

Inman shook his head and gave a wry, sad smile. "But then you know hospitals. They don't like getting involved in family dramas, particularly not with black folk. As Millicent was getting worse, Thelonius kept asking questions and interrogating everyone.

While the lab technicians were running tests and trying to figure out what antigens the baby lacked and where to get the blood, I went to the immunologist—the doctor overseeing the transfusions. I told him that I thought I had a rare blood type. And then I asked him to test my blood and see if Henrietta could receive it without the baby getting any sicker."

"Did he suspect you were the father?" Anna asked.

"I could see it in his eyes. And from the look on his face he *knew* I was the father. I'd been at the hospital every day since the obstetrician had admitted Henrietta. And now *I* had come to him and was *hinting* that I might have this rare blood type that the baby needed. He thanked me."

"So much so that he said nothing," Anna said.

"Not to anyone. It was no skin off his back. With all the drama going on—Thelonius wanting answers, and Henrietta acting as if she had no idea—both the immunologist and I just wanted to save the baby. Within hours of my visit, he called wanting more of my blood. Henrietta had received what I'd given him, and Millicent hadn't reacted."

"So how did Thelonius find out?"

"He didn't. Henrietta's obstetrician was black. Thelonius' real estate firm had helped him find a house then carried out the purchase. He and Thelonius became friends, played golf together. They belonged to the same country club. I figure he must have explained to Thelonius that he probably wasn't the father. A day after Henrietta had received the first full transfusion, Thelonius burst into Henrietta's hospital room and said he wasn't leaving until she told him the truth."

"Explained who the father was," Anna said.

Inman nodded. "He had considered Henrietta and me to be like sister and brother. I think he might have even suspected that we were intimate, but . . ." Inman's voice trailed off. "He just didn't count on her getting pregnant."

"But Henrietta's and Millicent's illnesses demanded that he know," Anna said.

"I suppose like Edward's cancer, it forced a lot of things to the surface."

Anna lowered her head into a hard silence. Several moments passed.

"Thelonius calmed down after Henrietta and I told him we'd planned to let him bring up baby as his own child. If Henrietta had never had the problem with her placenta, he wouldn't have known. Thelonius would have raised Millicent thinking she was his, which is what he said he wanted." Inman gave a bitter chuckle. His solemnity returned. "We never told Millicent."

"But what about Thelonius and his unfaithfulness?" Anna asked.

"That started after Millicent's birth. Henrietta said she didn't hold it against him, that it was her fault. She had hurt him, that Thelonius had sought affection outside the marriage to get back at Henrietta and me."

"But how would *his* infidelities hurt you and Henrietta?" Anna was confused.

"I loved Henrietta," Inman said. Anna's face warmed to a slow burn. "Thelonius knew that. He also knew I wanted the best for her, but I could never measure up to him."

"Would you have taken her had she left Thelonius?"

"I wanted to marry her, told her so." Inman then said, "But Thelonius knew that Henrietta would never leave him for me."

A momentary silence passed, Anna absorbing the raw truth of Inman's story. She then considered how close Inman had grown with Millicent. "Why didn't Thelonius demand you get out of Henrietta's life?"

"Thelonius and Henrietta didn't have much of a sex life." Inman flashed his palm. "Don't ask me what was going on there. When she made it clear to Thelonius that she'd never thought of leaving him, he seemed to settle down. He appeared complacent and unaffected by my being around Millicent. I was in Millicent's life until she was thirteen."

"You would have been married to Marilyn and had Dancia by then," Anna said.

"Dancia was six the last time I saw Millicent." Inman twisted his face. "Marilyn hated Henrietta. She thought I was still in love with her."

"Were you?"

"Possibly. But Henrietta certainly didn't love me. I came to see that. Though I couldn't blame her." Anna's heart sank another notch in awareness of Inman's self-loathing. "Every July I went back to Chicago for a week. I stayed in a hotel and spent most of my time visiting Millicent."

"As her godfather?"

"Yeah, but Marilyn maintained that Millicent was my excuse to remain connected with Henrietta."

"Did she know that Millicent was your child?"

"No." Inman shook his head. Even he had sworn himself to silence.

"What made you stop visiting?"

"Thelonius' complacency was short-lived. He started having mood swings when Millicent entered adolescence. He'd get really angry then sink into these deep depressions. By then Henrietta was fed up with his affairs."

"What do you mean?"

"The spring before I came that last summer, Henrietta threatened to leave Thelonius and take Millicent with her if Thelonius didn't stop his ways. Thelonius said he'd stop only if—"

"You stopped visiting Millicent." It all came clear to Anna.

Inman's eyes receded. He said, "Thelonius told her he wanted me out of Millicent's and Henrietta's lives forever. Millicent turned thirteen the week I was in Chicago that last summer. Henrietta was hosting a birthday party for her. I was really excited to be there that week."

Inman continued. "It had been hard for me to get away that particular week, the one of her birthday, in recent summers. Millicent was turning thirteen and I really wanted to be there.

After Millicent had opened all her gifts, Henrietta said she wanted to talk. While Millicent and the kids were dancing downstairs in the game room, Henrietta explained what had been going on with Thelonius, his affairs, the mood swings, her threat to leave and take Millicent."

Inman turned away, his gaze receding even farther. He tapped his fingers upon the table.

Chapter 55

Despite her frustrations, Anna felt sorry for Inman. Henrietta had used him.

Inman said, "I left the house that afternoon having promised never to come back. Since Millicent's wedding I've come to believe that it was Henrietta, and not Thelonius, who wanted me out of Millicent's life. I'm sure Thelonius was relieved.

But I was a stain on her life. She, perhaps more than Thelonius, was afraid of what I might tell Millicent, or what Millicent might discover as she got older. I left that summer and Millicent thought I'd come back next summer as usual. I didn't. A year later, Marilyn left me and Dancia."

"How did you learn Millicent was getting married?"

"It was kind of freaky, sort of a glitch. I was in Los Angeles Airport waiting for my flight back up here when Millicent saw me. She had been visiting friends from college who then lived in L.A. She was on her way back to Chicago. Both our flights had been delayed for three hours. We spent the time catching up. She wanted to know where I lived, asked for my e-mail address and phone number. I couldn't refuse her. She was in graduate school, an adult."

She's also your daughter," Anna said. "Did she tell Henrietta and Thelonius of having met you?"

"I figured that out when I called to say I was coming to the wedding. Millicent and I kept in touch after having met at the airport. A year later, she told me she was getting married. I was a little shocked. We talked every two or three weeks. She'd said nothing about dating or anything. But she wanted *me* at the wedding to walk her down the aisle and give her away. I should have known something when she assured me that she'd settled everything with Henrietta and Thelonius," Inman lamented.

"You didn't call them?"

"Yes, but Henrietta was shocked when I did. It was two months before the wedding. I called Henrietta to see if Millicent had told her that she wanted me at the wedding and to give her away. I also wanted to find out about the person Millicent was marrying," Inman said.

Anna was somewhat taken aback that Millicent had not discussed Theo with him, that he'd had to ask about him.

Inman took a breath. "Millicent had said little of her fiancé. Instead, she focused more on her soon-to-be mother-in-law." He looked at Anna. A lump formed in Anna's throat as she recalled having shared with Inman her frustrations concerning Millicent. Anna had referred to Millicent as a *b-i-t-c-h* for which she now felt imminently sorry. But Anna had held no inkling of the possibility that Inman could be, never mind, *was* Millicent's biological father.

The depth of Anna and Inman's predicament, coupled with the various discoveries Anna had made about him during the past few weeks, tugged at Anna's nerves still raw from Edward's death. Not only was he Mrs. McGrath's nephew. He was also father to the daughter-in-law with whom Anna least felt comfortable and safe. Again she felt exposed. She interwove her fingers.

Inman said, "Millicent was worried that you didn't think she was good enough for Theo." Anna lowered her gaze. Inman stared at his hands. "You were right," he conceded. "Millicent can be a lot like Thelonius. That's one of the things that bothered me. As she grew older, Millicent looked up to him. I told Henrietta so. As for the call to Henrietta about Millicent wanting me at the wedding, Henrietta refused to tell me anything. I told her I didn't want Millicent marrying a rendition of Thelonius. She asked if I'd rather have her marry someone like myself."

Anna's heart pounded with pain. "Henrietta told me not to come to the wedding."

"So Millicent hadn't told her or Thelonius that she wanted you there?"

"No, she hadn't. And I didn't want to cause any problems," Inman said. "It was Millicent's wedding. I left it to Henrietta to tell Millicent that I wasn't coming."

Anna read In

man's downcast eyes. "But she didn't."

A thick air of dread washed over Inman's face as he recalled, "The day of Millicent and Theo's wedding, I was in Maui with Dancia. I'm on the beach and I get this call. It's Millicent wanting to know where I was, why I hadn't come to Chicago for the wedding." Inman sighed. "Henrietta had been reassuring her I'd be there."

"Just like Millicent had told you she'd made everything right with her parents," Anna interceded. "That they were okay with you giving her away."

"Exactly. It was a mess. I hated doing it, but I told Millicent that I had spoken with her mother two months earlier and that Henrietta had suggested I not come to the wedding."

"What happened then?"

"Henrietta stonewalled Millicent again, like she had me." Inman then said, "I heard about the fiasco that nearly took place the day of the wedding with Thelonius threatening to call off the ceremony if I showed up, and then Millicent saying she was going to elope. When Millicent called, I asked her about Theo. She'd said nothing of him. I told her I didn't want to hear anymore about Theo's mother. I needed her to tell me about Theo. She said he was nice and kind, was always concerned about her happiness. She began to cry. I asked why. She said she didn't think she deserved him. She was afraid his mother was right about her. That she would hurt him".

Inman said, "I told Millicent, 'You need to marry him and you need to treat him right. If you can't do that, then call it off. He'll be hurt now, but later, he'll thank you.' I'd been thinking about me and Henrietta during the entire phone conversation. I know that Millicent can be better than her parents. I knew it then; I know it now. But how could I say that without speaking badly of them and letting her know what kind of man I'd been? A person who'd had an affair with a married woman, *her* mother. There was no way I was going to tell Millicent how she was conceived."

"What does she say now that she knows?"

"It's a shock. But she's older. Five years of marriage has provided a padding of experience. That and the fact that I revealed the truth to save her life."

Anna momentarily considered all that Inman had endured. The loss of a fiancée, and then his wife, Marilyn. Fixed between those events stood his affair with Henrietta, a married woman wherein Inman had suffered as a casualty. However wrong he was in sleeping with Henrietta, she was an adult. As such, she bore half the responsibility for the affair having taken place.

And then to order Inman out of Millicent's life despite the fact he never wanted Millicent to know he was her father, to believe and see Thelonius in that role. Anna shook her head in recognition of how ruthless Henrietta had behaved.

Briefly, she met Inman's gaze. And for a moment Anna saw the eyes of Stella, Esther, and the other unnamed women with whom Edward had lain. Perhaps it was her imagination. Anna then beheld the reflection of her own self. No longer pursuing the divorce, and she having brought Edward home to die, she had slept with Inman.

Anna said, "You never came to visit Millicent even after she and Theo married."

"I told Millicent she needed to get to know her father and see who he was beyond his affairs," Inman said. "By this time she knew of Thelonius' unfaithfulness. I told her I wanted her to do this for herself and Theo and their marriage. I added that like always, she could call me anytime, night or day. I wanted Millicent to be happy with both Theo *and* Thelonius. The best way to do that was to make myself available only to Millicent, and to not ask anything of her."

Nor of Henrietta. Anna bristled. "So you did that by staying away? What about Dancia? When do you plan to tell her about Millicent? And does Millicent know about Dancia?"

Inman lowered his head. "Having Dancia made me respect what Thelonius had done for Millicent, loving her as his own daughter. Losing Marilyn showed me what Thelonius must have felt when he learned that I was the father of the child Henrietta was carrying. I didn't want to lose Dancia by her learning about my sordid past. Same as with Millicent."

"Surely you don't think Dancia will judge you? Millicent hasn't."

"Perhaps. And you're right about Millicent," Inman said. "But then again, you have."

Chapter 56

Inman's story left much for Anna to ponder, least of which were her feelings of having been exposed due to revelation and discovery. Yet again, Inman held much in his past for which he felt ashamed.

They had been intimate, thus making Anna's life like a glass house with pristine windows through which Inman could see her soul. Wrinkles and spots dotted the way; Anna's foibles of intense self-judgment had inevitably shaped her opinion of others.

Unlike it had been with Edward and his shortcomings, Anna found herself exercising more criticism of Henrietta than she was willing to level upon Inman. He had needed protection, Anna thought. And then, *If only I could have . . .*

She shot down the idea. It bore too much hope and possibility concerning her relationship with Inman. Though she felt sorry for him, deeply empathized with his hurt, Anna could not, *they could not,* continue their involvement. Inman was Millicent's father. Anna was Theo's mother. Anna and Inman were in-laws, soon to be grandparents to the twins Millicent was carrying. Things could not continue as they had.

Anna spent Thanksgiving following Edward's death with Linda and Brad in Los Angeles. At Anna's invitation, Bryce accompanied her on what she termed a working vacation during which he could bring her up to speed on more matters involved in the running of Manning Ventures.

For Bryce, whose mother had died when he was in college, the request offered the perfect excuse to see Serine, Anna's secondary motive for asking him along.

After Thanksgiving dinner Anna, Bryce, Serine, and Brad asked Linda to play her violin. Linda had confessed to having returned to playing the instrument after performing at the gravesite.

"It was beautiful, what you played," Anna said as Linda opened her case on Thanksgiving day. Her stomach round and full with life, she had yet to deliver.

"It soothes me," Linda said upon lifting the wooden instrument, with its European finish smooth and clear, from the case.

Anna said, "Your father was so excited when he found it in Austria. I remember the day he called me." Anna's heart grew full, her chest warm. Linda embraced her. Only then did Anna realized herself about to cry.

"I feel he hears me when I play," Linda whispered.

"It's how we talk, how I remain close to him." Anna squeezed her daughter's hand and patted her stomach.

During the family's mini concert, Bryce reached for Serine's hand, and Serine let it rest in Bryce's palm. Anna grew hopeful as Linda played.

Later that night, Anna joined Serine in the kitchen for a late night snack.

"I see I'm not the only one hungry," Anna said on entering.

"Oh, I'm making a sandwich for Linda." Serine continued to cut one more slice of turkey then spread mayonnaise over the bread. "She's hungry again. And Brad was asleep. I told her I'd make it and bring it up."

"That's good. You're not eating, and since I hate eating alone, I have less incentive to snack."

"It's all healthy," Serine looked up from the sandwich that she had placed on the plate.

"But I'm not getting any younger." Anna patted her abdomen. She needed to get back to exercising. Better yet, find a new gym. Memories of Inman, filled the one in Amory Village down from the house.

"You look fine." Serine slid the pan containing the turkey back onto the top shelf of the refrigerator then closed the door. "You can't imagine how the mothers of some of my colleagues look. You're way ahead of them." Her words were sweet and comforting, encouraging.

Anna drew near. "Thank you."

Serine looked to her. Anna met the gaze of her youngest daughter. Serine's accusation came to mind. *I can't believe you sat across from him for fifteen months and never noticed how sick Daddy was, that he was dying. Or did you know and not care?*

"I'm sorry for abandoning you, not calling to check up on you while your father and I were divorcing," Anna said.

"You were going through a lot." Serine returned to the counter, was about to lift the plate holding the sandwich she had made for Linda when Anna again drew near. "I should not have pushed you away. Perhaps if I had been there, this mess with Grant and Matthew would have never—"

"I'm a grown woman. And I knew better." Petite and inches shorter than Anna, Serine was penitent.

"Why did you do it?"

"I was angry and scared. You and Daddy were divorcing. I couldn't hold onto the lie."

"What lie was that?"

"That he loved you. I mean truly loved you."

The truth of Serine's words hit Anna's face and burned her cheeks.

"Daddy cared for you. He gave us all we ever needed. And he took care of us, and you. But he never gave of himself."

"He was hurting. Your father carried a lot that he just couldn't shar—"

"That maybe. And believe me I love him. But I don't want to die like him. That's where my life was headed, and where I was going with Grant and Matt."

"Surely you're not going to refuse to let yourself grow close to someone, send people away, those who might love you."

"Both Grant and Matt loved me," Serine said. "But I couldn't love them."

"Why not?" Anna felt hope slipping away.

Serine breathed in. "I don't know. It's going to take some time figuring that out." Serine grew somber then, "I'm just thankful for Bryce."

"Oh?" Anna remained calmed against a surge of hope.

"He told me a lot about Daddy in those last two years. Bryce and I've been talking a lot. He wants to talk, and I'm eager to hear. I need to hear of the man Dad truly was."

"What sort of things is he saying?" Anna grew anxious.

Again Serine grew reflective. Her gaze receded as if recalling Bryce's words, and she, while appreciative of Bryce's sharing, also regretful.

"They're not things you would want to hear, nor do you need to." The attorney in Serine spoke, not unlike Grant, what Anna surmised Serine had inherited from him during her time working under his tutelage. "Hold onto the Edward that you know. But I'm a person of truth. Neither will I stop loving him." Anna's youngest daughter grew wistful. "Call it compassion. But learning about the real Edward Manning helps me love him more."

Serine's words moved Anna. They also reflected Anna's need for illusions. Softly, she kissed Serine's cheek then said, "Your sister needs her sandwich."

Serine kissed Anna then headed for the doorway. On reaching it she turned back and said, "You're a good person." She then left.

Once again Anna stood pondering the shifts and changes Edward's life and death had wrought.

Accepting David's invitation to spend Christmas with him and Heather in Detroit provided Anna more encouragement and evidence of her children's ability to move beyond their father's death. It also left Anna feeling somewhat guilty of having ignored Theo and Millicent.

Anna coaxed herself to remember that Inman had been with them for Thanksgiving. By way of Linda, she had also learned that Inman's daughter, Dancia, would be accompanying him to Chicago for Christmas. Inman needed time and space to introduce his daughters to each other. Christmas would be their first time meeting. Inman would finally tell them the truth.

On Christmas Eve, Anna spoke to Theo privately. "How are things with Millicent and Dancia?" she asked.

"It's slow going," Theo said, the energy of hope filling his voice. "They're warming to each other. The prospect of the twins helps. That and the fact that Inman keeps emphasizing that he met Henrietta *before* marrying Dancia's mother."

"I hope Dancia remembers that fact when considering Inman's annual trip to a July business conference—the guise he used when visiting Millicent in Chicago," Anna said.

Inman's concerns that Dancia would level negative judgment upon his past actions reminded Anna of how she had, during those last weeks of Elena's life, thought of her father. Anna had concluded the Reverend Elijah to have been unfaithful.

Now having heard Inman's story, having gained another perspective on how human individuals log these clandestine occasions into the filing cabinets of our hearts and minds, Anna wondered of the phenomenon of unfaithfulness, the experience of infidelity, and also the act of betrayal.

Anna considered herself having been unfaithful to Edward. More than that she had lied to herself when asking for the divorce. Anna had betrayed herself and her heart, all that she believed and hoped when declaring that her love for Edward had died, and was no more.

~*~*~*~

Again Bryce accompanied Anna for her holiday travels. The two arrived for Christmas at David and Heather's home in Detroit, and found Serine already present. David eagerly welcomed Anna seeing to her every need, and what he thought she might desire.

After dinner David came to Anna and quietly stated he had received the deed to the house. "I own it in name only," he emphasized. "In my heart it will always be yours. I speak for everyone else."

Anna's smile, and gracious "Thank you," did little to comfort him.

Later that night, the children, Heather, Serine, and Bryce in bed and the house quiet, he suggested, "Why don't you just buy it back from me. For $1? I'll even give you the dollar." Anna and David had been sitting on the couch, the fireplace aglow before them and casting warmth upon their legs.

"That's not what your father wanted," Anna said.

"And we know Dad was having a hard time of it those last few weeks."

"You forget," Anna said. "Your father made out his will months before he died." She reached over and touched David's hand, which was trembling like his lips.

"I want you to be happy. I *need* you to be happy," he whispered.

"I am happy," Anna said. David felt heartily sorry for how he behaved. But like many men and *women*, he did not know how to ask for forgiveness.

"The house," he continued. "It's yours. It belongs to y—
"

Anna placed her forefinger upon his lips.

"This is what gives me joy." She turned to the Christmas tree decorated with white lights flashing and standing by the window. She then pointed to the stockings hanging from the mantle over the fireplace. Anna had brought five with her, one for David and Heather's children, Emily and Josh, two more for

372

David and Heather, and one also for Bryce. Seeing Serine present, she had rushed out to the mall and purchased a sixth that she filled with bath gel and Godiva chocolates for her youngest.

"I'm your mother and always will be," Anna said to David. "I'll always love you. No matter what. Don't ever forget that."

David breathed in. His hands began to tremble as he held back tears.

Chapter 57

Anna and Bryce remained with David until the New Year, then returned to Oakland. By the end of January, Anna was back in Los Angeles, this time for the birth of Edward Manning Oliver, Linda and Brad's first child and Anna's third grandchild.

Life picked up speed in early March when Millicent gave birth to Anna Hayes Manning and Inman Regarde Manning. Anna allowed Inman time to visit with them before she scheduled her trip to see Theo, Millicent, and the twins at the end of March.

Two days before she was to leave for Chicago, she called Theo. He confirmed that Inman was returning to Oakland before she arrived.

Yet when driving her from O'Hare to his and Millicent's home, Theo carefully pointed out, "He asks about you all the time."

Anna thought about Inman, too. But Edward had died. And with that had gone much of her hatred toward him. She now held him in compassion, wished for him a better life in the world he had entered, a place she was trying to reach.

Anna did not want to run from the hurts of her marriage with Edward, and those she had felt while watching him die in her arms. Neither did she want to sulk and give way to feelings of desperation that often overtook her.

More times than she cared to admit, particularly to herself, Anna wished for Inman's arms to wrap her and kiss her neck as he had done on that night in the bedroom of his house atop Grizzly Peak and overlooking UC Berkeley. Yet the longer she remained from him, the more Anna feared losing all hope of life and possibilities of love that the future could deliver.

In her efforts to remain grounded, Anna refused to push away the reality that Inman was Millicent's father. Much came with that fact, most specifically how Anna had felt about Millicent before learning that not only was Inman her father, but how that came about.

Anna would not return to Inman unless she could show him compassion, love and respect for what he had endured as the result of his actions and Henrietta's. And yet Millicent remained her daughter-in-law, the two of them connected by Theo.

"I haven't been avoiding you," Anna said on arriving at Theo and Millicent's home ten days after the birth of the twins. She felt the need to explain her absence during Thanksgiving and Christmas. "You needed time with your father," Anna said to Millicent. "And by that I mean Inman." Anna wanted no confusion. Millicent smiled.

Some minutes later, she thanked Anna not only for her ability to give her and Theo space and time to integrate Inman and Dancia into their lives, but also for, "Your honesty."

In explaining, Millicent said, "Mama and Daddy, Thelonius, can't get used to me knowing the truth. They've held so long to the lie that Thelonius Regarde was my father now that the truth is out they don't know what to do."

376

"But Thelonius is your father," Anna said. "That's why I clarified about whom I was speaking in this instance, Inman. There'll be other times when I say your father and I'll be speaking of Thelonius."

Millicent looked to Anna. With Inman Regarde nursing at her breast, Millicent had been sitting in the recliner with Anna holding Anna Hayes. Seeing that Inman Regarde, the younger of the twins, had fallen asleep at her nipple, Millicent lifted the infant and asked for his elder sister.

Daughter-in-law and mother-in-law exchanged infants. Millicent settled into nursing Anna Hayes at her other breast, the one over her heart.

With Inman Regarde fast asleep in her arms, Anna smiled upon her granddaughter sucking at Millicent's breast.

"David always liked sucking from the nipple over my heart."

"I save this one for Anna," Millicent smiled knowingly. "Inman doesn't seem to care. He just wants the milk."

"He's like Theo, just wants to be close." Anna then said, "He always liked my right breast." She smiled. A warm feeling of closeness overcame her.

"He's good like that." Millicent beamed her eyes again and held that glow of recognition. "I love your son. I would never do anything to hurt him, ever," Millicent said.

"Thank you." Anna wished to say the same to Millicent regarding her father, Inman. And yet she feared she had done that very thing. "I'm sorry for how I've treated you."

Millicent said, "I'm sorry for not giving you the chance to love me the way I've always wanted. And for envying you the ability to do what I feared I never could." Millicent explained how from the first moment of meeting Theo, and then hearing about Anna she had prayed for Anna's acceptance.

Again, Anna felt truly sorry for the way she had behaved to Millicent over the years. "I felt like such a failure to the children, that their father's and my marriage had burdened them with a hurt that my love could not heal."

Cradling Anna Hayes with one hand Millicent extended her other to Anna. On Anna grasping it, Millicent said, "I

377

always felt you were the perfect mother, despite all that Father Manning did." Hearing Millicent say Father Manning soothed the loss of what Anna had hoped to share with Edward, at least in this lifetime.

Millicent said, "You have a wonderful family. *All your children*. I'm so thankful to be a part of this it. Having you as my mother-in-law and knowing what you endured gave me the strength to forgive my mother and to open my heart even more to Papa Inman."

Anna's heart grew full. She felt herself about to cry. Clutching Millicent's hand she looked into the eyes of her infant grandson, Inman Regarde Manning.

The world that had moments earlier threatened to careen out of control slowed to a rhythm moving in time with her heart and breathing. Anna ebbed closer to the shores of peace and calm.

Chapter 58

In late April, five months after Edward's death, Anna's children gathered at the house in Oakland. At dinner on the first night after their arrival, she took her seat at the end of the table opposite where Edward had sat throughout her marriage and during the meal where Serine and David had made their outbursts. On this evening Edward's chair stood empty.

The children occupied the seats they had filled when Edward had last been among them. Theo to her left held Anna Hayes Manning barely three weeks old while Millicent next to him held Anna Hayes' twin brother, Inman Regarde Manning.

To Anna's right was David with Heather beside him. Next to Heather sat Linda, holding Edward Manning Oliver with Brad at the end across from Serine and Bryce, whom Anna had asked to join them.

Anna was hesitant to interrupt the peaceful hum of conversations encompassing the table as everyone enjoyed first and second helpings of rice pilaf, and sautéed chard with either baked tilapia or braised chicken.

So much was different since she had last eaten with her children in this house. The presence of Heather beside David; the two of them smiling as they spoke to those around and across from them, gave Anna hope that their marriage would survive.

That Millicent had insisted on coming despite having just given birth, emphasized her commitment not simply to Theo, but that as she had stated, "I need you in my life. However you decide to leave things with Papa Inman. I hold no hard feelings."

And then there was Linda and Brad, also proud parents and beaming. Serine beside Bryce had lost interest in the drama surrounding her relationships with Grant and Matt.

Perhaps it was Bryce's close relationship with Edward as his mentor that so attracted her to Bryce whose presence had a calming effect. She was learning much about her father from Bryce.

Anna tapped the spoon to her water glass several times then stood. All eyes turned from those with whom they had been speaking.

"It's good to have all of you here." Her heart warmed as they smiled. "Thank you for coming. And at such short notice." The smiles around the table widened. Unlike when she had announced that she was seeking to divorce their father, Anna had, after Edward's death, not retreated into a shell.

She had instead kept in touch, calling all four of her children each week. She would do the same in the future. "It's been great running your father's company, Manning Ventures," Anna started once more.

"Don't you mean *your* company?" David asked.

"Perhaps," said Anna. "But as I was about to say, in so doing I've learned a lot. First of which is how great a choice Edward made in having Bryce as his right hand man."

She looked to Bryce at the far left end of the table, and said, "There's no way I could have done any of this without you. I'm now certain that had Edward not had you, he would never have entertained the idea of me running the company. Which brings me to my second point. Much of what I've learned in these last six months at the helm of Manning Ventures has been exciting and eye opening."

Anna paused. Seeing that she was about to cry, Theo lifted her left hand, David her right. She thanked them.

"As I said, I've learned a lot." She started once more. "Your father worked very hard. *Very hard.* I don't know how he did it. Despite his shortcomings, I'm very grateful for what he provided this family. Manning Ventures was his world, and he knew it inside and out. Bryce has shown me that." With tears threatening to spill into her throat once more, she again thanked Bryce.

"I've learned a lot," Anna reiterated. "And one of those things is that I'm not cut out for running a company, certainly not the size of Manning Ventures. Neither do I want to do it."

Smiles around the table faded. Anna turned to David on her right. "I'd like you to go and sit in your father's chair." Startled, but obedient, and penitent, he did as Anna requested. "How does it feel?" she asked.

"Scary." His face held a sense of wary caution as he grasped the side arms to the chair.

"Well, you're going to have to get used to it," Anna said. "I want you to sit there when you and Heather and the children eat here in the dining room." David and Heather would be moving into the house in two months. Anna then said, "I've decided not to take the apartment I looked at over in Alameda."

"So you're going to take me up on my offer to buy the house—for a dollar?" David assured everyone. His face at the other end held an aura of hope.

"We could all live here together," Heather said.

"Thank you," Anna said. "It's good to know that your children and their spouses like to have you around, need you." She smiled at Millicent now once more nursing Inman Regarde and a warm feeling of freedom spread over her.

She said, "I'm moving to France. And I want—no, I'm asking—David if you will run Manning Ventures." For a moment Anna thought David would cry. In his hesitancy, she feared he would decline.

"Well come on, man. It's Mom," Theo said. "You can't refuse *her*."

David lifted his head to Linda who was beaming and turned to Serine, also smiling. To Anna he said, "Of course. I'd be glad to." Against everyone clapping, the little boy inside the man, David, then mouthed, "Thank you."

Joy filled Anna.

Chapter 59

At the outset of May, the week after Anna had hosted the children, Anna met Elise for breakfast. They had begun eating at the Amory Village Egg Shoppe when she said, "I'm putting David in charge of the company. He and Bryce work well together."

"Have you told Inman?" Elise said.

"Bryce notified him like all the other board members and trustees."

"But I thought you said Inman had stepped down from representing his aunt." Elise screwed her face. "Does Inman know that you're moving to France?"

"He'll learn soon enough." Anna bit into her toast.

"I can't believe you're leaving him." Elise challenged Anna. "The man loves you." They had discussed the topic several times in the last months.

"I don't know what more you could want, and that he could give," Elise said. "Are you mad? The man loves you."

"A marriage takes more than love," said Anna.

"And who said anything about marriage?" Elise's eyes widened.

"That's what Inman wants." Anna gave a shrug.

"Did he say that, ask you to marry him?"

Inman's words returned to her. *I'll take you any way that feels safe for you. Time's over for people making demands on you and your life."* Inman's desire to be with Anna, his declaration of love, "I need you, want you in my life. I promise to make you happy, more than Edward ever did," left Anna feeling trapped. *"I'm free now,"* Anna said.

"To do what, be alone?" Again Elise frowned this time in frustration. She reached across the table and grasped her hand. "I've watched you give everything to your marriage and your children. When are you going to give something to yourself?" Elise then said, "I've stopped blaming Edward for all your hurts. If I can do that so can you. I'm asking you, pleading. Think of your own happiness."

"And why is my happiness so important to you? I'm moving to Paris. That's what'll make me happy."

"Ha!" Elise angled her head. "And what will that be without Inman?"

"He had an affair with Millicent's mother. He's Millicent's father and Theo's father-in-law."

"And you're grandmother to his grandchildren," Elise rebutted. "It's not like the two of you are going to have any children."

"Still, it's not right." Anna shook her head.

"What's not right?" Elise asked.

"The nature of these relationships. It's too *incestuous.*"

"And to think," Elise quipped, "you had accused Millicent, figuratively speaking, of having an affair with Thelonius."

Anna resumed eating her eggs.

On finishing her eggs, Elise said, "I get it. If you continue with Inman, you'll have to make amends with Millicent."

"We've done that," Anna said. "She's innocent in all of this."

"So you admit you were wrong about her?"

"Yes. And I told her as much. But he was unfaithful, her father."

"Which father?" Elise asked. "Thelonius or Inman?"

"Both."

"So you've let Millicent off the hook but not Thelonius or Inman."

"They were like Edward."

Elise stared at her. "And you?"

"I was like them too. I slept with Inman while I was still married to Edward." Anna lifted her last strip of bacon.

Some minutes later, Elise confessed, "I'm the one who told Serine about your plans to move to France. She called me complaining about how you were divorcing Edward. Ten minutes into listening to her, I lost it. I told her that she was a spoiled brat thinking only of herself."

Elise grew sad, as if regretful, said, "I wish I hadn't done it. I heard about how she and David attacked you during dinner that first night they were all home before Edward died. I'm sorry but—"

"It doesn't matter." Anna flashed her palm. She was long past her anger at Elise. "I suspected she learned it from you."

"You said nothing."

"You're my friend. And Edward was dying. The children were going to learn about my time with Inman sooner or later."

"You still can't get over it, forgive yourself for sleeping with Inman while Edward was dying," Elise said.

"I made love with Edward, too," Anna said. "Two nights after I'd been with Inman."

"So what?" Elise shrugged while lifting her hands.

"What kind of woman am I?" Anna's heart sank. "I was no better than Edward. And to think I had such a hard time forgiving him."

"Have you ever considered that maybe everything happened the way it did to let you see how both Edward *and*

Inman felt? You've experienced betrayal and you've been the one to *betray*, since you insist on looking at what you did with Inman in that way."

Anna reviewed her actions with Inman and then Edward. Yet Elise's conclusion, hard to grasp, remained at bay.

"I need to be sure that I'm not angry at him, Inman," Anna said. "That in some flash of the moment when Millicent calls about Henrietta or Thelonius I won't remind him of him what he did."

"And just what did he do?" Elise fired another interrogative.

Again Inman's words resurfaced. *I loved Henrietta. I wanted the best for her and Millicent. And that meant I needed to be out of their lives. Millicent needed to see Thelonius as her father.*

"What do you hope to accomplish by living alone in Paris?" Elise asked.

"I'll be on my own, not dependent on anyone else to make decisions for me."

"That's what white people do, live alone, pretending that they don't need anyone."

"You're one to talk." African American and fifty-three years old, Elise Simpson had yet to marry. She had never even been pregnant.

"I know all too well how lonely this life gets," Elise said. "Like Edward, I've made a lot of money in real estate. I have a nice house. All my accounts are in order. I can take a vacation when I like and visit almost any place I desire. Like you—" she smiled, "I could even move to another country."

Elise's humor dissipated. She said, "One thing separates us, me from you. I have no one who wants to go with me. There's no one willing to pick up and start afresh and stand beside me. The saddest part is that I wouldn't even know how to behave if someone wanted to, or did."

Elise's eyes glistened with tears. She offered a second confession "The reason I've been so angry with Edward all these years is that he took a place with you I could never fill. You and I were simply girlfriends. But he became your husband. I can't be that close to anyone. All I know is work. *Competition. Accomplishment.* And *myself.*"

"That was Edward," Anna said astonished.

"We weren't that different. But he had you beside him. I envied him that." Elise continued as if perplexed by her own self-discovery and revelation. "Despite everything he did—the women, the traveling—he never left you, and you stayed with him. The two of you remained with each other until the end. You should be proud of that, what you did, taking him in. It took strength."

Let the dead bury the dead.

Of Marilyn's death and being left with Dancia, Inman had said, "It showed me what Thelonius must have felt when he learned that I was Millicent's father and not he." Inman had rubbed his temple. And then of Millicent's illness while pregnant that demanded the truth, "She needed to know. I'm glad I was here to help her and the babies. They're my grandchildren."

"You saved them," Anna had said.

"Perhaps." Inman had again pulled at his temple. "But I hope it wasn't at the expense of losing Dancia."

"She won't judge you. She loves you," Anna had urged.

"And how can you be so sure? You have."

In the coffee shop Anna drank some water then said to Elise sitting across from her, "I don't want to hurt Inman anymore than I already have."

"Then let yourself love him. So he can love you." With that Elise grasped Anna's hand once more.

Chapter 60

Less than a month beyond Anna's breakfast with Elise, everyone returned to Oakland and gathered in St. Maria's Chapel where Father Richard baptized Linda and Brad's son, Edward Manning Oliver.

Later that night and with everyone asleep, Anna and David sat on the patio by the pool and discussed plans for David, guided and supported by Bryce, as the leader of Manning Ventures.

Having addressed basic housekeeping issues, David once again thanked Anna for the gift of trust she had shown by making him CEO of what had been his father's, now her, company.

"It means a lot, that after everything I've done you still have faith in me. Knowing that you still love me has given me the strength to be a better friend and husband to Heather."

"Oh, David," Anna reached out and hugged her eldest child, "I never stopped."

"But there was a point where I thought I had stopped loving you. And Dad too." David leaned back in his chair. "I never understood why Dad was away all the time. I knew he was working.

But why did he have to be gone so much? And why did you have to cry? Even when I was little I knew something wasn't right. It hurt that I couldn't make it better."

He gave a slight sigh. Anna sensed her elder son coming to terms with his father's death. David was surviving Edward's passing.

David said, "When you told us you were divorcing him, I felt like I had during all the times he had been away." David then said, "I knew Dad was sick and dying. He told me before he let Bryce know. I wanted to tell you. Dad made me promise not to."

"So that's why you filed papers to have me declared insane." It was all making sense.

"I wanted to get your attention." David lowered his head then lifted it. Anna met his gaze. "I'm sorry, so sorry," he said. Again she opened her arms and embraced him. "I'm going to miss you," he said.

With her bags packed and downstairs, David would drive Anna to San Francisco Airport the next day. She was leaving for France.

~*~*~*~

Elise kept Emily and Josh the following afternoon while David and Heather drove Anna to SFO airport.

"I wish you would reconsider calling Inman," Elise whispered into Anna's ear when hugging her.

Anna simply thanked her for being such a good friend, then got into the back seat of David's sedan. She had already kissed and hugged, said her good-byes to Emily and Josh. With Heather seated in the front passenger seat, and Anna behind her, David drove off.

At the airport and about to walk through security, Anna kissed David's forehead. Again she wished him well at the helm

390

of Manning Ventures. She turned to Heather, and as with David, she kissed her daughter-in-law's forehead.

"Thank you for not giving up on my son."

"How could I?" Heather said, "You've entrusted me with your house." David and Heather had returned to Oakland and would be living in the house.

Anna smiled bittersweet. "I hope you and David create wonderful memories in it."

"We will. I promise," said Heather. "With Dad and Papa Edward looking down on us, I speak to them all the time," she explained. "Everything will be fine."

Anna touched Heather's hand. Then, after grasping David's palm and bringing it to Heather's, she left to board her flight.

Chapter 61

Anna experienced greater awe in her elder son when Bryce informed her that David, three months into leading Manning Ventures, had retained Inman Hayes as a full-time consultant. She wanted so much for David to succeed at what she had no desire, and in her opinion little to no acumen, at accomplishing. Anna called from Paris to voice her approval of his decision to bring Inman on board.

"Your father would be, no, he *is* proud of what you're doing," she said to David. "So am I."

"The man knows his stuff," David said of Inman. "I'm just an attorney who spent ten years doing wills, trusts, and estate planning."

"You're much more than that. Much more."

"I'm glad you're not bothered that I hired Inman." David sounded relieved.

"Of course not. He's good at what he does. Like your father."

"Yes, he is." David agreed. With sadness in his voice, he asked. "Is Dad still alive for you?"

"Like I said. *He's* proud of you," Anna said.

"Then why can't I connect with, or feel him? Heather says she talks with her father all the time, even with Dad. She feels their presences. Why does Dad talk to Heather and not me?"

"Are you calling out, asking him to come?" In David's silence, Anna suggested, "Perhaps you should."

Chapter 62

October brought Anna from Paris to Chicago for the christening of Theo and Millicent's twins. Minutes after she disembarked the plane, David greeted her inside the terminal of O'Hare Airport.

"It's good to see you." He kissed her, and then explained on the way to the baggage carousel, "Linda, Brad, little Edward Jr., along with Serine, Heather, Josh, and Emily are back at the hotel. Even Aunt Elise came."

"Is that what we're calling him now, Linda and Brad's son?"

"Seems so," David smiled. Or maybe it's just me."

Anna smiled too. She loved the name little Edward Jr. She was also comforted that her move to France had not signaled, nor had Elise translated it as an abandonment of their friendship. Anna hoped to one day convince Elise to stop working so hard and live a little, maybe even visit Paris.

During the drive from the airport to their hotel in Chicago, David provided an update. "Dad's contacts in Beijing and Rio have given us a solid base in China and Brazil. They've also been eager to help with the transition of my taking over the leadership of the company. After the holidays we'll be moving into Indonesia."

"Indonesia," Anna mused. "That sounds exciting."

"There're some great start-ups in Jakarta that Inman wants me to look at. He and I are flying over in January after the new year." Anna stared at David. "We're only going to be there for four days," he said.

"Can't you get someone else?" Memories of Edward being away from the family flooded her with worry.

"I tried to get Heather to come with me," David said, "— let Aunt Elise keep the kids. She's made herself their adoptive grandmother while you're away."

"She probably doesn't want to upset the children's schedules," Anna said of Heather. "Unlike Inman, you have a wife to attend." After a momentary silence, she offered, "Perhaps I should come and stay with Heather while you're there."

"Ma. It's only four days," David assured. He had returned to addressing her as *Ma,* his term of endearment and familiarity during childhood and adolescence. Only after returning home from college had he resorted to calling her *Mama,* and then *Mother* when anxious or perturbed about a matter.

David had consistently called her Mother during the fifteen months she had fought to divorce Edward and sell the house. Early adulthood had been a time when David had battled to assert himself beyond the effects of Edward's clandestine relationships with women other than Anna.

This period in David's life, she now realized, had extended into his mid-thirties, most specifically until Anna had handed him control of Manning Ventures.

"Things must be better," Anna, now calmer, said.

"Why do you say that?" David lifted his eyebrows.

"You're back to calling me *Ma.*"

David smiled.

"But don't get too comfortable," Anna said. "I can always fire you if I find you're not spending enough time with your family. Remember, you have Bryce. Don't try doing too much. Your family needs and loves you."

"Well, I don't know how much longer I'll have Bryce," David said.

Anna knitted her brows. "He's not leaving, is he?"

"Only for weekends to visit Serine in L.A." David continued driving.

"She resists him, says she's not good for him. But he won't have any of it," Anna said. "She's still thinking about what happened with Grant and Matt.

"I told her to forget it. Thank God she hadn't married either one of them."

"They were nice young men."

"Not very bright," David said, his eye focused on the freeway ahead.

"They were desperate like us all."

"Desperation's not a good way to start a marriage."

Anna turned to David.

He said, "I told Serine she should treat Bryce well, that he was Dad's right hand man and that he only deserves the best from us."

Anna smiled feeling proud.

"Serine already knew that. I think the only way she can hurt him is by not marrying him."

"Does she love him?" Anna grew serious.

"I told her love would come as long as there's respect and mutual desire for a common goal."

"And what goal might that be?" Anna frowned. David's words sounded sage like. They also bore deep questions.

"They both loved Dad, I mean the real man that he was. I know you've been worried about her, felt like you failed her. I'll see to Serine. Between me and Bryce she'll be fine."

Anna's heart settled. And despite her concerns of Serine not loving Bryce who clearly cared for her, she warmed to the possibility of having Bryce as a son-in-law.

David then said, "As for traveling in the service of the company, after Bryce, there's only Inman." He turned to Anna for a split moment then back at the freeway. "But thanks for reminding me to keep it under control."

On a lighter note, David gave a smooth smile as he drove. "And how are things for you in Paris?"

"They're fine," Anna said.

"And you don't mind being there alone?"

"Well, if you and Heather would come to visit or let me have the kids for a couple of weeks so that the two of you could travel, then I wouldn't be—"

"Don't they call it the City of Love?" David said. Again he smiled.

"You sound like Elise." Anna said in the face of David's smile that remained bright. "I'm enjoying being there." She then fell somber. "I especially love wandering the museums with no constraints on time."

"Were we so bad that you feel the need to live like a pauper?" David turned serious. Anna had taken a tiny flat near Montmartre, despite his urgings that she get something more spacious for when one of the kids came to visit. "Aren't you lonely?" he asked.

"What's this with the twenty questions?"

David chuckled. "I don't know.

"Always the attorney." She smiled.

David continued driving. His smile returned, lit his face, and soothed Anna's heart.

Chapter 63

The next afternoon, Anna entered the narthex of Trueblood African Baptist Church of Chicago. Others stood talking as she continued to the front of the empty sanctuary. Anna sat on the pew she had occupied six years earlier during Theo and Millicent's wedding.

A fleeting passage of time swept her face. Memories of Edward, his life, their hurts, and his death drew near and hung as close as her breath. *Moments in time . . . An eternity.*

Anna then heard laughter. Serine and Bryce had entered the sanctuary. Smiles lit both their faces as Bryce, with Serine looking on, held Linda and Brad's son, Edward Oliver Manning. Enraptured with the soon to be, nine-month-old, the two of them remained unaware of Anna's presence at the front of the sanctuary. Guided by hope, Anna said a prayer. *Help Serine to forgive herself. I do.*

Everyone entered and took their places at the front of the church. As requested, Grandma Anna stood to the left of Millicent, Theo to Millicent's right. To the far right, on the other side of Theo, was Inman. Millicent held baby Inman, and Theo held Baby Anna.

Both babies were dressed in white. David, Heather, Josh, and Emily, formed one part of the half circle behind Theo and Millicent. Then there was Elise, Linda, and Brad, who was holding Edward Manning Oliver. Holding hands, Serine and Bryce formed the other part of half circle.

Seven-month-old Inman Regarde Manning, with eyes wide and bright, turned his head as if recording the scenery and event in his mind never to be forgotten. His tiny fingers pulled at Millicent's breasts.

Anna considered how much time, if any, her husband had experienced at his mother's breast, and if so, had they been empty and trembling, or full of fear and the struggle to survive. Her heart ached for all the times Edward must have hungered for what his mother never possessed.

Violet had loved him as best she could. That was the way it was for black mothers. Loving despite all. Giving even when empty. Moving forward without seeing a path. Good intent.

A *house*. A *home*. Only now did Anna realize how truly desperate and hungry Edward had been. She wiped tears from underneath her eyes.

Anna lowered her head along with all the others, as the minister standing before them offered a prayer.

"We ask, oh, Lord, that you hold Anna Hayes Manning and Inman Regarde Manning forever in your grace and protection. May they always be mindful of your presence and seek to do your will in whatever ways they can."

"Fill their hearts with right purpose and good intent," said the minister. "Place them with individuals who are able and willing to bring into fruition your will for them and your desire for their lives."

"Please, Lord," Anna whispered. Her heart beat in rhythm with the minister's words.

The minister then said, "Those who would be godparents to this Anna Hayes Manning and Inman Regarde Manning please come forward."

Millicent turned to Anna and handed over Inman Regarde. Anna stepped forward. Inman, having received Anna Hayes, joined Grandma Anna in facing the minister. Anna looked to Inman as he held their granddaughter—Anna's namesake. Likewise, she held his namesake, seven-month-old Inman Regarde. The elder Inman was finally receiving what Henrietta had denied him.

Inman kissed little Anna Hayes Manning's brown cheek. The clarity of atonement graced with the fire of redemption pulsated through Anna's heart. In that moment she recalled that Bryce and Serine had accepted the roles of godparents to Linda and Brad's son, Edward Oliver Manning.

Slowly Anna turned back, and met Serine's warm gaze. Serine's lips formed the words, "I love you," as Bryce looking on, patted Serine's shoulder. He sent Anna a smile.

In an effort to stave back tears Anna lowered her eyelids. Gently she brushed the side of Inman Regarde's brown face. The steam of forgiveness flooded her chest.

Feeling her attention pulled to the right, she angled her head, and turned toward Inman.

"I'm sorry," she whispered.

Inman pulled little Anna Hayes Manning deeper into his chest. The words, *I forgive you* ebbed from his eyes. Imbibing more of his gaze, Anna recalled Edward's words. *Moments in time. You. An eternity.* A second heady and more intoxicating wave of warmth filled her heart. It spread through her body. The words, *I love you*, filled Anna's heart. She smiled.

Chapter 64

Tuesday following the christening, David escorted Anna into O'Hare Airport where she would fly back to DeGaulle in Paris. She checked in and David walked her to the line forming at the security gate.

"I guess this is it for a while," he said.

"I'm serious about you, Heather, and the children visiting me in France for Christmas. It'll be good for Josh and Emily, and you, too." She patted his shoulder.

"We'll definitely be coming. I just want to make sure everything is in order with the company. I may be CEO, but you own majority stock."

"Yes, and I demand that you delegate the work, or else . . ."

"I know; you'll fire me." David smiled. He then hugged Anna. I appreciate you reminding me to keep my priorities straight. His voice then lifted. "On another note, I have a message for you."

"From whom?"

"Dad. He spoke to me. I called on him like you suggested. And he came. We've been talking for a while," David said. "He told me things about the company and how to work with potential investors. We discuss other things, too." Anna's elder son gave a solemn smile.

He then slid an envelope from within the breast pocket of his jacket. "Dad didn't tell me to do this, but from some of the things he's been saying, I know it's time, the right thing."

David extended the envelope to Anna. "None are secure until all are saved," he said. Startled by his words, she tore it open.

"A ticket to Paris? But I have my own."

David said," We all hold regrets and need forgiveness. You gave me mine. Now I'm giving you yours. The ticket's not for you." David turned and waved. In the distance, stood Inman. He started toward them.

As tears slid onto her cheeks, Anna's fingers found their way into her coat pocket. Carefully, she lifted out the dried and shriveled petals now cracked and brown like the earth in which Edward lay.

She offered David what had once been a succulent orange and pink Ecuadorian rosebud. Having opened and died, it had now separated into many pieces.

A symbol of her life, it had bloomed during reconciliation with Edward. In his death it reflected the man he had become. Anna considered the possibilities that new life held surrounding her—her and Edward's children and grandchildren—flowers blossoming from the old family stem.

"I laid this on your father's forehead moments after he died," she said.

David accepted the petal, kissed her, said, "I love you," and left.

Inman walked toward her.

404

"I'm told you've become a fan of the Tunisian artist, Atman Khattab," he said.

"I have." Anna was quaking within.

"Well, he's having an exhibit next month in Vienna." As had David, Inman pulled two tickets from the jacket pocket over to his heart. "Would you care to go?"

"Well, I do live in Paris." She smiled. "Will you be around?"

"Only if you'll have me." Inman's lips trembled.

"I'd be more than honored." Anna reached up and kissed him.

Bibliography

"Death needs a strong heart."—Uganda (Ganda, Lugbara) p. 213

" The goat says, 'Nobody willingly walks to his own death.' —Ghana p. 213

"If one could know where death resided, one would never stop there." —Ghana (Ashanti) p. 213

"Death does not sound a trumpet."—Congo, Liberia p. 213

" When death holds something in its grip, life cannot take it away."—Ghana (Akan) p. 213

" Death is one ditch you cannot jump."—United States, South Carolina (Gullah) p. 211

" Whatever you love, death also loves."—Ghana p. 213

" Lie down and die and you will see who really loves you." —Niger, Nigeria (Hausa) p. 213

The proverbs recited by Father Richard in Chapter 13, p. 59, and listed above were taken from:

Hodari, Ashkari Johnson and Sobers, Yvonne McCalla. <u>The Book of African Proverbs</u>, Broadway Books: New York, 2009. pp. 211-214

Acknowledgments

The reason this novel has come to print is due to the love and support of one person, my husband. After reading it, he said, "This needs to be published." That he consistently refers to himself as a non-literary person, his words touched my heart immensely. Like his words to me, mine of the novel had reached beyond the confines of committed readers and moved him.

My one, true desire as a writer is to not only provide engaging and entertaining fiction that touches the heart and moves the soul, but to pen, craft, and shape words that affect those who for whatever reason have felt that no stories have been written to which they can relate or identify.

Beyond the central love of my life, stand three more jewels, no less important. Mascot and leader of the pack, Samantha. Meredyth, affectionately known as "Mimi." And tall Naomi who will always be my little baby.

Accept my apologies for all the endless hours, days, and nights during which I have worked on the computer, seemingly oblivious to your presence. I have not forgotten you. Rather, as an astrologer, now deceased, pointed out over a decade earlier, I am writing for and because of you.

It is out of your love for me that I pen these words. Hopefully, when I am gone, you can read them and know the person I truly am, and gain fuel to find the deepest roots of who you are.

On a more practical note, if you ever find yourself up late at night and toiling when others have made their way to bed do not feel foolish or stupid. Instead, reclaim your images of me at the computer, writing, thinking, working. Follow your passion. Make your dreams into a living reality. And know you are never alone.

To Joy, the sister for whom I have always longed, "Thanks so much," for your probing questions. They pointed me in the direction of uncovering who Inman really was, and therein lay the last third of this book. I love you.

To Father Leo, as always, thanks for continually reminding me that we are all afraid, and that love, forgiveness, and compassion are the only antidotes to fear.

To Linda Beed, Yvonne Perry, and Shonelle Bacon my editors, "Many, many thanks." A writer can only achieve what good editing makes possible. And for what words can never achieve, "Thank you," Audria Gardner, for creating a book cover that went beyond all expectations. All of you gave me 110 percent.

To authors Yvonne McCalla Sobers and Askhari Johnson Hodari, thank you for allowing me to use eight African Proverbs from your book, *The Black Book of Proverbs*.

To those whose encouragement and support has come through reminders that you were waiting to read this novel, "This is it. Enjoy."

May all in whose hands these words land know that I gave my personal best.

I also love connecting with readers.

E-mail me @: anjuelle@anjuellefloyd.com